D1616926

Inside the Natchez Trace Collection

INSIDE THE
NATCHEZ TRACE
COLLECTION

New Sources for Southern History

Edited by
KATHERINE J. ADAMS
and LEWIS L. GOULD

F
217
·N37
I5X
1999
West

*Published in Cooperation with the Center for American History
at the University of Texas at Austin*

LOUISIANA STATE UNIVERSITY PRESS • Baton Rouge

Copyright © 1999 by the Center for American History, University of Texas at Austin
All rights reserved
Manufactured in the United States of America
First printing
08   07   06   05   04   03   02   01   00   99
5   4   3   2   1

Designer: Michele Myatt Quinn
Typeface: Goudy
Typesetter: Coghill Composition
Printer and binder: Edwards Brothers, Inc.

Library of Congress Cataloging-in-Publication Data

Inside the Natchez Trace Collection : new sources for southern history
    / edited by Katherine J. Adams and Lewis L. Gould.
        p.   cm.
    Includes index.
    ISBN 0-8071-2363-3 (cloth : alk. paper)
    1. Southern States—History—1775–1865—Archival resources.
2. Southern States—History—Colonial period, ca. 1600–1775—
Archival resources.   3. Natchez Trace—History—19th century—
Archival resources.   4. Natchez Trace—History—18th century—
Archival resources.   5. Mississippi—History—19th century—
Archival resources.   6. Mississippi—History—18th century—
Archival resources.   7. University of Texas at Austin. Center for
American History. Natchez Trace Collection.   I. Adams, Katherine J.
II. Gould, Lewis L.
Z1251.S7I57   1999
026.975—dc21   98-53364
                                                            CIP

The paper in this book meets the guidelines for permanence and durability of the Committee on
Production Guidelines for Book Longevity of the Council on Library Resources. ♾

CONTENTS

ILLUSTRATIONS

PREFACE

Since the University of Texas at Austin's acquisition of the Natchez Trace Collection (NTC) in December 1985, the Center for American History has made organizing and describing this vast and important southern history collection a top priority. With few exceptions, the various components of the NTC have been processed and are open for research use. Bibliographic records for individual subcollections, books, and newspapers are entered on an ongoing basis into OCLC, an online computer library database that is accessible over the Internet. Future plans call for inventories to NTC subcollections to appear on the Center's website.

As the person who was primarily responsible for the acquisition of the NTC, I have strongly believed that proper stewardship of this collection required the Center to promote its use and share its content through lectures, publications, exhibitions, and microfilming projects. Toward that end, I described the collection to the Natchez Literary Conference in 1988, a talk that subsequently was published in *Natchez Before 1830* (University Press of Mississippi, 1989); the Center in 1991–92 hosted a public lecture series featuring southern history specialists who have used the Natchez Trace Collection, including John Hope Franklin, John Guice, and Morton Rothstein; and we showcased the collection in exhibitions in 1992, 1996, and 1998, including "Windows to the Old South: Social History and the Natchez Trace Collection," and "Natchez-Texas: A Historic Nexus, 1705–1865," both of which were viewed by thousands of visitors to the Center as well as by participants in the biennial Historic Natchez Conference and annual meetings of the Texas State Historical Association. Substantial portions of the collection are now also available on microfilm. The Center has microfilmed the NTC's Provincial and Territorial Records, and University Publications of America features NTC plantation-related collections in its microfilm series *Records of Ante-Bellum Southern Plantations from the Revolution through the Civil War*, series G, parts 3–5.

Inside the Natchez Trace Collection: New Sources for Southern History continues the Center for American History's commitment to bringing the Natchez Trace Collection to the attention of the research community. Although the Center has published circulars and inventories describing the content of specific parts of the collection, this volume will acquaint students of southern history with its extraordinary research potential in several important areas.

This book would not have been possible without the support of many of my colleagues, including the very fine staff at the Center for American History. Their expertise in cataloging and exhibition preparation has made the Natchez Trace Collection highly visible and eminently accessible. In particular, CAH Exhibits Curator Lynn Bell and CAH Head of Archives Sara Clark have made major contributions to this effort. CAH Associate Director Alison Beck played a key role in getting the NTC moved to Austin, and has skillfully directed its cataloging. CAH Associate Director Kate Adams has not only written an essay for this volume but has managed this book project from the beginning. Her organizational and editorial skills have been invaluable. Noted Civil War historian Michael Parrish and Richard Holland, formerly southern history bibliographer for the University of Texas General Libraries, provided much help in the acquisition phase of the NTC's history. I am especially indebted to Lewis L. Gould, Eugene C. Barker Centennial Professor Emeritus in American History at the University of Texas at Austin, whose skillful and persistent editorial direction brought this book to life. Lew's support for the Center and for our acquisition and promotion of the Natchez Trace Collection has been unfailingly beneficial. I appreciate, too, the hard work of each of the other authors. Their visits to the Center graced us all, and we learned much from their research.

Finally, I am enormously grateful to my friends and colleagues Harold Billings, director of the university's General Libraries, and Sheldon Ekland-Olson, dean of the university's College of Liberal Arts, for their willing and generous financial support for this publication. It is my belief that they stepped forward because they recognized the importance of this volume.

DON E. CARLETON
Director and J. R. Parten Fellow
in the Archives of American History

Inside the
Natchez Trace
Collection

LEWIS L. GOULD

Introduction

In his evocative and powerful book *Mississippi: An American Journey* (1996), Anthony Walton recounts his visits to the state where his parents were born and from which they moved north in the 1950s. They had left in search of a better life than the segregated South then provided to young African Americans. As Walton searches for his roots, his ancestors, and the meaning of slavery, violence, and racism in American life, he ponders the troubled and turbulent history of Mississippi. The state, he finds, is "a baffling place, a dedicated consumer of human dreams." Its name is "the most loaded proper noun in American English." In the end, Walton concludes that "there is something different about Mississippi, something almost unspeakably primal and vicious; something savage unleashed there that has yet to come to rest."[1]

Historians, scholars, and novelists have been grappling with the meaning of southern history and the place of Mississippi in that history for most of the twentieth century. The roster of distinguished writers on the state's past is long and impressive. Their efforts have depended upon the existence of primary sources from the people and institutions of nineteenth-century Mississippi and the Lower South. Accordingly, any discovery of

---

1. Anthony Walton, *Mississippi: An American Journey* (New York: Random House, 1996), 4, 46.

untapped original documents sets off a flurry of new research and writing in the field.

During the past decade, researchers have begun exploration of a vast and rich treasure trove of primary information about Mississippi and the South, the Natchez Trace Collection, now housed at the Center for American History at the University of Texas at Austin. The university acquired the collection from an anonymous individual in 1986, and the way in which the Natchez Trace material was originally assembled itself represents a fascinating episode in the preservation of southern history.

The impetus for the amassing of the collection came during the years following World War I. Anxious to preserve the historical heritage of the South, an amateur collector used knowledge of the local community to acquire legal records and plantation documents throughout the 1920s. Weekend journeys up and down the Mississippi River took this person to plantations, courthouses, lawyers' offices, and private homes. Sometimes the documents had to be purchased for modest sums. On other occasions, the collector's willingness to remove the materials proved sufficient inducement for their donation. As the years passed and the papers continued to accumulate, they were housed in shacks, old slave cabins, and other buildings at the collector's home.

In time, the collection became the property of the heirs of the person who had originally assembled it. Around 1980, the possibility of these materials being put up for sale reached the ears of Don Carleton, director of the Center for American History at the University of Texas at Austin. Over the next few years, negotiations went forward as the owners made clear their desire that the University of Texas at Austin should have the collection if the financial arrangements could be worked out.

University officials recognized the potential historical importance of these materials. The documents, business records, and court records, and the many fascinating personal letters, could provide new information on key aspects of the development of two regions of central significance for the history of the Lower South—the Natchez Trace and Natchez itself. The Natchez Trace was a people's highway into the Old Southwest that flourished from the 1780s to the 1830s. Beginning in Nashville, Tennessee, it moved southwestward across a corner of Alabama and through the heart of Mississippi to Natchez on the Mississippi River. Along the Trace, as many authors have noted, came such persons of historical prominence as Davy Crockett, Andrew Jackson, and Gideon Lincecum. But through its woods and along its paths also traveled the plain folks of the westward migration. The untouched primary sources that were to become the Natchez Trace Collection offered the promise of telling the stories of the anonymous men and women—slaves, Indians, woodsmen, soldiers, capitalists, wives—who peopled the Southwest in the antebellum years.

Equally alluring was the prospect of new insights and fresh documents on the town of Natchez and its slave society in the decades of the Civil War and Reconstruction. Few cities captured more of the tone and spirit of the Old South than Natchez in its heyday, with its proximity to the Mississippi, its nabob aristocracy, and its dependence on the labor of men and women in bondage. The documents being offered to the Center for American History evoked the days when cotton dominated southern agriculture, slavery shaped the lives of black and white in Natchez and its environs, and a sense of sectional crisis loomed beneath every social exchange and business transaction. Names such as Wade Hampton, Jefferson Davis, and John A. Quitman jumped off the dusty pages. The inclusion of the papers of other individuals less well known but important in Natchez's history—such as Richard T. Archer, William L. Sharkey, and Josiah Winchester—suggested that the collection might facilitate a richer understanding of the real inner workings of the cotton culture in the Deep South.

The size of the monetary commitment that the University of Texas was being asked to make naturally prompted the school's higher administration to investigate whether the documents in the collection did in fact warrant such an expenditure of state funds.

In September 1984, I was asked to accompany Richard Holland (then the history bibliographer of the Perry-Castañeda Library) and Don Carleton to Mississippi to examine this collection at the home of its owners. The experience was one of those incandescent moments that historians dream about. There in room after room were original letters and documents, many of them like the ones described in William Faulkner's *Absalom, Absalom!*: "the paper old and faded and falling to pieces, the writing faded, almost indecipherable, yet meaningful, familiar in shape and sense, the name and presence of volatile sentient forces."[2]

Most of the papers were unknown to modern scholars. Tumbled together were letters from Stephen F. Austin, James Wilkinson, Wade Hampton, S. S. Prentiss, and John A. Quitman. A student at Washington and Lee College had his grade reports signed by Robert E. Lee. Plantation records, bank correspondence, songbooks, and family letters spilled out in a cornucopia of southern history. We moved from house to slave cabin, from shed to storage facility, in a day that became a panorama of the Old South in its original state.

The report I filed confirmed what Don Carleton and Dick Holland had also concluded. The material in this collection represented one of the great unexplored treasures of southern history, and the University of Texas at Austin should do all it could to acquire it at the earliest possible date. Negotiations went forward between the owners of the collection and the university administration, and these culminated in 1985 in an agreement to transfer the material. A portion was given outright, and the rest sold for $900,000. By now the documents had gained the informal title "The Natchez Trace Collection," which conveyed a sense of where the material focused geographically without offering any precise indication of the identity of the original owner and compiler.

In December 1985, the Natchez Trace Collection arrived at the University of Texas at Austin in a large moving van, and the task of organizing the papers got under way. On March 10, 1986, a press conference announced the acquisition of the collection. George C. Wright, a member of the history department, observed that "no serious student will be able fully to comprehend and write about slavery without coming to the University of Texas and devoting considerable time to researching the Natchez Trace Collection."[3]

During the decade that has followed the arrival of the Natchez Trace Collection, researchers have begun to explore its many facets and to publish books and articles based on their findings. The task of organizing and

2. William Faulkner, *Absalom, Absalom,* (New York, 1951), 101.

3. The University of Texas at Austin News and Information Service, "On Campus," March 17–23, 1986. This is a news story available from the Center for American History.

cataloging the large body of letters, documents, printed materials, songs, and other artifacts has gone forward as rapidly as the resources of the Center for American History have permitted. Staff members of the Center have organized conferences, spoken about the holdings, and otherwise sought to stimulate interest in the collection. In the process, awareness of the value of the collection has grown in the scholarly community.

As the Center considered ways of bringing information about the Natchez Trace Collection to an even wider audience, Don Carleton, Kate Adams, and I discussed the idea of a book of essays that would provide specific guidance to what the collection contained in the context of existing scholarly research on southern history. During the early 1990s, we invited scholars knowledgeable about the Old South and its history to prepare essays on topics relating to various parts of the collection. Coverage was designed to be partially topical and partially chronological. While the essays could not aspire to be exhaustive discussions of everything the collection contains relating to a particular period or subject, they could provide guideposts to other researchers about what might exist on such topics as slavery, women's roles, the Old Southwest, the politics of the Jacksonian period, the sectional conflict, and the role of businessmen and entrepreneurs in the antebellum period.

The resulting essays make up the body of this book. Working in consultation with Don Carleton, Kate Adams and I selected the authors to take part, and suggested a general topic or chronological period that should be addressed. After that, the authors went their own way and followed their own sense of what made the information in the collection historically significant. Wherever possible, the authors sought to connect the documents in the collection to current issues of historical interest and debate in their profession. They were also encouraged to point readers toward workable research topics and unexplored questions for which the collection might offer new insights and valuable hard evidence.

To discuss the holdings of the collection that bear on the early frontier period of the Old Southwest, John D. W. Guice of the University of Southern Mississippi was a natural choice. He has written extensively about the frontier experience and its ramifications for the history of the region, and he knows intimately the manuscript sources in other repositories that illuminate the newly discovered information in the collection.

His essay focuses on how historians can increase their understanding of this formative period by means of the private papers and government records that have been assembled in the Natchez Trace materials. Guice is especially effective in showing how government, the legal community, and entrepreneurs interacted on this frontier. He also throws light on the complexity of a society where Spanish, French, Native American, and African American influences operated in unexpected and fascinating ways to shape the early history of the Lower South.

Slavery was a pervasive part of life in the Natchez Trace region. Randolph B. Campbell of the University of North Texas brings to the collection's sources on slavery the insights gained from studying the peculiar institution in Texas and the rest of the South during this same period. The collection proves quite revealing of how whites in Mississippi and Louisiana viewed their slaves, ran their plantations, and used their power to maintain the framework of bondage. Despite the obstacles that confront any historian trying to reach the minds of the slaves themselves, Campbell demonstrates that the Natchez Trace Collection can offer additional clues for that vital analytical task.

Katherine J. Adams of the Center for American History has surveyed the Natchez Trace Collection for sources relating to the history of women. Her research indicates how rich a body of untapped material exists within the various subcollections of this archive for understanding the lives and minds of southern women. Family letters convey the rigors of daily life on the plantations, the fascinating interplay between white women and their slaves, and the many areas in which women exerted influence over the development of antebellum society. The range of documents that yield information about aspects of women's history underscores the value of such a cohesive body of primary sources from a single area housed in one place. Adams is especially perceptive regarding the social and familial interconnections that become clear as the component parts of the Natchez Trace Collection are surveyed with the history of women as a primary focus.

Capitalists and entrepreneurs were drawn to the Natchez region by the promise of profit and the lure of riches. With his deep knowledge of primary documents regarding the economic life of the antebellum South, Morton Rothstein of the University of California at Davis was an ideal choice to probe how the collection sheds fresh light on the role of business enterprise in the developing Mississippi economy during the nineteenth century. Ranging across the United States, his essay reveals how sources outside the Center for American History enrich the materials in the collection and emphasizes the value of these new materials for addressing existing historical problems in southern business history.

The last two essays in the book explore how the Natchez Trace Collection illuminates the issues surrounding the Civil War, its causes, and its consequences. Mississippi by the 1850s had become one of the bastions of anti-Union attitudes. Shearer Davis Bowman of the University of Texas at Austin looks at the ways in which people represented in the collection dealt with the breakdown of sectional harmony and moved toward civil strife. Bowman traces the responses of various prominent individuals to the events of the 1850s and 1860s. His work provides excellent guideposts to portions of the collection that contain evidence touching on a number of debated issues surrounding the Civil War and Reconstruction.

Although William G. Shade's essay on the Jacksonian period deals with the 1830s and 1840s, it comes last in the book because it provides a striking example of how research and analysis in the collection can shed new light on substantive issues involving the economic, political, and cultural history of the Old South. In surveying Mississippi in the age of Jackson, Shade, of Lehigh University, finds that the state was more an entrepreneurial frontier in its politics and outlook than a fountain of presecession sentiment. His essay examines in detail how three prominent figures in the state, whose papers are contained in the collection, embodied the turbulent factionalism and "politics of place" in Mississippi. Shade finds that the Natchez materials depict a region with cosmopolitan tastes and attitudes, at least among its ruling elite. His absorbing work suggests the ways in which the collection will modify the perennial debate concerning the genesis of the mindset of the Old South. In so doing, it also offers a superb example of how the information in the collection can inspire new interpretations and provocative insights.

This book does not begin to exhaust the riches of the Natchez Trace Collection. Rather, the essays are designed to hint at the possibilities it contains for fruitful investigation. The original collector, who spent so many days finding and preserving these fragile documents and unique records, did so from a healthy impulse to safeguard a vital aspect of the state and region whose history the person knew so well. The materials that were thus gathered did not reach a scholarly audience for more than half a century, but the Natchez Trace Collection, as it now exists at the University of Texas at Austin, manifests the constructive vision that first impelled its assembler to embark on those journeys of historical excavation and retrieval in the 1920s. The next step is for scholars to explore, classify, and utilize the documents in the collection in the same adventurous spirit. This volume is designed to facilitate and promote that process in the years ahead.

JOHN D. W. GUICE

Windows on the Old Southwest

The Natchez Trace Collection demonstrates anew that the Natchez District was a microcosm of the southern frontier.[1] Slavery and the Civil War so dominate the history of the region that it is not generally viewed as a frontier. In reality, however, the Old Southwest—as historians now designate the southwestern quadrant of the young republic—was as complex a frontier as any in North America.[2] There Britain, France, and Spain expended their final efforts to thwart the growth of the United States. A source of grave concern to the early federal administrations, the presence of these foreign powers led to the purchase of Louisiana and the occupation of Florida. The Old Southwest was also the site of the Creek War and the final battle of the War of 1812—both of which were related to foreign intervention.

1. During the colonial era, Spanish and British authorities used the term *Natchez District* (sometimes just *the Natchez*) to denote a triangle of land with Vicksburg (Walnut Hills) at its apex and the thirty-first parallel at its base. The western side of the triangle was the Mississippi River; the eastern, a line drawn from Vicksburg down to the intersection of the thirty-first parallel with the Pearl River. More precisely, the northern edge of the Natchez District was the mouth of the Yazoo River.

2. As used here, the term *Old Southwest* refers to present-day Mississippi and Alabama, southern Tennessee, western Georgia, western Florida, and southeastern Louisiana. Often northeastern Louisiana and southern Arkansas are also viewed as part of the Old Southwest.

Though these events occurred on the periphery of the Natchez District, within the district itself resided every type of settler, and virtually every type of frontier activity took place there except mining.[3] It was, for instance, the location of incredibly complex land grants and of the nation's most enormous and most corrupt land speculations, the Yazoo Land Companies. The region was home to some of the South's most prosperous planters and merchants as well as some of the nation's most cantankerous squatters and pioneer farmers. There Celtic cattle raisers watched their herds of cattle and swine multiply in the piney woods region and on the Gulf coastal plains. Atop the bluff at Natchez developed one of the most urbane, sophisticated, and cosmopolitan towns in the American West; beneath the bluff emerged one of the roughest and raunchiest but also economically significant ports on any western river. Well into the nineteenth century, Natchez-under-the-Hill was second only to New Orleans in trade and probably its equal in debauchery.[4]

Though the Natchez District bordered the Choctaw Nation and was across the Mississippi from numerous smaller tribes of American Indians, there were relatively few encounters with large numbers of Indians within the district itself. Such activity was limited to small bands of discontented Choctaw occasionally roaming the region. Regarding the African American slaves, Randolph B. Campbell discusses the extent to which the Natchez Trace Collection pertains to them, but their role as frontiersmen is seldom recognized. Although they may have played such roles only reluctantly or involuntarily, they made untold contributions to the clearing and cultivation of land, and functioned as cowboys and Indian fighters. Of course, the relationship between African Americans and American Indians was an intricate one, which has generally been ignored by scholars. Nor has much attention been paid to the role of free blacks in the Old Southwest, except perhaps in the cities of Natchez and New Orleans.[5]

3. Eventually, iron, coal, and a few other minerals were mined in Alabama and Tennessee, areas outside of the Natchez District.

4. Michael F. Beard, "Natchez-Under-the-Hill, 1790–1840: A Reinterpretation" (honor's thesis, University of Southern Mississippi, 1971); Beard, "Frontier Port on the Mississippi: A History of the Legend of Natchez-Under-the-Hill, 1800–1900" (master's thesis, Louisiana State University, 1981).

5. Many of the above topics are developed more fully in Thomas D. Clark and John D. W. Guice, *Frontiers in Conflict: The Old Southwest, 1795–1830* (Albuquerque: University

What is the usefulness of the Natchez Trace Collection in the writing of the history of the Old Southwest during the early national and antebellum periods? While many of the large subcollections may appear to relate to relatively narrow fields, each of them contains an astounding array of primary sources. Below are brief descriptions of some papers that were surveyed in preparation for this essay.

Among the richest and most varied collections is the Winchester Family Papers, which contains sources for social, intellectual, legal, and economic history as well as an abundance of genealogical and biographical data. This collection also reveals much about the contacts between Natchez and the Eastern Seaboard, particularly New England. In addition, from George Winchester's correspondence with family members one can glean insights into the attitudes toward and roles of women in the society.

Similarly, the papers of banker Gabriel Tichenor (in the Bank of the State of Mississippi Records) also relate to an impressive array of topics. In particular, this collection discloses much about the national significance of Natchez and the economic interrelationships between the Natchez District and eastern cities. Another set of papers important to students of the economic history of the region are those of James Campbell Wilkins. In addition to casting light on business activities in general, this subcollection contains information on the role of the army in improving the Natchez Trace, the important road connecting Natchez on the Mississippi River with Nashville on the Cumberland. It seems reasonable to hope that the Natchez Trace Collection will stimulate interest in the economic history of the Old Southwest, a topic largely neglected except as it pertains to agriculture and slavery.

A key section of the collection for this period is the Provincial and Territorial Records, which pertain to a wide range of topics. One portion of these records consists of French documents of the late colonial and early national periods, relating primarily to settlements at Avoyelles, Baton Rouge, Iberville, Natchez, Natchitoches, Ouachita, Opelousas, and Pointe Coupée.[6] The balance of the subcollection includes a variety of important

of New Mexico Press, 1989). The bibliography in this work is extremely useful to researchers in the Natchez Trace Collection.

6. For a reasonably detailed preliminary inventory of the Louisiana colonial documents, see *Le Racenteur, Le Comité des Archives de Louisiana*, vol. 14 (April 1994).

records, primarily in English, such as land grants, correspondence of Spanish governors of Natchez, sundry petitions regarding the governance of Natchez, and other assorted documents relating to such topics as the cattle industry, slavery under the Spanish regime, Spanish policies toward British and American settlers, the powers of Spanish governors, and economic conditions in Natchez. Although copies of some of these documents are in French and Spanish archives at Paris and Seville, their availability here provides another measure of the importance of the Natchez Trace Collection.

The B. L. C. Wailes Papers, though consisting of only two folders, are of great value for filling in missing pieces in the history of Jefferson College, an institution of higher education in Washington, about six miles northeast of Natchez. Many of the papers concern the financial structure of the college, which, to an extent, was based on land holdings around the territory.[7] Others, however, deal with academic matters and board politics. It is unfortunate that Charles Sydnor did not have these papers when he wrote his biography of Wailes.[8] The even smaller file of Levin Wailes papers pertains primarily to matters before the Jefferson College Board.

The Minor Family Papers, owing to the prominence of Stephen Minor, contain considerable information concerning governance, litigation, and business. A native of Pennsylvania, Minor migrated to New Orleans during the Revolution, and in 1781 became adjutant to the commandant at the Natchez post. There he served as an effective subordinate to Natchez commandants and, after 1789, to the governor until 1797, when he became the last Spanish governor of the Natchez District. After the formation of the Mississippi Territory, Stephen Minor remained active in Natchez business and politics, as would his descendants.

While the strength of the NTC resides in the major subcollections, a

---

7. Now property of the Mississippi Department of Archives and History, Jefferson College is undergoing restoration. On the grounds there is a library of primary and secondary sources relating to the college. The B. L. C. Wailes Papers, Box 2E514, also contain letters relating to the sale of Jefferson College land.

8. Charles S. Sydnor, *A Gentleman of the Old Natchez Region: Benjamin L. C. Wailes* (Durham, N.C.: Duke University Press, 1938). Sydnor relied extensively on the Benjamin L. C. Wailes Papers at Duke University in his research for this excellent commentary on the social and intellectual climate of the Natchez District.

myriad of subjects are covered in a host of smaller subcollections. Though time consuming to search, these manuscripts contain important tidbits of data that one can easily overlook. Hence, researchers should at least examine the papers of persons and organizations connected to their studies. Some of the files useful for the study of the Old Southwest include Jefferson College; Jenkins; Lafayette; Lintot; Marshalk; McCabb; McCall; The Nashville, New Orleans, and Felicia Mail Company; Norrell; Nugent; Turpin; Oakland College; Phillips; Pinckneyville, Mississippi, church records; Poindexter; and the Port Gibson Herald and Correspondent.[9]

The first category of history to be explored with regard to the collection is biography. Though a researcher can learn much about women from the collection (as Katherine Adams has demonstrated in her essay), the documents relate primarily to men—whether they were powerful, famous, infamous, or obscure. Obviously, George Winchester himself is the personality about whom most is revealed in the papers bearing his name. They provide a nucleus for a short monograph, a master's thesis, or a series of articles that would reflect a considerable amount of Natchez legal, financial, and social history. Indeed, there is hardly an aspect of Natchez history not touched upon in this collection.

Moreover, Winchester's poetic prose stands in marked contrast to the style of most professional and business people today. Although his literacy permeates his entire written record, Winchester's prose is particularly moving when he philosophizes on the death of a friend whose "soul was conversing with the visions of eternity." Winchester remarks:

> How grand is the rapid departure of so great a soul! When I contemplate it, I scarcely know in what course the imagination should pursue. Is he now hovering around our Earth, accompanying her in her swift course and viewing at a glance all the pursuits and busy scenes of her inhabitants. Does he perceive at a distance the storms of war brooding across the ocean . . . , or has his soul mingled in the

9. Because many of the manuscripts pertain to the territorial period, 1798–1817, researchers will find helpful Robert V. Haynes, "A Political History of the Mississippi Territory" (Ph.D. diss., Rice Institute, 1958). Also see his "Historians and the Mississippi Territory," *Journal of Mississippi History* 29 (November 1967): 409–28.

throng of Heroes & Statesmen & Philosophers who graced with him the early dawnings of American greatness, and departed before him to eternal mansions, or is he swallowed up in an eternity whatever he may now do, . . . however amazing the scenery behind the curtain where he has withdrawn for eternity, to his society who remains, to his townsmen, to his citizens of America and to many Philosophers of Europe, there seems the loss of a vast luminary blotted from our literary Hemisphere, and the broad beams of light which he has left behind, serve to draw our eyes to the path of his departure, and arouse the startling inquiry, where is he!

Winchester closes with the benediction "Bless be with him for eternity."[10]

Stephen Minor is one of the numerous men of prominence mentioned in the George Winchester Papers. Others include George Poindexter, Stephen Duncan, Andrew Marschalk, and Isaac Guion. Many well-known names also appear in the Bank of the State of Mississippi Records, among them Stephen Duncan and Thomas Freeman. Both of these large collections, however, include references to literally hundreds of persons.

The Provincial and Territorial Records also contain significant biographical material. Some of the easily recognizable personalities include—in addition to many of those already listed—Daniel Clark, Charles de Grand Pre, Manuel Gayoso de Lemos, and Reuben Kemper. Neither is it any surprise that numerous important figures are noted in the B. L. C. Wailes Papers. A few of these are David Holmes, George L. Gaines, and Silas Dinsmoor. Many smaller subcollections contain references to most of the familiar personalities in the other sets.

Whether the papers are those of an attorney, a banker, a planter, or a merchant, it is likely that the files can aid social and intellectual historians in studying how various types of people in the Old Southwest lived and thought. Scholars interested in such topics as modes of living, health, religion, and the intellectual climate in the Old Southwest will find the Natchez Trace Collection a valuable resource. A variety of documents reveal how homes were furnished, what people wore, and the kinds of diets

10. George Winchester to unidentified "Friend Stevens," January 29, 1820, Winchester Papers, Box 2E903.

they enjoyed (or endured, as the case may be), as well as how much many of these things cost them.

Another universal characteristic of the collections is the extent to which they illustrate the closeness of family ties. Virtually every personal letter offers news about parents, siblings, cousins, uncles, and aunts. Correspondents invariably requested similar information in return. The frequent references to the pain of separation from loved ones make evident the emotional cost of migration into the Old Southwest and underscore the economic potential that nevertheless lured pioneers of all classes to distant lands.

Correspondence throughout the NTC shows that much of the Old Southwest was not a healthful place to reside. It was a rare letter to family that did not contain references to illnesses, death, or the oppressive climate. A frequent complaint was fevers, the yellow fever being the most dreaded. Many families traveled to their country estates or visited relatives away from Natchez during the fever season.[11] So did natives of New Orleans, who vacationed annually along the Mississippi Gulf coast or to the north of Lake Pontchartrain.

Researchers will also find in the collection commentary on religion, some of which addresses the problematic realities of frontier life. For instance, a letter to George Winchester from Pascagoula in 1846 refers to the custom of legitimatizing a de facto marriage and to the Spanish law which recognized the legitimacy of the offspring of marriages consummated prior to the benefit of clergy. The writer asked Winchester to locate witnesses who then resided in Natchez and who could testify to the existence of a particular marriage. As the frontier moved across the South, most settlers were Baptists, Methodists, or Presbyterians, while the Episcopal Church remained strong among the upper class, especially in Natchez, where George Winchester was a vestryman. Writing to the Reverend Edward Read of Grahamsville, South Carolina, Winchester judged that "an increase in the congregation and the renting of pews" would provide "a more liberal salary." Unfortunately, records in the file do not indicate

---

11. For example, Gabriel Tichenor wrote James C. Wilkins, "I am glad to find that you left town at the beginning of the fever & hope you will remain in the country until it entirely disappears." Tichenor to Wilkins, October 21, [year illegible], postmarked Port Gibson, Bank of the State of Mississippi Records, Box 2E971.

whether or not the Reverend Mr. Read accepted the call to become rector, but the letter does offer a measure of the optimism and vitality of Natchez Episcopalians in the 1840s.[12] Correspondence indicates that Winchester may have given a large donation in Jackson, Mississippi, for the construction of Saint Andrew's Protestant Episcopal Church. Sprinkled through the Natchez Trace Collection are numerous other references to the importance of religion in the Natchez District.

By the opening decade of the nineteenth century, a rigorous intellectual climate existed in Natchez. D. Clayton James, William B. Hamilton, and Charles Sydnor are among the historians who have emphasized the literacy of the privileged classes there.[13] Winchester was among their number. One of the first documents encountered in his vast papers is the long 1820 letter, quoted above, in which he waxes poetic about the soul of a departed friend. Today one would expect to find such contemplations of the afterlife only in a theological journal. Clearly he loved to write, and it would be interesting to discover if he availed himself of the columns offered by newspaper publishers. Like many cultured men in the antebellum South, Winchester occasionally used Latin for emphasis. William M. Green, who chided Winchester for resorting to Latin, wrote, "I always tho't you were intended by nature for a schoolmaster." Green then described himself as "a mere countryman, a clod hopper, a man who has been deprived of the advantages, all important advantages, of a collegiate education."[14] Among the many pieces of evidence of Winchester's continuing academic interests are his subscriptions to the *New England Historical & Genealogical Register* and the *Antiquarian Journal*.

12. George Winchester to the Reverend Edward Read, Natchez, March 26, 1846, Winchester Papers, Box 2E903. There is a collection of records of Trinity Episcopal Church of Natchez in the Mississippi Department of Archives and History.

13. D. Clayton James, *Antebellum Natchez* (1968; rpr. Baton Rouge: Louisiana State University Press, 1993); William B. Hamilton, "American Beginnings in the Old Southwest: The Mississippi Phase" (Ph.D. diss., Duke University, 1937); Sydnor, *Benjamin L. C. Wailes*. Also see Hamilton, "The Southwestern Frontier, 1795–1817: An Essay in Social History," *Journal of Southern History* 10 (November 1944): 389–403. Hamilton also wrote other articles on social history, and his vast collection of papers in the Duke University Archives contains thousands of notes on the subject. His outstanding dissertation (listed above) remains one of the most authoritative sources on the Old Southwest.

14. Wm. M. Green to George Winchester, Greenville, Miss., March 2, 1836, Winchester Papers, Box 2E903.

One of the best-known intellectuals of the Natchez District was Benjamin L. C. Wailes, whose papers substantiate that reputation. He complained to D. Appleton & Co. when issues of the *Journal of the Academy of Science* failed to arrive, and also subscribed to *Silliman's Journal*, published in New Haven, Connecticut. Of his varied academic activities, none seems to have brought him more pleasure than the promotion of Jefferson College through his role as a member of its board of trustees. His papers include numerous copies of correspondence by other trustees. Frequent subjects include the curriculum, the faculty, and the lands, which were an important source of revenue.[15]

Jefferson College accepted its first students in 1811 and kept its doors open—finally as a boys' prep school—until the 1960s. One wonders if its curriculum was ever more demanding than it was in 1811, when students studied Latin, Greek, ancient classics, mathematics, geography, and natural philosophy. For the privilege of studying these subjects students in 1830 paid a tuition fee of twenty-five dollars per academic year.[16] Correspondence indicates that some students were neither bright nor highly motivated.

Applicants for faculty positions at Jefferson College generally boasted degrees and certificates from New England institutions, though one of the applicants had graduated from the United States Military Academy at West Point. Letters on the subject of college lands contain more information regarding land prices and methods of financing than about the college itself. Depending on the circumstances, purchase offers ranged from two to over six dollars per acre. One buyer offered to pay for the land over three years at 8.5 percent interest. Some of the college lands were in Choctaw cessions.[17]

15. The Levin Wailes Papers also contain information relating to the Jefferson College Board of Trustees.

16. William T. Blain, *Education in the Old Southwest: A History of Jefferson College, Washington, Mississippi* (Washington, Miss.: Friends of Jefferson College, Inc., 1976); Charles M. Newton to David Holmes, Washington, Mont., August 11, 1811, B. L. C. Wailes Papers, Box 2E514; Receipts signed by Levin Wailes, Bank of the State of Mississippi Records, Box 2E976.

17. Letters in the B. L. C. Wailes Papers show that in 1832 the college advertised for sale 23,000 acres of land in a Choctaw cession, but they do not indicate when and for what price the land was sold. The Jefferson College Records, Box 2E562, also contain correspondence concerning Jefferson College lands. The Ezra McCall Papers, Box 2E567, contains records of the Board of Land Commissioners West of the Pearl River.

                              *   *   *

Business history, a topic to which Morton Rothstein's essay in this volume
is devoted, is another field that will be rewarded by work in the Natchez
Trace Collection. Considering that Natchez for decades was second in importance only to New Orleans as a Mississippi River port, it is not surprising that the collection abounds in records of business activities in the Old
Southwest. While the Wilkins Papers are rich in business-related documents, no collection reveals as much about the profession of banking as
the Bank of the State of Mississippi Records. To a large extent, this bank
was a barometer of economic activity of the entire region, including Louisiana. Researchers unfamiliar with the history of banking will be surprised
at the number of transactions between this institution and banks throughout the Mississippi and Ohio River Valleys. Clearly, the Bank of the State
of Mississippi was a major provider of credit for the entire Natchez District, but only competent business historians can ascertain the degree to
which it accelerated economic growth. To what extent did it provide
credit for crops? How lucrative was it to its stockholders?

In a sense, it is impossible to consider the history of banking in Natchez
apart from its economic and urban history. The Bank collection is virtually a mirror of the community's business activity. These documents also
indicate the close association of Natchez with Concordia and Pointe
Coupée Parishes across the river in Louisiana, a fact often noted by students of the region's planter class.[18] As mentioned above, the Bank Records are complemented in this regard by several other collections, such as
the Wilkins Papers and Winchester Papers. Many of the documents in the
Provincial and Territorial Records, especially petitions to the Spanish
governor, also reflect the early economic development of the region, as do
several documents in smaller subcollections.

Heavy indebtedness is one of the themes of plantation history, and
ample evidence of the financial embarrassment of the gentry is not difficult to uncover in the Natchez Trace Collection. Among the Bank Records in particular are many letters from farmers and planters who complain of a variety of financial exigencies in their requests for an extension

18. Documents throughout the Natchez Trace Collection also substantiate the considerable social and economic exchange between the Natchez District and the Feliciana Parishes of Louisiana below the thirty-first parallel.

of time for the repayment of their loans from the bank. In a letter to Bank of the State of Mississippi cashier Gabriel Tichenor, for example, C. B. Green thanked the bank board "for the indulgences they were pleased to extend to me," and then he asked Tichenor to quietly sell some of his bank stock. "Do not for God's sake," Green pleaded, "mention that it is my stock you are offering." After inquiring of stock prices, Green concluded by begging Tichenor to "keep the secret, if you please." A few weeks later, when he mailed Tichenor certificates for thirty shares of bank stock, Green wrote, "I have made a totally great crop, but not a lock of it is ready for market, nor cannot be for some time." After further news of improvements on his place, Green pleaded again, "Do what you can for me."[19] As one would expect, records illustrate that it was not uncommon for the bank and other creditors to foreclose and that on occasion protracted litigation ensued.

Throughout the Natchez Trace Collection one finds invoices, inventories, and receipts showing retail and wholesale prices of virtually every type of item and commodity marketed in the region: groceries, utensils, hardware, tools, machines, notions, cloth, clothing, jewelry, books, office supplies, liquor and wine, medicine, agricultural commodities, timber and lumber, and livestock. And of course there are records indicating the value of slaves and land. Significantly, various collections, especially the Provincial and Territorial Records, indicate that a cattle business thrived in the Natchez District, thus supporting the recent recognition of a significant cattle industry in the antebellum South. A strong case has been made that more people sustained themselves in the Old Southwest by raising cattle than by any other means until the emergence of the cotton kingdom and the removal of the American Indians after the War of 1812. Historians Forrest McDonald and Grady McWhiney contend that the value of livestock in the South in 1860 exceeded the value of cotton.[20] The Natchez District cattle business reflected by the NTC included a

19. C. B. Green to Gabriel Tichenor, November 25, December 2, 1819, Bank of the State of Mississippi Records, Box 2E951.

20. Forrest McDonald and Grady McWhiney, "The South from Self-Sufficiency to Peonage: An Interpretation," *American Historical Review* 85 (December 1980), 1095–1118. Also see Grady McWhiney, *Cracker Culture: Celtic Ways in the Old South* (Tuscaloosa, Ala.: University of Alabama Press, 1988).

lively trade with Louisiana and Texas. During the colonial and early national periods, planters raised so many cattle that one could argue their plantations were actually ranches.

Not often do historians consider the impact of the U.S. Army on the economy of frontier communities. Perhaps this is because most of the data are buried in the records of the War Department, records used primarily by military historians mainly interested in strategies, tactics, and logistics. Although supplies and equipment are extremely important logistic concerns, military historians seldom show interest in the extent to which an army post affected the local economy. Both the Bank Records and the Wilkins Papers help bridge this gap by shedding important light on how individuals and communities profited from the military presence.

In 1801 and 1802, troops from Fort Adams were assigned to improve the road from Fort Adams to Natchez and the Natchez Trace up to Grindstone Ford on Bayou Pierre.[21] Though the Trace ran from Natchez up to Nashville, the road along the Mississippi from New Orleans to Natchez was actually an extension of it. Some of the cargoes from Mississippi and Ohio River boats were sold at Natchez, but New Orleans was the ultimate destination of most. After the sale of the cargoes and boats there, the boatmen walked or rode up to Natchez and from there to Nashville and points beyond. Because of more favorable prices and the availability of the preferred ponies from the Opelousas region of Louisiana, many of the boatmen purchased mounts in Natchez.[22] Often, however, groups of boatmen walked up the Trace.

The merchant under contract to supply army troops for the improvement of this heavily trafficked route was Charles Wilkins of Lexington, Kentucky, an uncle of James Campbell Wilkins.[23] His contracts, which included Fort Stoddard, Fort Deposit, and Fort Adams, were quite lucrative.

21. Grindstone Ford on Bayou Pierre was the northernmost point on the Natchez Trace before it entered the Choctaw Nation. It is not far to the east of present-day Vicksburg. For years Daniel Burnet operated a stand there.

22. A significant livestock industry thrived in the Opelousas region of Louisiana, to the west of Baton Rouge. The Opelousas pony should not be confused with the appaloosa, a breed of saddle horse developed in the Pacific Northwest.

23. A small collection of the papers of Charles Wilkins is in the Filson Club Library in Louisville, Kentucky.

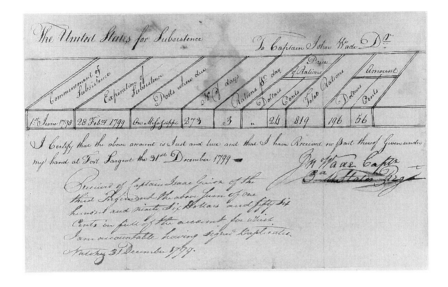

An account for provisions used by United States troops from June 1, 1798, to February 28, 1799, while they established forts for the protection of the Natchez Trace. *From the James C. Wilkins Papers, NTC, the Center for American History, the University of Texas at Austin.*

Letters to and from Nathaniel Evans, agent for Charles Wilkins at Fort Adams, contain inventories, orders, and receipts that disclose considerable information regarding the equipment and supplies used at Fort Adams and on the road project.[24]

These papers reveal much about army life at Fort Adams and about the work of the soldiers on the Trace, since they indicate both the kinds of supplies and equipment used and how much they cost. Though some of the supplies were shipped from the Ohio Valley, significant quantities were also purchased in the Natchez District and in New Orleans. Such purchases clearly had a positive impact on the local economy. Though army pay, especially for enlisted men, was not high, expenditures by the officers and soldiers provided another welcome source of cash flow. When used together with records of the War and Treasury Departments, the Natchez Trace Collection provides a more complete record of the impact of the army on the Old Southwest. Moreover, War Department records indicate that in a frontier setting the military often provided a wide variety of assistance in addition to building roads and bridges.[25] Thus besides the purely economic issues, the overall relationship between the military and civilian populations in the Old Southwest bears closer scrutiny, and the NTC should prove a valuable resource in that regard.

Until quite recently, historians of both the early frontier and the trans-Mississippi West paid little attention to the persistent economic and family contacts between those regions and the older states, particularly along the Atlantic seaboard. Numerous documents in the Natchez Trace Collection verify that the Natchez financial and legal communities maintained frequent associations with their counterparts back east, especially in New England, New York, and Philadelphia. As one would expect, they also had associates in southern cities such as Lexington, Louisville, Nashville, and Mobile.[26]

24. Nathaniel Evans to Charles Wilkins, Fort Adams, December 20, 1801, January 30, May 19, June 10, 1802, James Campbell Wilkins Papers, Box 2E540.

25. Cynthia Ann Meade Sullivan, "An Analysis of Letters of the Secretary of War as Sources for the Writing of Mississippi History, 1800–1814" (master's thesis, University of Southern Mississippi, 1987).

26. During the last decade the self-styled New Western Historians have emphasized the

Of the collections searched in preparation for this essay, the manu-scripts in the Winchester files best illustrate the importance of East-West connections. There is ample correspondence to and from all of the areas mentioned above. Although he moved to Natchez from Massachusetts in 1820, George Winchester maintained an active association with family and business interests in his native state throughout his career. As much as twenty-five years after his arrival Winchester continued to receive nu-merous letters from home regarding financial and legal matters. A good example is an inquiry of November 1845 from a Salem businessman who employed Winchester to collect payment on a mortgage of a steam engine located in a Natchez cotton factory. The Salem financier who held the $1,200 mortgage described the machine as "one Steam engine of twenty horse power, manufactured by Steleman and Co. at the Novelty Works, New York."[27] Judging from the number of inquiries in the Winchester pa-pers, much of the machinery used in the Natchez District was manufac-tured in New York and New England.

Because his files contain so many requests for Winchester to collect various notes and mortgages for Salem creditors, one wonders whether he generated those investments or whether New England simply was a pri-mary source of finance in the South during the antebellum period. To what extent was Winchester a broker for Massachusetts creditors? Did he enjoy an advantage because of his New England connections? The answer is a definite yes. On the other hand, in what situations and to what extent did Winchester's Yankee contacts place him at a disadvantage in a south-ern community?

Winchester also maintained business relationships with other financial

---

continuing relationship between the older states and the territories and states of the trans-Mississippi West. This theme, however, was introduced over twenty years ago. See, for ex-ample, Lewis L. Gould, *Wyoming: A Political History, 1868–1896* (New Haven, Conn.: Yale University Press, 1968) and John D. W. Guice, *The Rocky Mountain Bench: The Territorial Supreme Courts of Colorado, Montana, and Wyoming, 1861–1890* (New Haven, Conn.: Yale University Press, 1972). In his extensive study of large slaveholders, my colleague William K. Scarborough also finds that these families were in frequent communication with business associates and relatives throughout the United States. Scarborough attempts to identify every person in the country who owned at least 250 slaves for his forthcoming book, *The Planter Dynasty*. The Natchez Trace Collection is included in Scarborough's sources.

27. Geo. F. Chever to George Winchester, Salem, November 10, 1845, Box 2E905.

centers. Among other examples, his files contain correspondence with Isaac Phillips, a New York merchant with a Wall Street address. Phillips was a dealer in British, French, and German firearms, cutlery, jewelry, and sundry other products. Other letters indicate that Winchester was often retained by distant businessmen to collect mortgages, notes, and other debts. His clients had addresses in such distant cities as Philadelphia and Richmond. Correspondence from Richmond probably reflects the impact of the Panic of 1837 as well as the extensive nature of Winchester's practice. "We are extremely desirous of closing up our unsettled accounts in the South," wrote Lancaster, Darby, and Company in the opening line of their letter, which indicated that they had extended credit to a number of individuals in Natchez. It is a safe assumption that Natchez, with its numerous Virginia connections, was a natural market for Richmond creditors. Was the Lancaster firm simply cleaning up its accounts receivable in Natchez? Or was the letter an indication that Natchez was feeling the impact of the Panic of 1837? In his authoritative study of antebellum Natchez, D. Clayton James states that the Natchez economy did not recover from that depression until the mid-1840s.[28]

Though the Winchester Papers are representative of the truly national connections of the Natchez business and professional community, they are by no means unique in this respect within the Natchez Trace Collection. The Bank of the State of Mississippi Records, for example, also contain letters originating in a long list of distant localities. Indeed, virtually all of the subcollections reflect the attention focused on the Old Southwest by residents of all parts of the country.

It is impossible to discuss the national connections maintained by Natchez District inhabitants without emphasizing the pervasiveness of the American view of the Old Southwest as a land of opportunity, particularly after the War of 1812 ended and after millions of acres of Indian land were opened to settlers. During the postwar decade there was such a stream of migrants into the Mississippi Territory that the attraction to the region became known throughout the nation and even in Europe as the "Ala-

28. Isaac Phillips to George Winchester, New York, April 18, 1837, Winchester Papers, Box 2E903; Lancaster, Darby, and Company to George Winchester, Richmond, November 11, 1837, Winchester Papers, Box 2E904; James, *Antebellum Natchez*, 166.

bama Fever." Joseph G. Baldwin, who participated in this boom, describes it in his *Flush Times of Alabama and Mississippi*, which stands as one of the great classics in the field of southwestern humor.[29]

The lure of the Old Southwest as a region ripe for exploitation is illustrated by a revealing letter from I. W. Proder written in Danvers, Massachusetts, on January 13, 1820. A young student of the law, Proder sought advice from Winchester regarding prospects at the bar in Natchez. Obviously, the lad had read and heard of the opportunities in the Old Southwest, but he was a bit apprehensive. Perhaps he could work as a tutor while attempting to establish a practice.

Proder explained that he was also considering Huntsville, Alabama. "But then," he wrote, "the number of lawyers already there, compared with the number of inhabitants in the vicinity, is rather appalling. On this account I should not hesitate much, were all other circumstances favorable." After relating that one of his friends in Huntsville had already left that city for Savannah, Proder continued, "Could I obtain a situation to instruct either in an academy or respectable private family with a handsome compensation (say about 1000 dollars), I should be willing to accept it, not with a view of making it a permanent business, but as a convenient means in aiding me in my view of the Country."[30] The aspiring young attorney evidently recognized that opportunities abounded in Natchez and its environs.

In addition to its potential usefulness for the major historical inquiries thus far discussed, the Natchez Trace Collection contains material relating to a host of other subjects. One of the most interesting is legal history, several aspects of which are brought to life by documents in various sections of the archive.

Even during the Spanish dominion, settlers in the Natchez District were a litigious lot. And after the organization of the Mississippi Territory, lawyers had a field day unsnarling the incredible tangle of land titles.[31] On

29. Joseph G. Baldwin, *The Flush Times of Alabama and Mississippi* (1853; rpr. Baton Rouge: Louisiana State University Press, 1987).

30. I. W. Proder to George Winchester, Danvers, January 13, 1820, Winchester Papers, Box 2E903.

31. The Provincial and Territorial Records contain innumerable references to litigation

no other frontier was there such an assortment of conflicting claims. Not only did the courts and land commissions have to contend with the confusion resulting from overlapping French, Spanish, and British land grants, but in some areas they also had to deal with the legacies of Georgia's abortive Bourbon County and two different sets of Georgia's Yazoo land companies. To make matters worse (or better, for the lawyers), just before transferring the Natchez District to American authorities, Spanish officials issued a number of land claims which they dated prior to the signing of the Treaty of San Lorenzo on October 27, 1795. Attorneys collected handsome fees from the resulting disputes as well as from everyday civil practices in a region of such intense commercial activity. Criminal cases provided a considerably less steady source of income.

While evidence of the litigious disposition of Natchezians is spread throughout the Natchez Trace Collection, it particularly abounds in the Winchester Papers. The thousands of documents there, representing dozens of types of legal actions, should prove tantalizing to legal historians. These files seem to prompt comparison of the importance of the bar and bench in the Natchez District with that of the Rocky Mountains. In both instances, the legal profession contributed to economic development and stability. The legal portions of the Winchester Papers are useful for biographers and genealogists as well. It is interesting, for instance, how frequently Stephen Minor appears as a litigant in the Winchester records.[32]

Winchester's practice was as varied as it was extensive. In addition to his real estate work, he represented many merchants, brokers, and financiers in a wide range of civil cases. He also settled estates and handled

during the Spanish dominion. Numerous petitions to the governor of Natchez enable scholars to compare Spanish administrative justice with British-American jurisprudence. To what extent, for instance, did Spanish administrative law influence decisions and codes after the formation of the Mississippi Territory in 1798? On the land disputes, see Clark and Guice, *Frontiers in Conflict*, 67–82.

32. William B. Hamilton, *Anglo-American Law on the Frontier: Thomas Rodney & His Territorial Cases* (Durham, N.C.: Duke University Press, 1953); Hamilton, "The Transmission of English Law to the Frontier of America," *South Atlantic Quarterly* 67 (1968): 243–64; Guice, *The Rocky Mountain Bench*; Winchester Papers, Box 2E903. It is interesting that Hamilton, who criticized Frederick Jackson Turner's frontier thesis at every opportunity, used the term *lodestone* to describe the power of Natchez to attract people from around the world. In many ways one can compare Natchez with a mining town.

many other matters in chancery. Judging by his correspondence, Winchester derived a considerable income from collection of debts, for which he received from 2.5 to 6 percent. Apparently, Winchester devoted little of his practice to criminal cases. Copies of statements to his clients for other types of cases indicate that his fees often amounted to one hundred dollars. Of course, he often received considerably more. "If Mr. Gayoso can afford it I think he ought to pay me a fee in advance of at least three hundred dollars," Winchester wrote. "This amount would be a small compensation for the labors, expense, and trouble I have already incurred in his suit."[33]

Besides revealing much about the nature of law practice in antebellum Natchez, Winchester's files contain documentation of his library. Receipts and other documents depict him as an avid student of the law who purchased a large number of books to satisfy his eclectic interests. Attorneys in Natchez, as on all of the nation's frontiers, relied heavily on the precedents established through case law in the older states. Winchester's library included codes and reports from throughout the nation. Considering both the library lists and the legal records, it seems likely that the Winchester collection constitutes the largest single set of papers of an attorney in Natchez and possibly in the entire South. Their sheer volume provides a challenge for scholars who wish to analyze them in detail, and raises questions regarding Winchester's representativeness among Natchez attorneys.[34] How many lawyers in the Natchez District enjoyed such extensive practices? Was his practice typical for Natchez and the South as a whole? Who among his peers were more learned students of the law?

Another topic addressable in view of the NTC is the role of the Spanish governor of the Natchez District. This subject, on which the Provincial and Territorial Records shed much light, is closely related to legal history because the actions of the governor amounted to administrative law. Though some of the documents are letters and decrees, many of them are petitions seeking resolutions for disputes and grievances of every imagin-

33. Winchester to unidentified addressee, Natchez, November 19, 1838, Winchester Papers, Box 2E903.
34. Dunbar Rowland, *Courts, Judges, and Lawyers in Mississippi* (Jackson, Miss.: Mississippi Department of Archives and History, 1935).

An indenture, dated July 8, 1794, by which James Smith bound his seven-year-old son, Prestwood Smith, to his brother William Smith until the age of twenty-one "to learn the Art or Mystery of a Silver-smith during which Term his Master's secrets he shall keep." *From the NTC Provincial and Territorial Records, the Center for American History, the University of Texas at Austin.*

able kind. Often petitioners sought the settlement of various types of business disputes, such as damages, property ownership, and debts. Indeed, from careful analysis of these petitions one can reconstruct to a significant degree the economy of Natchez during the late colonial period. At times, however, petitioners' concerns had to do with inheritance, paternity, and a wide range of other problems. Generally lengthy and detailed, the petitions impart quite a bit of information concerning virtually every aspect of life in the District. Because there are a number of extant Spanish censuses from the 1790s, it would be possible to calculate the percentage of residents who petitioned the governor.[35] Can one assume that the data contained in the petitions also describe the lives of the many settlers who did not sign petitions?

The Provincial and Territorial Records also facilitate a measure of the considerable power of the governor, since they contain hundreds of petitions to Manuel Gayoso de Lemos and orders signed by him which illustrate beautifully his exercise of authority. These documents depict him as a man of action and decision who was not reluctant, when the situation demanded, to incarcerate offenders. Some problems he resolved by decree; for others he ordered arbitration. The NTC items thus substantiate D. Clayton James, who describes Gayoso as fair, competent, tactful, and popular with both the elite and the common people, by offering tangible demonstrations of the governors' use of his legislative, administrative, and judicial powers.[36] The Provincial and Territorial Records also contain papers from a protracted legal battle over real estate between the heirs of Gayoso and the heirs of Stephen Minor.

Because Spain controlled the Natchez District for so long, most Ameri-

35. For an account of census material, see the Natchez Database Project prepared by G. Douglas Inglis at the Armstrong Natchez Library, Natchez. Inglis spent two years searching Spanish archives while writing his Ph.D. dissertation at Texas Christian University.

36. Jack D. L. Holmes, *Gayoso: The Life of a Spanish Governor in the Mississippi Valley, 1789–1799* (Baton Rouge: Louisiana State University Press, 1965); James, *Antebellum Natchez,* 32–33. Holmes, who dedicated much of his career as a historian to the Spanish rule of Louisiana and Florida, was a prolific contributor to periodicals in Louisiana and Mississippi. Many of his articles are edited Spanish documents relating to the Natchez District. Though Holmes probably discovered copies of some of the documents in the Colonial Manuscripts in the Spanish archives, it is unfortunate that he did not have access to the Natchez Trace Collection.

cans assume that many Spaniards lived there, when actually the vast majority of the population was British or British-American. Wisely, the officials attempted to govern the district in a spirit of accommodation, a policy beautifully illustrated by an order addressed to the families in Pensacola, Mobile, New Orleans, and Baton Rouge by the captain general of the Floridas on April 5, 1786. The order specified that residents must sign an oath of fidelity and obedience to Spain and must not move to a new location without permission, but its tone was not harsh.[37]

In November 1792, Governor Gayoso issued a ten-page decree spelling out with great care regulations governing the maintenance of the public roads of the Natchez District. For administrative purposes, the governor divided the region into six districts. The document is remarkable not only for its exposure of bureaucratic workings, but also for Gayoso's descriptions of each district, which are so detailed that the decree serves as a veritable historic geography.

My exploratory journey through the Natchez Trace Collection uncovered sources pertaining to a host of miscellaneous subjects whose depth and breadth of treatment is not great. The limited references to Indians in these collections are an indication of the limited contact that residents of the Natchez District had with them even though the Trace ran through the Choctaw and Chickasaw Nations. Small bands of Choctaw occasionally meandered through the District, and before the acquisition of Louisiana, some of the chiefs would occasionally pass through en route to conferences with Spanish officials in New Orleans. The Bank Records contain limited correspondence from the Choctaw agency regarding financial transactions. In the B. L. C. Wailes files are several letters from the fascinating Silas Dinsmoor, who for years was an unusually conscientious and effective agent to the Choctaw. And there are a few references in the Wilkins Papers to the negotiation in 1801 at Fort Adams of a treaty by which the Choctaw granted permission for the portion of the Natchez Trace that crossed their land to be surveyed and improved.

Although Katherine Adams's essay uncovers fascinating data regarding

37. Royal Order of Count de Galvez, Captain General of the Floridas, April 5, 1786, Provincial and Territorial Records, Box 2E988.

women and their activities, this is another area whose overall coverage is not large. Preserved within the Winchester Papers, however, are numerous letters written from Massachusetts by George Winchester's sister, E. W. Cook. Though their father referred to her as Betsy, she always closed her letters "Your affectionate sister, E. W. Cook." An extremely literate, well-educated woman who kept abreast of political, legal, and religious issues, Betsy unabashedly spoke her mind. In 1840 she boasted in detail of her endeavor, through correspondence, to convince church leaders that "in practice, the Policy of Congregationalism is despotic" even though they claimed a "truly liberal and catholic spirit." "I wish you were here," she concluded, "to see if I have succeeded in establishing my position."[38]

Like other family members, the obviously devoted Betsy often chided Winchester for not writing home more often. She was also a poetic soul who enjoyed discussing spiritual matters. One of her most moving letters speaks of the death of a sister: "Five weeks today since our dear Sister Smith's spirit took its flight to an eternal Sabbath in heaven." On this occasion, as on others, Betsy quoted poetry: "Death is the lightest evil we should fear; Tis certain, 'tis the consequence of life; The important question is not that we die, But how we die."[39]

In recent years historians have recognized that Mississippi was one of the first states to grant women the right to own property. Hence, it is not surprising that the NTC contains quite a few references, especially in the Winchester Papers and the Bank Records, to women owning property and conducting many types of business.

Aside from the Civil War itself, the most intriguing and important topic for historians of the South is slavery. While this is the subject of another essay in the present volume, certain references warrant mention here. One is a petition for the governor of Natchez to decree the return to slavery of a woman who claimed to be free; according to the heir of the woman's former owner, the papers of manumission were forged. Other documents reflect the high monetary value of slaves. In 1786 a buyer paid four hundred dollars for a female African. Until after the War of 1812, the

38. E. W. Cook to George Winchester, Danvers, August 30, 1840, Winchester Papers, Box 2E904.

39. E. W. Cook to George Washington, Danvers, November 24, 1849, Winchester Papers, Box 2E905.

possibility that their slaves might escape into the Indian nations was a
constant source of concern for owners. In the Natchez area, the Choctaw
Nation was the destination of many fugitive slaves. While some fled up the
Natchez Trace, others undoubtedly preferred to take their chances on less
frequently traveled trails.[40] Considering the value of slaves, it is not surprising that the collection houses many records of their being the subject
of various types of litigation, especially relating to purchases and rentals.

The collection seems to contain surprisingly few specific references to
the trail for which it was named, the Natchez Trace. Nevertheless, the
name is not inappropriate, since most of the papers were the property of
men and women who resided in the region known as the Natchez District
and bound together by the Trace. As mentioned above, the James Wilkins
Papers include important information regarding the improvement of the
Trace in 1801 and 1802. Details in the Nathaniel Evans letters to Charles
Wilkins, an uncle of James, are particularly valuable because War Department records in the National Archives contain few references to the
army's improvement of the Trace. Evans describes the progress of troops
who cut the road from the Florida line up to Natchez in late 1801 and
early 1802. After reaching Natchez, the troops worked to make the Trace
more passable in the northern end of the District near Grindstone Ford on
Bayou Pierre. The best-maintained portion of the Trace was that which
ran through the center of the District. Except in that area, little of this famous route was improved sufficiently to be accurately termed a road. Until
after the War of 1812, the portion of the Trace from Bayou Pierre to above
the Tennessee River was actually just a path or trail through the wilderness.[41]

Family historians and genealogists should not feel slighted by the present essay's inclusion of their fields among the miscellany. Indeed, for too
long historians have either ignored or soft-pedaled the value of genealogical research to history. In terms of its genealogical treasures, the Natchez

40. Petition of Joseph Barnard, Provincial and Territorial Records, Box 2E986; undated
certificate of William Walton and statement of January 28, 1785, witnessed by Stephen
Hayward, Minor Family Papers, Box 2E515.

41. Clark and Guice, *Frontiers in Conflict*, 83–97. Another purpose of using troops on
the Trace was to inhibit outlaws who terrorized travelers in the early 1800s. See John D. W.
Guice, "A Trace of Violence?," *Southern Quarterly* 29 (summer 1991): 123–43.

Trace Collection might be compared to an entire mountain range full of gold mines. In the not-too-distant future, it is likely that ambitious and diligent genealogists armed with computers will comb these files and generate a mammoth database. While every collection is of value, some of the larger ones such as the Wilkins Papers and the Bank Records reveal the names and activities of hundreds, perhaps thousands, of individuals. Similarly, many of the smaller subcollections include various types of membership and subscription lists.[42] From a genealogical standpoint, the number of families touched upon is truly exciting.

I should like to close with a bit of trivia that illustrates why Natchez was not just another frontier town, why it is still known as a city with style. It seems that its very transition from Spanish dominion was tempestuous.

In the Marquis de Lafayette Papers are the minutes of the steering committee that planned the celebration surrounding the visit of the marquis during his triumphant tour through the South in 1825. The celebration appears to have been quite a nabob affair. Levin R. Marshall, who owned nearly 850 slaves and some 25,000 acres of land, participated.[43] So did James C. Wilkins. Every town vied for a special place in Lafayette's memory, but did every town have a steering committee with at least a dozen subcommittees? Four prominent men were dispatched to New Orleans to confer with Lafayette prior to his arrival. Other subcommittees were formed to write a welcoming address, to supervise military arrangements, to receive him at the state line, to greet him at the city limits, to oversee the harmony and good order of the city, to solicit funds for a public dinner, to solicit funds for a public ball, to oversee newspaper publicity, and to procure a band from New Orleans at a cost not to exceed $150. The city appropriated $500 in support of all aspects of the gala except the dinner and ball. Trivial? Perhaps. But does it not tell much about Natchez and the Natchez Trace Collection?

42. For example, the Pinckneyville, Miss., Church Records, and the hundred-page *Port Gibson Herald and Correspondent* subscription book, Box 2E572.

43. Marquis de Lafayette Papers, Box 2E564. Levin R. Marshall was a grandson of Stephen Minor.

RANDOLPH B. CAMPBELL

Slavery in the Natchez Trace Collection

The Natchez District," writes Michael Wayne in his outstanding study, *The Reshaping of Plantation Society*, "was the richest principality in the domain of King Cotton in the decades leading up to the Civil War." Planters and slaves constituted an overwhelming presence in the district, which according to Wayne included Warren, Claiborne, Jefferson, Adams, and Wilkinson counties in Mississippi and the Louisiana parishes of Concordia, Tensas, and Madison.[1] In 1860 the five Mississippi counties had a population of 21,580 whites and 363 free blacks, while the slaves numbered 65,879, or 75 percent of the total. The population of the three Louisiana parishes (44,016) was 90 percent slave. The five counties and three parishes had 224 slaveholders who owned 100 or more bondsmen in 1860.[2] Not surprisingly, then, the Natchez Trace Collection, which cen-

---

1. Michael Wayne, *The Reshaping of Plantation Society: The Natchez District, 1860–80* (Baton Rouge: Louisiana State University Press, 1983), 1, 6–7. For an excellent account of the development of the slaveholding society in one of the Natchez District counties, see Christopher Morris, *Becoming Southern: The Evolution of a Way of Life, Warren County and Vicksburg, Mississippi, 1770–1860* (New York: Oxford University Press, 1995).

2. U.S. Bureau of the Census, *Population of the United States in 1860: Compiled from the Original Returns of the Eighth Census* (Washington, D.C., 1864), 194, 270; U.S. Bureau of the Census, *Agriculture of the United States in 1860: Compiled from the Original Returns of the Eighth Census* (Washington, D.C., 1864), 67, 85, 230, 232.

ters on this district but also contains materials from other counties and parishes where large slaveholders ruled (especially Holmes County and the parishes of East Feliciana, West Feliciana, East Baton Rouge, and West Baton Rouge), is rich in untapped resources for study of the antebellum South's peculiar institution.

Researchers using the Natchez Trace manuscripts will find papers on slaves and planters concentrated in two subdivisions of the collection. First, there is a "slaves and slavery" subcollection comprising more than two feet of material on varied subjects, including the slave trade, runaways, court cases involving bondsmen, manumissions, and the condition of free blacks. Many of these manuscripts are the originals of documents that were copied for record in Mississippi and Louisiana courthouses. Barring fires and various other threats to local record preservation, the copies of these manuscripts and others like them should be available in county seats across the two states. The Natchez Trace Collection, however, offers researchers the convenience of a sizable, well-preserved body of such material in one location. Second, there are the private papers of individual planters, including several highly useful collections such as the James Campbell Wilkins Papers, the Basil Kiger Papers, and the Chamberlain-Hyland-Gould Family Papers. One manuscript collection in particular, the Richard Thompson Archer Family Papers, is a truly spectacular find for scholars interested in the lives and minds of the Deep South's large slaveholders and their families.[3]

The Natchez Trace Collection's holdings related to slavery, like all materials on the subject, reflect the fact that there were always two perspectives on the institution—that of the planter and that of the slave. Although planters owned the slaves, they could only view slavery from the outside, never really knowing what it was like to be a slave. Slaves, in contrast, lived inside the institution, and their testimony is the only source that can reveal what it was like to live in bondage.[4] Materials in the

3. Each of the major subcollections in the Natchez Trace Collection has an extensive inventory. In the case of family papers, the inventories contain biographical and genealogical information as well.

4. This distinction has been made by many historians of slavery. For example, the titles of two of Eugene D. Genovese's studies nicely indicate the polarization: *The World the Slaveholders Made: Two Essays in Interpretation* (New York: Pantheon Books, 1969), and *Roll, Jordan, Roll: The World the Slaves Made* (New York: Pantheon Books, 1974).

An 1851 agreement between two owners that their slaves Gilbert Jones and Ellen Anderson can marry. *From the NTC Slaves and Slavery Collection, the Center for American History, the University of Texas at Austin.*

Natchez Trace Collection provide direct evidence regarding slavery largely from the outside and testify only indirectly by inference to life on the inside. These manuscripts describe the slaves physically, but beyond that, as the following examples will indicate, even the most revealing items present the peculiar institution far more from the perspective of the planters than of the slaves.

Evidence in the form of bills of sale and letters concerning the slave trade during the first six decades of the nineteenth century is found throughout the collection. These materials do not support systematic investigations of important questions such as the extent of the slave trade and its impact on slave families, but they provide much new documentation concerning the nature of the business. While on a slave purchasing trip to Virginia during the summer of 1828, Samuel Cobun wrote several times to Abram Barnes at Port Gibson, Claiborne County, Mississippi, to complain about competition and high prices. "There are very large sums to be invested in negroes this year," he wrote from Charlottesville on July 10, "which will keep prices up until late; but I think they will certainly decline in the fall." He had made a few purchases on favorable terms but expected trading to become more difficult unless he waited to buy until the first of September. "Traders generally try to get off by 20th August," he explained, "and I am sometimes tempted to by bye until the competition is lessened. The labor of the negroes would be worth considerable if the cotton crop proves abundant, but if it should not be, it would be of very little value compared with the difference which I think there will be in late & early purchases."[5] The interstate trade in human property was indeed a cold and calculating business.

Some of the slave trade documents provide intriguing glimpses of bondsmen as individuals as well as property. The commissioners of the Southern Railroad of the State of Mississippi, who bought nearly one hundred slaves in Richmond, Virginia, in 1848, kept a receipt book that contained personal comments on many of their purchases. "Benjamin," they noted, was "heavy made, speaks quick and pleasantly, has been running James River as a boat hand for several years." He was five feet four inches

---

5. Samuel Cobun to Abram Barnes, July 10, 1828, Barnes-Willis Family Papers, Box 2E529.

in height and had "a very remarkable scar above the knee on the right leg cut with a broad axe." "Wilson" they described as "yellow with hair inclined to be straight he is sprightly and intelligent, 5 ft. 10 inches high." A woman named "Nancy" somehow received special consideration, as her receipt read, "She is started this morning on the Lynchburg boat so as to meet Mr. Batte at Campbell Courthouse, Va. who has her husband on the way to Mississippi."[6] What happened to the couple when they reached their destination we can only wonder.

The collection of bills of sale constitutes a strong reminder that slaves were hardly immune to transfer among owners even after reaching a Deep South state such as Mississippi or Louisiana. A sizable minority of the sales were local or intrastate, arising especially from the settlement of the estates of deceased persons. Doubtless such transactions did not work hardships on bondsmen as severe as those created by sale from the Upper to Lower South, but any change of owners must surely have disrupted family relationships to some extent. Even family members living on neighboring plantations likely could be together only on weekends.[7]

Ironically, the Natchez Trace Collection's most interesting documents on the slave trade in Louisiana were generated by an effort to regulate and restrict the importation of bondsmen. In 1817, as slaves from the Upper South poured into Louisiana, the state legislature passed an act barring those guilty of serious crimes. Such a minor restriction had little effect on the trade, and in 1826 the legislature, concerned about the amount of money leaving the state to pay for slaves, prohibited the importation of bondsmen for two years. Prohibition proved so unpopular, however, that it was repealed in 1828 before running its two-year course. Louisiana's legislature then attempted to strengthen the 1817 law against importation of criminals by an 1829 act requiring that every slave brought into the state have an affidavit of good character signed by two men in the county from which the slave was sold and certified by the county clerk. The affidavit,

6. Slaves and Slavery Collection, Box 2E775, File 4.

7. Ann Patton Malone, in *Sweet Chariot: Slave Family and Household Structure in Nineteenth-Century Louisiana* (Chapel Hill: University of North Carolina Press, 1992), 213, points out that local private sales "did not often divide nuclear family members, but they always separated the slaves from their community."

which was attached to the bill of sale, had to have a description of the slave in terms of age, color, height, and distinguishing characteristics. Violations of this law meant penalties for both the buyer and seller.[8]

Three files of affidavits from Concordia Parish and one from West Feliciana Parish in the Natchez Trace Collection reveal how quickly slave traders adapted to the 1829 requirements of Louisiana law. Printed forms for compliance appeared immediately in Virginia, Kentucky, North Carolina, Tennessee, and South Carolina. (The Virginia form had the state's name printed on it; the others had a blank in which to write the name of the state.) Two men in the slave's home county swore that they knew the bondsman in question and that he "has not within our knowledge been guilty or convicted of any crimes, but hath a good moral character; and is not in the habit of running away." This part of the affidavit was followed by an oath from a local justice of the peace to the effect that he knew the two men attesting to the slave's good character; then the county clerk swore that he knew the two men and the justice of the peace; and finally, the presiding magistrate of the county swore that he knew the county clerk. The whole process was wonderfully bureaucratic, but there is no way of saying how many "undesirables" it kept out of Louisiana. The affidavits, however, contain quite a bit of information that could be used to create a profile of slaves being imported into the state during the late 1820s and early 1830s. Many of the bondsmen were, as would be expected, men in their prime working years, but at times less valuable slaves were purchased too. One group of fifteen slaves from Adams County, Mississippi, were described as "nearly all family slaves" and included "Old Lucy" who was forty-eight years of age, "4 feet 10 inches high, yellow complexion her teeth lost and near sighted." The same group included Leonard, a fifty-year-old male who was described as slender and having "red eyes."[9]

Nat Turner's rebellion in Southampton County, Virginia, in August 1831 led to further tightening of Louisiana's restrictions on the slave trade as the state joined others across the Deep South in passing legislation aimed at preventing the importation of bondsmen who might be infected

---

8. Joe Gray Taylor, *Negro Slavery in Louisiana* (Baton Rouge: Louisiana Historical Association, 1963), 39–40.

9. Slaves and Slavery Collection, Box 2E776, Files 5–7, Box 2E777, File 1.

with the insurrectionary virus. Meeting in November, a special session of the legislature in effect eliminated professional slave traders from the state. Only residents and new immigrants could import slaves, and even they could not buy bondsmen in neighboring states. (This provision was to prevent slave traders from operating just across the state line.) Individuals who imported slaves under these new regulations had to appear before a parish justice within five days of the arrival of their bondsmen and swear that they would not for five years "sell, mortgage, loan, hire, exchange or in any other manner dispose of or effect said negro slaves so as to contravene the provisions of the law" of November 1831 regulating importations. These affidavits, like those required under the 1829 law concerning good behavior, included information on the age and physical characteristics of each slave.[10]

The 1831 law eliminated professional slave traders from Louisiana, but affidavits from Concordia and West Feliciana Parishes in 1832 and 1833 indicate that bondsmen continued to pour into the state. Immigrants brought bondsmen with them, and in some cases large slaveholders who owned plantations in other states simply transferred their hands into Louisiana. Other slaveowners went on slave-purchasing trips themselves. For instance, Mrs. Ann Fort of West Feliciana Parish swore in September 1833 that the eleven slaves she was importing had been "purchased by her own self in person" in Kentucky.[11]

No systematic analysis of the information on the many slaves described in these affidavits has been attempted here; anecdotal examples, however, suggest the possibilities therein for studying matters such as the physical characteristics of slaves and the slave family. All sixteen of the bondsmen moved by D. C. Michie of Adams County, Mississippi, to Concordia Parish in January 1832, had surnames as well as given names, such as "Sophia Gross, 4 years old, 2 feet 10 inches high, of black complexion." Laura Green described one of the slaves she brought from Claiborne County, Mississippi, to Concordia as "Becky, a bright mulatto girl, say three-fourths white, fifteen years old, and of ordinary stature." Another affidavit provided a useful comment on a slave's physical stature by referring to

---

10. Taylor, *Negro Slavery in Louisiana*, 41–43.
11. Ibid., 44; Slaves and Slavery Collection, Box 2E776, Files 5–7, Box 2E277, File 1.

nineteen-year-old Watt who was "near six feet high" as a "tall . . . fellow." Jon Routh imported twenty-nine men and thirteen women in October 1833, none of whom was younger than fourteen and none older than twenty-six years of age. A different system of classification was followed in an affidavit from January of the same year, which arranged thirty-three slaves by family.[12]

By 1834 the demand for slaves in Louisiana was so great that the legislature repealed all restrictions. Professional trading resumed, and detailed documentation of slave importations, except for those bondsmen moving through the New Orleans market, ended.[13] For the period from 1829 through 1833, however, as the Natchez Trace Collection amply demonstrates, Louisiana's regulations created extremely rich sources of evidence on the purchase and importation of bondsmen into parishes throughout the state.

Researchers will find that the collection also has valuable material on runaway slaves. The Natchez District was so far removed from Canada or Mexico as to limit greatly any hope of running for freedom, but bondsmen regularly ran away anyhow. This is evident from the presence in the Wilkins Papers of a printed form summarizing the fees to be paid to the jailor of Adams County, Mississippi, for capturing and returning a runaway. The charges for returning a slave named Margaret in 1837 included a $6 reward for capturing her, $2 for committing and releasing her from jail, $2.80 for seven days of "sustenance" at the jail, 25 cents for entering the case on a docket, 75 cents for executing a warrant of commitment to jail, 87$\frac{1}{2}$ cents as the justice's fee for the commitment process, and 50 cents for four miles' "conveyance." Runaways thus were common enough to warrant printed forms and standardized fees in dealing with their capture.[14]

It seems likely, however, that many did not leave the area and had little chance of escaping slavery forever. For example, ten slaves ran away from a plantation owned by Wilkins in Holmes County, Mississippi, in 1842. Thomas E. Helm investigated for Wilkins and blamed a discontented overseer named Wise who intended to quit immediately upon being paid.

12. Slaves and Slavery Collection, Box 2E776, Files 5–7, Box 2E277, File 1.
13. Taylor, *Negro Slavery in Louisiana*, 44–45.
14. James Campbell Wilkins Papers, Box 2E545.

EXTENSIVE SALE OF

CHOICE SLAVES

Comprising Field Hands, Mechanics and House Servants,

AT THE ST. LOUIS HOTEL.

By C. E. GIRARDEY & CO.,

OFFICE, 37 MAGAZINE STREET.

ON SATURDAY, OCTOBER 22, 1859,

At the ST. LOUIS EXCHANGE, commencing immediately after the succession sales,
will be SOLD AT AUCTION, the following valuable Slaves to wit:

1. AUGUSTIN, black, creole, aged 17 years, very likely, No. 1 field hand.
2. HENRY, black, aged 21 years, very likely, No. 1 field hand.
3. FRANK black, aged 32 years, and his wife
4. CELIA, black, aged 30 years, both field hands.
5. BILL, black, aged 19 years, No. 1 field hand.
6. LOUISA, black, aged 16 years, good child's nurse and house servant, speaks French and English.
7. JUDY, black, 24 years, good cook, excellent washer and ironer, country raised.
7. JOE, black, 21 years, fair engineer, and practical Saw-Mill man.
9. JANE, black, 18 years, Seamstress and House Servant.
10. MARIA, black, 15 years, Field Hand and House Servant.
11. PRESCILLA, black, 16 years, Field Hand and House Servant.
12. KIZZIE,   do. 17 do.   do.   do.
13. DAN,   do. 16 do.   do.   do.
14. BARRY,   do. 16 do.   do.   do.
15. EMILY,   do. 19 do.   House Servant.
16. ISAAC,   do. 26 do.   Field Hand.
17. LOUISA,   do.   9 do.   Orphan.
18. BURWELL, do. 15 do.   Field Hand, Runaway.
19. HENRY,   do. 21 do.   do. do. } These two are sold subject to the certificates of Dr.
20. NED,   do. 19 do.   do. do. } B. H. Moss and the late Dr. Graham, pronouncing them sound, but guaranteed in title only.
21. JOHN, mulatto, aged 16 years, raised by T. J. Casey, Esq., an accomplished House and Dining Room Servant.
22. JANE, black, aged about 25 years, a firstrate Seamstress and good Washer and Ironer, and her son
23. BEN, black, aged 3 years.
24. THERESA, black, aged 22 years, Creole, speaks French and English, good Cook, Washer and Ironer.
25. MATILDA, dark griff, aged about 40 years, excellent child's Nurse, also good Cook and Ironer, has absented herself once, otherwise fully guaranteed.
26. EDWARD, black, aged about 28 years, Creole, general Laborer.
27. BAILY, black, aged about 35 years, a superior Woodman and general Laborer.
28. JOHN, dark griff, aged about 23 years, a first class Waiter and House Servant, Creole, speaks French and English.
29. RACHEL, black, aged 19 years, a superior House Servant, good Seamstress, and fair Cook, Washer and Ironer, and Hair Dresser, raised in the city. Her menus are irregular, otherwise fully guaranteed.
30. BOB, black, aged 43 years, No. 1 Field Hand, and his wife
31. JANE, black,   36 do.   do.   do.   do.
32. WINNEY, do.   14 do.   do.   do.   do.
33. MARY,   do.   12 do.   do.   do.   do.
34. HENRY   do.   9 do.   do.   do.   do.
35. BOB,   do.   6 do.   do.   do.   do.
36. ALEXANDER, black, aged 24 years, an accomplished Carriage Driver, House and Dining Room Servant,

One Family.

The above are all fully guaranteed, with exceptions stated.

TERMS.—12 mos. Credit for approved City Acceptances, bearing 8 per cent. interest—or cash if the purchaser prefers.

Acts of Sale before E. BARNETT and W. J. CASTELL, N. P., at the expense of the Purchasers.
N. B—Slaves will not be delivered under any circumstances until terms are fully complied with.

Broadside announcement describing "choice slaves" for sale at auction in New Orleans, 1859. *From the NTC Broadside Collection, the Center for American History, the University of Texas at Austin.*

"I can account for it in no other way," Helm wrote, "than they being aware of Mr. Wise's intention of quiting [sic] as soon as he was paid they concluded to run off untill that took place." Helm had thought, he wrote Wilkins, that "by telling the Negroes no that they would not be whiped [sic] if they come in that the driver or some of the others would see them and they would come in but Mr. Wise remarking that he thought they ought to be whiped I declined giving out the flag of truce thinking that if I did make such promises they ought to be strictly obeyed."[15] Apparently Helm had no fear that the runaways had left the neighborhood or that getting them back was anything but a matter of time and policy.

Runaways in the Natchez District probably had little hope of full freedom, but there were a few blacks in the region who escaped servitude by voluntary emancipation and remained as permanent residents. Louisiana had a significant free black population before it became a state (8,000 in 1810), and additions to that number from a variety of sources including manumissions brought it to more than 18,500 by 1860. Most of the state's free blacks lived in New Orleans rather than the parishes of the Natchez District, but there were enough emancipations in those parishes to generate several files of records in the collection. Mississippi had a much smaller free black population (363, according to the census of 1860), but 225 lived in Adams County, the site of Natchez.[16] Thus the collection also has a file on free blacks in Mississippi.

The files of emancipation actions in Louisiana contain cases dating from 1808 to 1850, dates that coincide almost exactly with the passage of laws regulating the practice. The territorial legislature first acted on the subject in 1807, and manumission remained legal until 1857, albeit with numerous changes in the law. Researchers will have an interesting time matching emancipation documents with the legal requirements in effect at that date. For example, until 1827 a slave under the age of thirty could be freed only if he or she saved the life of the master or a member of his family. After that date, slaves under the age of thirty, if native to Louisi-

15. Thomas E. Helm to James C. Wilkins, October 24, 1842, Wilkins Papers, Box 2E546.

16. Ira Berlin, *Slaves Without Masters: The Free Negro in the Antebellum South* (New York: Pantheon Books, 1974), 110–18, 251; U.S. Bureau of the Census, *Population of the United States in 1860*, 194, 270; Slaves and Slavery Collection, Box 2E773, Files 4–5.

ana, could be freed with the approval of three-fourths of the members of the parish policy jury. These restrictions likely explain the fact that many of the emancipation documents specify that the slave in question was thirty.[17]

Some of the emancipation materials indicate the tremendous variety of slave experiences and challenge historians to flesh out the stories of the individuals involved. Thomas R. Purnell of West Feliciana Parish, for example, freed a thirty-year-old woman named Mary and then appealed to the police jury to permit him to emancipate her three children, aged seven, five, and eighteen months, on the grounds that their mother was free. He also said that the children were "very bright mulattos or quatroons and petitioner is desirous to educate them and give them a trade and thereby to better their condition both . . . to themselves and to society." In 1850, a "free man of color" in West Feliciana, Henry Connor, petitioned to be allowed to free Ann and her six children for "fidelity and valuable services." Lambert Jacob of Iberville Parish sought to emancipate forty-five-year-old Julienne and her daughter, sixteen-year-old Marguerite, in 1833 on the grounds that he had been blinded and would have died but for their help. The police jury accepted his petition on the mother but refused in the case of the daughter.[18]

Thus the Natchez Trace Collection is rich in detail on the slave trade, runaway slaves, and emancipation. Other materials in the Slaves and Slavery subcollection, although less extensive, will reward researchers with excellent examples of the severe punishments given slaves who threatened the system and of just how many functions slavery performed for white society. When one John, a slave in Concordia Parish, ran away and resisted a white person who sought to capture him, he was sentenced by a justice court to thirty lashes each day for ten days "to be well laid on" and to wear an iron collar weighing eight to twelve pounds around his neck for the next twelve months. A ledger entitled "Slaves Subject to Road Duty," kept in Adams County from 1850 to 1857, reminds us that roads were built and maintained by slaves at no cost except for the time lost from work for their owners. All bondsmen aged fifteen to fifty were liable for work on the

17. Taylor, *Negro Slavery in Louisiana*, 154–7.
18. Slaves and Slavery Collection, Box 2E773, Files 4–5.

The names of slaves and their owners from "Slaves Subject to Road Duty, Adams County," a ledger covering the period from May 4, 1850, to March 21, 1857, and listing slaves from the county's residences and plantations. *From the NTC Slaves and Slavery Collection, the Center for American History, the University of Texas at Austin.*

roads, and in a Natchez District county such as Adams there certainly was no shortage of labor. Frank Surget, Sr., alone had 338 slaves (on five plantations) subject to road duty.[19]

The slaveholders' world that is documented in so many ways in the Natchez Trace Collection was perfectly personified by a Claiborne County, Mississippi, planter named Richard Thompson Archer. Heretofore unknown to historians of either antebellum Mississippi or planters and slavery, the papers of Archer and his family alone render the collection a major contribution to the writing of southern history. A sketch of Archer's life and extensive planting operations is essential to understanding what his papers reveal about the peculiar institution from the perspective of a prominent planter.

Richard Thompson Archer was born in 1797 in Amelia County, Virginia. He attended the College of William and Mary and moved to the Natchez District in 1824, living for about five years on rented land in Adams County, Mississippi. During the late 1820s his widowed mother and older brother, Stephen C. Archer, also moved from Virginia to Mississippi. They likewise rented land at first, but then Stephen married Catherine Barnes, the daughter of a North Carolina–born planter named Abram Barnes who had established Oaken Grove plantation in Claiborne County. Barnes died in 1830, and his son-in-law took over the plantation. Three years later, Richard T. Archer married Ann Barnes, the younger sister of his brother's wife. He was in his mid-thirties, and she was fourteen or fifteen years old. The younger couple lived at Oaken Grove until 1837 and then moved to their own plantation, Anchuca (meaning "my house" in Choctaw), near Port Gibson in Claiborne County. On an elevation overlooking the plantation, Archer built a two-and-one-half story house with a double veranda across the front. Cedar-lined drives marked all ap-

19. Ibid., File 1; also Box 2E777. Another vitally important "function" of the peculiar institution that could be explored in the Natchez Trace Collection is the use of slave assets as the collateral for loans. See Richard H. Kilbourne, Jr., *Debt, Investment, Slaves: Credit Relations in East Feliciana Parish, Louisiana, 1825–1885* (Tuscaloosa: University of Alabama Press, 1995).

proaches to the house. Anchuca would be the Archers' homeplace for the rest of their lives.[20]

Richard and Ann Barnes Archer had nine children who survived infancy. The eldest they named Abram Barnes Archer for his maternal grandfather; the youngest, Branch T. Archer, for a relative who had played an important role in the Texas Revolution in the 1830s. After Stephen C. Archer and his wife both died at an early age, Richard and Ann Archer in effect adopted their son, Edward S. Archer, and reared him as their own.[21] Undoubtedly, the plantation house at Anchuca had few quiet moments during the late antebellum years.

During the late 1820s and the following decade, Richard T. Archer laid the foundations for one of the greatest plantation dynasties in the Natchez District. He not only acquired Anchuca in Claiborne County but also bought a large tract of land located in Holmes County, in central Mississippi north of Jackson. This tract, situated in the highly fertile area between the Yazoo River to its west and a riverlike body of water called Tchula Lake to its east, was called Honey Island. Archer's correspondence is filled with references to "the island" where he eventually established three plantations: Walton's Bend, Archerlita, and Inno Albino. Tchula Lake was navigable until the late nineteenth century, and each of the three plantations had a steamboat landing. Finally, Archer bought another plantation in Claiborne County called Pine Woods. Not far from Anchuca, Pine Woods gave him a total of five plantations located on some of the best cotton land in the world.[22]

The spreading out of his real estate holdings among five plantations, two in one county and three in another, masked the magnitude of

20. *Biographical and Historical Memoir of Mississippi*, 2 vols. (1891; rpr. Spartanburg, S.C.: The Reprint Company, 1978), 1:309–10. The meaning of "anchuca" or "anchuka" is found in Cyrus Byington, *A Dictionary of the Choctaw Language*, ed. John R. Swanton and Henry S. Halbert (Washington, D.C.: Government Printing Office, 1915), 42.

21. *Biographical and Historical Memoir of Mississippi*, 1:309–10.

22. Ibid., 309. Harry P. Owens, in *Steamboats and the Cotton Economy: River Trade in the Yazoo-Mississippi Delta* (Jackson, Miss.: University Press of Mississippi, 1990), 5–6, 200, describes Honey Island and gives the names of the steamboat landings for the three plantations owned there by Archer.

Archer's planting empire from the census taker and hence from historians. Published returns of the U.S. Census of 1860 for Mississippi, which summarized the size of slaveholdings county by county, indicate only one owner of more than five hundred slaves in the state. An examination of the 1860 manuscript slave schedule for Claiborne County, however, shows that Archer owned 188 bondsmen on Anchuca (listed by the census taker as the "Home Place") and 83 on Pine Woods. The manuscript returns for Holmes County did not give plantation names, but Archer appeared as the owner of 85 slaves in one unit and as co-owner with his nephew, Edward S. Archer, of 88 slaves in another. Oldest son Abram B. Archer, who was living on "the island" by this time, was reported as the owner of 76 bondsmen. The exact nature of ownership arrangements with Edward S. Archer is not known, but it is clear that in 1860 Richard T. Archer owned outright 432 slaves and partly owned or effectively controlled 88 more. The total slave force at his disposal numbered 520, and the value of his real and personal property far exceeded $500,000. In good years, his lands and slaves were tremendously productive. For example, he reported in July 1857 that he expected to make 1,700 bales of cotton on the five plantations, and when he switched from cotton to corn during the Civil War, his Honey Island plantations alone produced 84,200 bushels in 1862.[23]

Richard T. Archer's widespread planting operations and his large family created the circumstances for writing numerous letters, almost all of which dealt in some way with slaves and slavery. He took regular trips from Anchuca to Holmes County to oversee the plantations there and also traveled frequently on business to New Orleans. On several occasions during the 1850s, he accompanied some of his children to schools that they attended in Virginia, Maryland, and Pennsylvania. In every case, he wrote

23. U.S. Bureau of the Census, *Agriculture of the United States in 1860*, 232; Eighth Census of the United States, 1860, Schedule 1—Free Inhabitants and Schedule 2—Slave Inhabitants (microfilm, National Archives, Washington, D.C.); Richard Thompson Archer to Edward S. Archer, July 20, 1857, Richard T. Archer, undated note on corn production in 1862, Richard Thompson Archer Family Papers, Boxes 2E646, 2E648. Because the Archer Family Papers, which contain the manuscript material necessary to reveal his slaveholding status, were not available, Archer is not mentioned in Wayne, *The Reshaping of Plantation Society*, or Charles S. Sydnor, *Slavery in Mississippi* (New York: D. Appleton-Century Company, 1933).

frequently to his wife. Ann Barnes Archer sent letters to her husband while he was away from Anchuca, and she also corresponded during the 1840s with her mother-in-law, who had returned to Virginia. When her children and nephew, Edward, went east to school during the 1850s, she wrote to them regularly. The children, especially the oldest three, Abram, Mary Catherine, and Ann Maria, wrote regularly to their parents and younger siblings while they were away at school. Abram and Edward attended the University of Virginia in 1854–55; Mary Catherine (who was twenty-two in 1860) and Ann Maria (twenty years old in 1860) went to school in Philadelphia and at Patapsco Institute in Maryland during the late 1850s. There are also a few antebellum-era letters from Jane and Lizzie Archer, both of whom were still in their teens in 1860. The correspondence of the Archers thus provides a rare opportunity to view slavery from the perspectives of the father, mother, and several children of a distinguished planter family.[24]

Richard T. Archer recognized from the outset what slavery could mean in terms of effort and reward for the aspiring planter. "I have placed myself in a situation," he wrote to his brother from Honey Island in 1833, "that requires persevering effort or I shall be ruined. The total inexperience of our overseer, the much that must be done and the dangers from sickness all press on me. I shall probably be rich but I have had much irritation and bad health." As this letter indicates, Archer saw slaveholding as a business with financial success as the primary objective, and he acted accordingly. He frequently expressed a seemingly paternalistic concern for the care and supervision of his slaves—their health, housing, clothing, and management—but it was a "bottom-line" paternalism worthy of any great twentieth-century corporation. Consider, for example, his explanation for building new slave quarters at Walton's Bend in 1854. "My expenses will be very heavy," he told his wife, "but I have lost too much by bad negro houses to defer building longer." The same sort of paternalism showed through his frequent expressions of concern about the management of his slaves. "I wish you to tell Mr. Nolly," he instructed his son about the new

24. Eighth Census, 1860, Schedule 1. Jane Turner Censer, in *North Carolina Planters and Their Children, 1800–1860* (Baton Rouge: Louisiana State University Press, 1984), 135–49, comments on the relationships between slaveholders' families, including children, and their slaves but has limited evidence of the kind found in the Archer Papers.

overseer at Walton's Bend in 1856, "that I wish the negroes treated kindly and that he endeavor to get on with as little whipping as possible. . . . I wish no night or Sunday work, no marking or bruising when he has to correct, and shall be greatly pleased if he makes the negroes love him and work cheerfully. I want good work done but no overworking either negroes or teams."[25] It seems that slaves, although more difficult to handle, stood on the same plane with livestock in Archer's view of good management. William G. Shade's essay in this volume discusses in detail the "bourgeois capitalism" of Archer and other Mississippi planters.

As Michael Wayne has pointed out, the paternalism of great planters such as Archer also had a basis in racism. No doubt he believed that blacks needed a "father" because of their inferior and childlike natures and that all whites were inherently superior to blacks. At the time of the secession crisis in Mississippi, Archer wrote, "By the abolition of slavery we all lose our property, our vocation, and our higher social position of the master race or class." He thus appealed to racial solidarity when necessary, but much of the time he had considerable difficulty in accepting the idea of equality among all whites. A belief in the social supremacy of the planter class shone through many of his letters. Speaking of the family of an overseer on one of his Honey Island plantations in 1853, he wrote, "They may like most people who have few negros allow them to be too familiar about the house. His negros seem as part of his white family, and I had to tell him none must enter the house and yard but those who wait in the house. They have a dirty pet negro which they have kept in the house, this I will not allow." Four years later, he confessed to his wife that he had neglected business on Honey Island because he so disliked the discomforts of "a dirty overseers house."[26]

Archer's belief in planter supremacy meant great sensitivity on questions of honor, as witnessed in a spectacular dispute that he had with a

25. Richard T. Archer to "Dear Brother," March 18, 1833, Richard T. Archer to Ann Barnes Archer, January 9, 1854, Richard T. Archer to Abram B. Archer, November 18, 1856, Archer Family Papers, Box 2E646.

26. Wayne, *The Reshaping of Plantation Society*, 25–26; Richard T. Archer, undated speech concerning delegates to the secession convention in Mississippi, Archer Family Papers, Box 2E647; Richard T. Archer to Ann B. Archer, January 18, 1853, January 30, 1857, Archer Family Papers, Box 2E646.

local lawyer in 1858. In Archer's words, the lawyer, who was representing the defendant in a case involving the nonfulfillment of a contract, "appealed to the agrarian feelings of the jury on account of the high respectability of the gentlemen who were witnesses for me and on account of my wealth to rob me under a contract proved to be violated in every particular." Enraged, Archer threatened to "publish" the lawyer who, in return, promised to issue a challenge himself. "If challenged," Archer wrote, "I shall fight him at not exceeding six feet. (The standard dueling distance was twenty-four feet.) He is a practiced shot probably twenty years my junior and single. I am unable to see the sights of a pistol. . . . I scorn to ask apology or redress from a liar and endorser of perjury and one who under the protection of a court is no less a hired robber than the highwayman without his daring. But I will not refuse to fight if called on and shall do so with the purpose of ridding society of a demoralizer or by my fall leaving my example to society that it is a duty to arrest this evil."[27] There was no exchange of gunfire at six feet, but the dispute, although almost farcical in retrospect, clearly reveals Richard Archer's view of himself as a member of the master race's ruling elite.

Archer rarely spoke of individual slaves or expressed any concern about their thoughts and feelings. By contrast, his wife, Ann Barnes Archer, demonstrated considerable awareness of such matters. Her letters to the children who were away at school generally mentioned particular slaves who had inquired about them. An 1854 letter to Abram at the University of Virginia quotes a slave named Mary Ann as saying "Mistress, the boys at Pine Woods miss Mas. Abe & Ned [Edward] most as much as you do." Mrs. Archer sought to keep slave families together. When her nephew Edward settled his father's estate in 1855, she urged him to buy all the slaves who might go to anyone else in the settlement "even if you have to sell land to do it. It is very distressing to negroes to be sold at any time, but more so to be sold from their *old* family, or from their *own* families." Ann Archer also disliked extreme punishments of slaves. In 1847 she complained to her husband who was in Philadelphia on business that in his

27. Richard T. Archer to Charles Cocke, April 2, 1858, Archer Family Papers, Box 2E646. Archer's touchy sense of honor seems to fit well into the world discussed in Bertram Wyatt-Brown, *Southern Honor: Ethics and Behavior in the Old South* (New York: Oxford University Press, 1982).

absence an overseer had "whipped one of the women so badly that there was scars made half as long as my hand & very many as far as I could see down to the waist & he had the woman stripped of all clothes. Both of these things I know you would not allow." She had demanded that there be no such punishment and promised to bring in a male cousin to stop it if necessary. A month later she informed her husband of a decision to buy meat for the slaves beyond the supply that he had ordered. It was a matter of conscience, she wrote. "I had rather be a minister to the comfort of my servants (who give me the means of so much & perhaps are hastened to their graves & to woe for it) & see them cheerful & happy than to be in Victoria's place or any other public station & I would not make them work too hard to make my children live easy or any other friend but give to each their due attention."[28]

There was, however, a limit to Ann Archer's sensitivity and concern for the slaves, and she revealed it sometimes incidentally and sometimes deliberately. Writing to Abram in 1858, she complained about the quality of a half barrel of molasses that he had sent from New Orleans. "It has a rough coarse taste, and I shall use it for the negroes as soon as I can ascertain what kind is best to get for family use and get another half barrel." A more deliberately expressed view of where slaves really stood in Ann Archer's eyes came in 1860 when two bondsmen did not behave in a properly respectful manner. She directed Abram, who was managing one of the Honey Island plantations, to take the two slaves from Anchuca to his place. "They shall not remain here longer than the time you go up [to the island] again," she wrote, "and should both be made to work in the field and do good work and regular good work as any of the hands on the place. The mother is so *insolent* she shall feel *her* place the rest of her life as long as I live, or one of my children who loves me as they ought."[29] Apparently, as mistress of the house, Ann Archer had less experience with recalcitrant slaves than did those who managed the rest of the plantation. When faced with "insolent" behavior, she reacted like most other members of the ruling race—and took the opportunity to point out her son's obligations to her as well!

28. Ann B. Archer to Abram B. Archer, December 17, 1854, Ann B. Archer to Richard T. Archer, October 6, November 5, 1847, Archer Family Papers, Box 2E649.
29. Ann B. Archer to Abram B. Archer, February 20, 1858, May 2, 1860, ibid.

Abram B. Archer's letters indicate that as a child and youth he associated freely with the slaves and seemingly enjoyed playing them off against poorer whites. Writing from the University of Virginia in January 1856, he explained to his mother that one of their overseers, Mr. Watkins, disliked several young slaves because he (Abram) and Edward took them "possum hunting" and gave them, rather than Watkins's son who also went along, all the possums. "He also dislikes them," Abram wrote, "because we would always make them do anything we wanted done, and we would make them sing when he was about, because he told them once, that they should not sing in the field or horse lot, and another reason he disliked them was because we would not let them call Julien [Watkins's son], Mars. [Master] Julien, as he had told them to call him."[30] Abram may have been simply exercising the power of his position as any young man might do, but perhaps he already had his father's view of their family as the master class as well as race.

Abram frequently closed his letters from Virginia to his mother: "Give my love to pa, the children, all of my relations, friends, and our negroes." He "loved" the slaves, however, as childlike inferiors, and once he returned to Mississippi to take up managing several of the family's plantations, all expressions of affection disappeared from his letters. Indeed, he soon began to accuse his father and mother of failure to discipline their slaves properly. "As for my managing the negroes down there," he wrote his father from Honey Island in 1862, "it will be impossible unless I have entire control of them in every respect, as most of them I think will need close management and watching. Another reason is you & ma will not let Tom [apparently the driver, a slave serving as foreman, at Anchuca at the time] manage as I want him to do & on this account there is not discipline enough among them, and if I tell them to do any work you may give other orders which will interfere with all of my arrangements." Early in 1865 Tom ran away, and Abram again blamed his parents for poor management. "If I had been there," he wrote, "the trouble could have been rectified very easily & in a different way for I would have given him a slight brushing to sober him. . . . After this, if any of them show a disposition to misbehave & pa can't whip them, let them know that it will be left over for me

30. Abram B. Archer to Ann B. Archer, January 20, 1856, ibid.

to settle as soon as I get there & don't take any further notice of it, & you may rest assured they will not cut up any more if none of you interfere in the management of them—for they will not want a second brushing from me."[31]

Abram managed the family's interests on Honey Island throughout the war because he served in the state troops rather than in the regular Confederate Army. He seemingly had no illusions about the attitude of his slaves and never expressed the romantic notion shared by many masters that their bondsmen loved them and would not leave at the first opportunity. "I will . . . stand by the Negroes," he wrote his mother in May 1862, "so long as any of them will stay with me." When Union gunboats arrived at Honey Island in February 1864, Abram wrote his father:

> the first thing I heard on Saturday morning was the Yankee fleet . . . so I did not have time to do anything—nor could I, if I had tried as the negroes were expecting them up. The fleet landed at Mr. Tom Helms before I knew what they were up to, came over to Archerlita & got all the mules & horses & all of the men & boys who wished to go & most of those on the Bend [Walton's Bend plantation] slipped off to them as soon as they heard of their being there. Making in all between 25 & 30. Others will leave as soon as the fleet comes down again. They then went to Dr. Cochrans & got all of his negroes except 5 men & a woman. Not one of them were forced off. None have left here [Inno Albino plantation] yet. [If] I can I will take off the men that are left.[32]

The tone of Abram Barnes's letters remained very matter-of-fact as the planters' world collapsed around him.

Three of the Archer family's daughters, Mary Catherine, Ann Maria, and Jane ("Jennie"), wrote home regularly while they attended school in Philadelphia and at Patapsco Institute in Maryland during the late 1850s. Jennie, who appears to have especially enjoyed the social life open to a young woman of her class, had little to say to or about the slaves. Mary

31. Abram B. Archer to Ann B. Archer, December 30, 1855, January 17, 1856, ibid.; Abram B. Archer to Richard T. Archer, November 20, 1862, Abram B. Archer to Ann B. Archer, March 1, 1865, Archer Family Papers, Boxes 2E649 and 2E650.

32. Abram B. Archer to Ann B. Archer, May 6, 1862, Abram B. Archer to Richard T. Archer, February 16, 1864, Archer Family Papers, Box 2E650.

Catherine and Ann Maria, however, had the same pattern of reference concerning the "servants." Both expressed affection, often by name, for those who served in the house but at the same time sought to pressure the bondsmen into good behavior. A letter from Mary Catherine to Jennie, who was still at home in January 1856, concluded with the following unpunctuated stream of directions: "Give my love to all of the servants tell Aunt Olive that I have not eaten any good bread & biscuits like hers since I left home & tell Aunt H T that she beats all the northern cake makers making cake tell Aunt Louisa & Betty that I hope that they will have no more trouble with my clothes both for their sakes & Ma's as it gives them so much more trouble than is necessary tell Bet Tom uncle H C aunt H P Sharlote Ann Bob & hands in the cook howdy tell Ann she must learn to sew very nicely & Bob learn to be a good diningroom servant for Ma." A December 1855 letter from Ann Maria to her mother played on the same theme in less detail. "Give my love to all the negroes," she wrote, "and tell them that I say they must mind you and if they do not tell them you will tell us."[33]

Both young women also displayed their family's understanding of itself as part of the ruling race and class. "I assure you," Mary Catherine wrote her younger sister, Lizzie, from Philadelphia in 1856, "I had rather see one of my sisters go to any school in the South than come North. It is one of the last places to come to for the servants are as impudent as they can be particularly the black servants. I would not give one of ours for all that are in the northern states." While still at Anchuca, in early 1855, Ann Maria wrote her cousin Edward in Virginia, "Adaline has gone into the field. She and Ann have been stealing and Ma had to put them in the field. . . . We are all very well the horses and dogs and negroes are all well." When Richard T. Archer gave Ann Maria her own personal servant in 1856, she responded, "I hope she will like me. I am very glad she is not older than I am for I wish mine to be near my own age. I will be a kind mistress to her and do the best I know for her when I leave school."[34]

Of course, defeat in the Civil War and the destruction of slavery dra-

33. Mary Catherine Archer to Jennie Archer, January 11, 1856, Ann Maria Archer to Ann Barnes Archer, December 6, 1855, Archer Family Papers, Boxes 2E650 and 2E651.

34. Mary Catherine Archer to Lizzie Archer, January 22, 1856, Ann Maria Archer to Edward S. Archer, January 7, 1855, Ann Maria Archer to Richard T. Archer, February 16, 1856, ibid.

matically changed the Archers' world, but the extent of that change is a matter of perspective. Two family members died during the war. Stephen C. Archer died of typhoid fever while serving in the Confederate Army, and Edward, the cousin who had been reared as a family member, was killed at the Battle of Malvern Hill in 1862. Richard T. Archer quickly gave up his diehard southern views once the war ended, taking the amnesty oath at Port Gibson, Mississippi, in June 1865, but he died on October 30, 1867, at the age of seventy-one. All other members of the family, however, survived at least into the 1890s. Ann Archer still lived at Anchuca in 1891 with five of her children (Mary Catherine, Jane, Richard, Esther, and Branch). According to an account of Mississippi at that time, "She manages her home place in an admirable manner, and is noted for her many charities and her kind and Christian character. She has a fine library, many of her books being very rare and costly. . . . She also has some very valuable oil paintings, and her home is a model of convenience, order and comfort." Abram remained a planter on Honey Island in Holmes County in 1891. Ann Maria married Dr. C. R. Irving and returned to live on the Archers' original homeplace in Amelia County, Virginia. Lizzie married James Rowan Percy of Holmes County, Mississippi.[35] In short, it appears that although the great planters' antebellum world met with destruction between 1861 and 1865, Richard T. Archer's family adjusted and survived in the same relative position in society that they had enjoyed before the war.

The Natchez Trace Collection offers a rich variety of resources to historians interested in virtually any facet of the slaveholders' view of the peculiar institution in Mississippi and Louisiana. The Archer Papers alone make the collection invaluable to students of the Old South's great planters and their families. Some of the materials point the way to systematic examinations of such matters as the slave trade and manumissions; others provide information highly useful in more traditional narrative accounts. The manuscripts also invite comparative analysis of slaveholders in a region dominated by great planters with those in other areas of the South. Perhaps there were significant differences, but an overview reading sug-

---

35. *Biographical and Historical Memoir of Mississippi*, 1:310–11; Richard T. Archer, Amnesty Oath, June 27, 1865, Archer Family Papers, Box 2E657.

gests that slaveholders, regardless of their wealth and the size of their operations, saw slaves as essentially a valuable property to be managed to the
master's best advantage. Richard T. Archer learned the ways of the peculiar institution in Virginia, and it seems clear that his basic views of slaves
and slave management would have been the same had he remained in the
Old Dominion or moved all the way to Texas. Slaveholders undoubtedly
differed from one part of the South to another in the details of their treatment of human property, but the Natchez Trace Collection reminds us
that differences in detail did not affect fundamentals. When it came down
to basics, the great planters of King Cotton's richest principality, although
participating in the peculiar institution on a grand scale, remained simply
slaveholders.

Katherine J. Adams

Natchez District Women:
Voices of Southern Women in the Natchez Trace Collection

On December 4, 1849, Fannie Pugh, the young wife of a Louisiana sugar planter, wrote to her mother in Natchez, Mississippi. Fannie's three-page letter is by turns melancholy, cheerful, and dramatic. She wrote of her loneliness for her mother and sister; she missed them and worried she would "go mad" if either of them died and she could not see them again. Although Fannie professed contentment with her lot, she also complained that she was sometimes "hardly treated" and had "so much trouble." She would remain happy, she said, "as long as my husband treats me as he does now," but mused that it was sinful "to allow all happiness to depend on such a frail & capricious thing as human love."

The family, Fannie reported, suffered from various ailments. Husband James had experienced a "*warning* of the bilious colic," fevers, and cold sweats, though none so severe as to keep him from working at "the sugar house (where he lives now)." She herself had suffered fever and now her breast milk was drying up. Her eldest daughter, Cynthia, was "quite cross and contrary" from cutting teeth. Still, Cynthia and baby Frances were her joy, and Fannie wrote of their good nature and appealing behavior with affection and pride. And she happily announced that she had hosted a lively party the previous day at which her guests danced until dark while she played bayou tunes on the piano.

In the middle of her letter Fannie shared with her mother "all the particulars" of a recent "blow up" with Annie, one of her house slaves.

Last Thursday I spent the day at mother's [her mother-in-law]. When I left home I left a small basket full of pinders [peanuts] on the bureau in your room. The next day I went to get them and more than half were gone and the basket behind the door in the room next to mine. I was scolding about them and passed through the parlor saying that too many things had disappeared lately and no body knew what had become of them. Annie was standing at the piano looking at a book, she slammed it too and walked off down stairs grumbling and quarreling that "she hadn't taken the pinders 'cause her mouth was too sore to eat them" (I had not accused her and don't believe she did eat them for her mouth is full of blisters and boils from that spell of toothache she had) she talked and quarreled as loud as she could down stairs so that I could hear her. I sent her word to come to me, it was a quarter of an hour before she came up stairs and then she didn't come to me but went into the little room and threw a dirty diaper at Catherine [a house servant] and said "here take this dirty diaper" in the gruffest tones you ever heard. I spoke to her and she answered so insolently that I made Catherine take Frances and I told her to get on her knees and she wouldn't. I struck her four or five times and she caught the whip and wouldn't let me strike her. I sent for Mr. Pugh, he couldn't come just then for it was raining very hard. He came home in the night and next morning he took her and waled her. I can tell you ever since that she has been in a good humor and as humble as a dog—it has done her good.[1]

Fannie Pugh's 1849 letter is one of many in the Natchez Trace Collection that supports research in southern women's history. It is a detailed and vivid personal narrative that touches on some of the topics being explored by scholars in the field, especially with respect to the plantation mistress:

1. Fannie Pugh to Frances Sprague, December 4, 1849, Winchester Family Papers, Box 2E913, File 6. I am grateful to Richard Lowe, Vicki Betts, and the *Dictionary of American English* for information about pinders.

domesticity, female identity, isolation and loneliness for family, the complicity of white women in the slave system and the uneasy relationship between mistress and slave within the household, religion, health, marriage
and spousal relationships, child rearing, and social life. Fannie's testimony
is relevant to both discrete and collective histories of southern women, at
once challenging researchers to discover more about her life and to use
this evidence to help build the base from which we can gain a greater understanding of the diversity of women's experience in American history
and their important role in shaping southern history.

    As the voices and stories of Natchez District women find their place in
the literature on southern women's history, they will help build toward
the "deep and nuanced understanding of southern women" called for by
historian Drew Gilpin Faust in her award-winning *Mothers of Invention:
Women of the Slaveholding South in the American Civil War*. Discrete and
collective histories of Natchez District women will open new lines of inquiry in southern women's history just as they will challenge and support
theses posed and patterns identified in such studies as Anne Firor Scott's
The Southern Lady: From Pedestal to Politics, 1830–1930 (1970); Catherine
Clinton's *The Plantation Mistress: Woman's World in the Old South* (1982);
Deborah Gray White's *Ar'n't I a Woman? Female Slaves in the Plantation
South* (1985); Jean E. Friedman's *The Enclosed Garden: Women and Com-
munity in the Evangelical South, 1830–1900* (1985); Elizabeth Fox-Geno-
vese's *Within the Plantation Household: Black and White Women in the Old
South* (1988); Sally G. McMillen's *Motherhood in the Old South: Pregnancy,
Childbirth, and Infant Rearing* (1990); Victoria E. Bynum's *Unruly Women:
The Politics of Social and Sexual Control in the Old South* (1992); and Faust's
Mothers of Invention.[2]

    2. Drew Gilpin Faust, *Mothers of Invention: Women of the Slaveholding South in the Ameri-
can Civil War* (Chapel Hill: University of North Carolina Press, 1996), 257. Examples of
current scholarship of Natchez District women include such works as Suzanne Hurley,
"Change, Continuity, and Tradition in the Nineteenth-Century South: The Chamberlain-
Hyland-Gould Women of Mississippi" (master's thesis, University of Texas at Austin,
1994); Florence E. Cook, "Growing Up White, Genteel and Female in a Changing South"
(Ph.D. diss., University of California at Berkeley, 1992); Joyce L. Broussard, "Women
Alone in Antebellum Natchez," in *Natchez on the Mississippi: A Journey Through Southern
History, 1870–1920*, exhibition catalog for the Henry C. Norman Collection (Northridge,
Calif.: California State University, Northridge, 1995), 30–2; and Broussard, "Female Soli-

The Natchez Trace Collection contains abundant information concerning the lives and worlds of southern women. This 450-linear-foot collection of collections brings to life the history of the Lower Mississippi River Valley from 1790 to 1900, especially in the area known as the Natchez District. NTC subcollections include sets of family papers, groups of business records, artificial collections created around various topics or formats (e.g., the NTC Steamboat Collection, the NTC Broadside Collection), and hundreds of small personal-name collections established to accommodate documents that lack other evident associations. Significant windows into the world of southern women are provided by a considerable portion of NTC's manuscript collections documenting prominent citizens of the region, especially planters and the attorneys who managed their legal affairs, as well as by the thousands of recorded bits and pieces reflecting the lives of people, often inarticulate, who have been ignored.

Natchez Trace Collection materials on southern women tend to focus on females in planter or upper-class families and, of those, females able and disposed to write. Less substantial and more scattered, but still present in the collection, is evidence on bondswomen, free black women, and wage-earning women, providing at least glimpses of populations otherwise sparsely documented. The bulk of NTC information relating to women is found in the collection's abundant personal letters written by women and in family financial and legal records and plantation and business files. The NTC's photographs and printed resources, such as sheet music, pamphlets, broadsides, ephemera, periodicals, and newspapers, complement these materials and provide additional views of the world of southern women. Some of the planter families and institutions represented in the NTC are also referenced in other southern history collections held at the Center for American History and at other repositories. Substantial complementary collections are mentioned in the notes.[3]

---

taires: Women Alone in the Lifeworld of Mid-Century Natchez, 1850–1880" (Ph.D. diss., University of Southern California, 1997). In addition to the works listed in the text, see Suzanne Lebsock's excellent review essay of Fox-Genovese's study: "Review Essay: Complicity and Contention: Women in the Plantation South," *Georgia Historical Quarterly* 74, no. 1 (1990): 59–83. A helpful reference work is the Society of Mississippi Archivists' *Mississippi's Historical Heritage: A Guide to Women's Sources in Mississippi Repositories*.

3. For example, the Center for American History houses the extensive (ten-foot) Pugh

*   *   *

Fannie Pugh's 1849 letter is one of the several dozen she wrote to her mother and sister that are preserved in the NTC's Winchester Family Papers. Although this large collection for the most part reflects the professional activities of two prominent Natchez attorneys, it is likewise an excellent source of data on several Natchez District women. The documentation on women in this extensive collection can serve as a guide to the quality and range of the NTC's abundant resources on southern women.[4]

The women's correspondence in the Winchester Family Papers centers on Frances Sprague, Fannie's mother and the wife of Sturges Sprague, erstwhile law partner of George Winchester. Sturges and Frances Sprague had at least five children, including daughter Margaret, who married Josiah Winchester, George's nephew, sometime in or after 1845, and daughter Frances (Fannie), who in 1847 married James Pugh, a member of one of the wealthiest sugar planter families in Louisiana. Thus the Sprague, Pugh, and Winchester families were joined by both business and marriage connections, a common arrangement among Natchez District families. Women's correspondence in the Winchester Family Papers reveals the extent and influence of these connections.

The personal letters between Frances Sprague and her daughters are the most direct and substantial source of information on these women's lives to be found in the Winchester Papers. Additional correspondents therein include Mrs. Sprague's sisters Jane Kempe and Margaret Louisa Kempe Howell (Mrs. William), the mother of Varina Howell (who in 1845 married Jefferson Davis), and more distant relations and friends.

Additional evidence about family women in the Winchester collection is found in personal financial and legal records. The collection also documents women, including bondswomen and tradeswomen, who were neither relations nor friends, but who are known to us through both family financial papers and professional materials of George and Josiah Winches-

Family Papers, 1807–1907, which are also available on microfilm as part of University Publications of America, *Records of Ante-Bellum Southern Plantations*, Series G.

4. Two related collections are housed in the Mississippi Department of Archives and History: the George Winchester Letters, 1869, and the Henry K. Winchester Estate Records, 1894–1898.

ter, such as their legal and political correspondence, court case files, probate records, indentures, estate inventories, and business and financial records. The Winchester Family Papers thus contain, as do several of the NTC's largest collections, substantial information on women from both personal/family letters written by women and work-related materials produced by the men of the family (e.g., an attorney's legal records or a planter's plantation records).

Women's letters in the Natchez Trace Collection emphasize the importance that female friends and relations held for women. For the plantation mistress distant from family, isolated on a remote estate, and married to a man often absent on plantation business, letters sent and received served as the lifeline to loved ones. Such letters routinely disclose these women's loneliness. Certainly this is true of Fannie Pugh's letters. Separated from her mother and sister in Natchez, she wrote them both often. As the Christmas holidays approached in 1849, she told her mother longingly: "I wish I was with you but it is my lot to be placed here and I will try to do my duty and not give way to pining and gloomy thoughts."[5]

Ellen Hyland's letters in the Chamberlain-Hyland-Gould Papers echo such sentiments. Mistress of Boquedesha plantation near Vicksburg, she wrote frequently to her father, Jeremiah Chamberlain, president of Oakland College, and to her sister Mary, who lived in the North. Ellen regularly expressed her boredom and loneliness. Writing Mary in 1854, Ellen admitted to low spirits and confessed to "feeling a constant and almost a nervous anxiety to hear from you and Clara," her other sister. Dismal weather added to Ellen's melancholy, but when the skies cleared she began gardening with great energy and found "active employment a sovereign remedy for low spirits or temper."[6]

NTC subcollections also contain many letters written by women to their husbands away on business. Such letters attest to loneliness but also give evidence of both their ability to manage affairs in their mate's ab-

5. Fannie Pugh to Frances Sprague, December 4, 1849, Winchester Family Papers, Box 2E913.

6. Ellen Hyland to Mary [?], March 15, 1854, Chamberlain-Hyland-Gould Family Papers, Box 2E908. Two cubic feet of records documenting Oakland College, 1829–1914, are housed in the Mississippi Department of Archives and History.

sence and their exasperation at having to do so. Margaret Sprague Win-chester, whose lawyer husband was frequently away at court in Jackson, wrote him often of her busy days tending to sick children and overseeing the household. In one letter she scolded him about a house repair that had to remain unattended until his return. One night she had heard "a terrible rumbling . . . then . . . a crash that shook the house." Investigation showed that a portion of the ceiling in the parlor had fallen away "just over where the card table stands. . . . It is a real mercy it has not fallen while the chil-dren were dancing." She also noted with some asperity that "there has been no dancing in there since you may be sure" and that she would "just let it alone till you come home." Margaret was distressed further by a cow that "took a run" at her and made her "take to Calhoun's fence in fine style." The incident had given her a backache, but Margaret claimed she was fully recovered after indulging in a "good crying fit." In all, Margaret felt that she would be "quite a nervous fine lady by the time you get back."[7]

Like Margaret Winchester, Mrs. Saphronia Castleman was eager for her husband's return. Writing while he was away on business, she pleaded with him to return home as her "troubles are great . . . but my dear my only dear you are all my consolation you I depend on you I place my future happiness on and remember dear that you are all I love." The letter con-taining this vivid expression of emotional dependence is one of the hun-dreds of documents housed in NTC small subcollections.[8] These small personal-name collections range in size from one to nearly a hundred items. Such bits and pieces in the Natchez Trace Collection complement the many larger collections of NTC family papers and support research on myriad topics relating to southern women's history.

The letters to and from the Sprague-Pugh-Winchester women in the Winchester Papers provide rich detail on personal events important in any family's life, including courtship, weddings, and the births and deaths of children. The particulars, of course, invite comparison with evidence of other versions of such universal experiences. Letters from female family

7. Margaret Winchester to Josiah Winchester, February 25, 1854, Winchester Family Papers, Box 2E912.

8. Saphronia Castleman Letter, Box 3E553.

members and friends written prior to Fannie's and Margaret's marriages, for example, make clear their keen interest in seeing the Sprague daughters married to advantage. One friend noted with despair Margaret's "dilatory proceedings in the line matrimonial," an apparent reference to Margaret's extended courtship by Josiah Winchester. Other correspondents reflect the invitation to Frances Sprague and her daughters to visit the Assumption Parish plantation of Colonel Sparks for the purpose of introducing Fannie and Margaret to eligible bachelors. One of the eligibles was James Pugh, whose superb credentials were trotted out for inspection: "son of a planter worth half a million . . . anxious for a wife . . . quite a good looking young man . . . would build a fine mansion when married . . . exquisite smile . . . pearly teeth . . . bowed legged, but that is only perceptible when he walks." Margaret's affections were elsewhere, however, and she eventually married Josiah Winchester. It was Fannie Sprague who married James Pugh in March 1847, thus fulfilling her mother's wish that "Frances Louise" accept "the best offer she ever will have."[9]

In another Winchester collection document, the marriage in 1866 of Frances ("Frank") Pugh, daughter of Fannie Pugh, is captured in a wonderfully detailed description of the wedding joining her to W. L. Mitchell. Cynthia Pugh (Fannie's oldest daughter) conveyed to her aunt Margaret S. Winchester the details of the lavish ceremony, including all the fashion particulars. "I assure you," Cynthia wrote, that

> we all looked "killing" with our hair all curled and puffed, almost entirely on the top of our heads. . . . I did not see Frank until we reached the Church; she was beautifully dressed and looked beautiful besides. Her dress was tarleton over white silk—the silk waist cut low, but the tarleton high in the neck, the sleeves were no sleeves at all, being merely a fall of lace. Her hair was dressed beautifully with curls, a thule veil falling almost to her feet, and a half wreath of orange blossoms and other delicate white flowers. . . . Frank behaved beautifully and controlled herself admirably until we proceeded to

9. Eliza Ann Dupuy to Frances Sprague, March 20, 1845, Ellen Cornell and Mrs. Sparks to Frances Sprague, May 18, 1845, Frances Sprague to Margaret Winchester, January 5, 1847, Winchester Family Papers, Box 2E913.

the vestry to sign her name, when she burst into tears . . . some time elapsed before she was sufficiently composed to write her name.[10]

In stark contrast to Cynthia's letter describing a joyous family wedding ceremony is the three-page indenture recording the divorce of John and Sarah Burns of Ouachita, one of many legal documents housed in NTC small manuscript collections. The indenture states the "unhappy difference" between the two, their agreement "to live separate and apart from each," and the restoration of Sarah's *femme sole* status as an unmarried woman. It supplies some interesting details of the life of a yeoman woman in the Natchez District. The division of property required John to give Sarah a mare and colt, a saddle, household furniture, beds, and bed-clothes; alimony for Sarah was set at three *sous* yearly for the remainder of her natural life; and custody of the couple's children was divided, with John retaining care of their son and Sarah keeping the two daughters.[11]

Family letters in the NTC testify to the toll that pregnancies, childbirth, and child rearing took upon southern women, as well as their ambivalence toward their maternal roles. Fannie Pugh, for example, routinely laced her letters with joyous news of her children while also expressing her fears of repeated pregnancies. Pregnant within months of her March 3, 1847, wedding, she wrote her mother in December of that year that her "time is drawing near." The birth of her first child, Cynthia, was quickly followed by the birth of Frances in 1849, then that of a third daughter, Augusta, in 1850. By March 1853, Fannie wrote her sister in Natchez that she feared she was again pregnant, and added, "but I hope not, as I have as many children as I can take care of." She was in fact pregnant; however, Harry died in his infancy, a loss that so affected Fannie that even months later she wrote, "Sometimes now at night and in the day too I could scream in agony." Still, in that same 1854 letter, Fannie wrote that she believed her-self pregnant once again.[12] Her sister Margaret could empathize with Fannie's situation; in all, she would give birth to twelve children.

10. Cynthia Pugh to Margaret Winchester, December 4, 1866, Winchester Family Papers, Box 2E912.

11. John and Sarah Burns Contract, December 19, 1806, Box 2E552.

12. Frances Pugh to Margaret Winchester, December 7, 1847, March 4, 1953, February 12, 1854, Winchester Family Papers, Boxes 2E913 and 2E912. Readers should consult Sally

An altogether different form of evidence reflecting pregnancy and childbirth is found in the NTC's James Rowan Percy Record Book of Obstetrical Cases. Percy's day book is an information-rich resource that provides the specifics on childbirths for a small sample of southern women and which can support research on medical practice in the South. Percy kept records while a medical student at Charity Hospital in New Orleans in the late 1850s. While working in the "Lying In" department in 1857, he listed the childbirths of thirty-four women, recording their names, ages, and dates of admission, as well as information on the duration of pregnancy, number of children, length of labor, type of presentation at birth, and sex of the newborn. Percy also set down his brief "observations," which indicate the time of delivery and any complications during birth. In addition, the record book contains his ten-page description of the medical causes, diagnosis, and treatment of miscarriage, and in one remark he recorded the apparent planned abortion by a sixteen-year-old. The woman "gave birth to her child while in the privy—she says she did not have any pain at all, but as she is a suspicious-looking character, and I think [she] would not tell the nurse in order that her child might be killed."[13]

Letters written by the female members of the Sprague-Pugh-Winchester circle and other women in NTC subcollections indicate an almost obsessive concern with illness and disease. Such evidence attests to the frailty and physical hazards of life in the nineteenth-century South and invites continued inquiry into the extent to which responsibility for care of the sick fell upon the shoulders of women when no professional medical care was available. Fannie Pugh's letters regularly report ailments that spanned both mundane and serious—even life-threatening—conditions, including measles, yellow fever, cholera, scarlet fever, boils, worms, colic, mumps, small pox, and bladder problems. Her letters also detail her specific treatments, including home vaccination. When nearly all her children were ill with scarlet fever, she administered salts and soda and treated their throat sores with a caustic wash made of sage tea, honey, and borax.

G. McMillen, *Motherhood in the Old South: Pregnancy, Childbirth, and Infant Rearing* (Baton Rouge: Louisiana State University Press, 1990), for an excellent in-depth study of what the author calls "the intimate lives of southern mothers."

13. James Rowan Percy Record Book of Obstetrical Cases, Box 2E515.

And in 1854 she reported that she treated her baby for a bad cold and
cough by vaccinating her, but noted that she suspected she "did not do it
right as it did not take . . . however I will try again."[14]

The NTC's Chamberlain-Hyland-Gould Family Papers also present evidence of the role of the plantation mistress as caregiver to the sick. One
of the strengths of this collection, which consists of approximately eight
inches of documents relating to three Mississippi families joined by blood
and marriage, is its letters written by Ellen Marie Wheaton Chamberlain
Hyland (1823–1863) and her daughter Martha J. (Pattie) Hyland Gould
(born 1849). The letters of these two women during the Civil War reveal
how the war affected the attitudes, experiences, and opportunities of two
plantation mistresses.[15]

Married to William S. Hyland in 1849, Ellen Hyland bore eight children before her death in 1863. She wrote often from her Boquedesha
plantation home south of Vicksburg to her sister Mary, who lived in the
North. Explaining that the care and responsibilities of her large family
"press heavily" upon her, Ellen regularly noted the ailments and injuries,
and even deaths, of family and friends—chills, fever, backache, sprained
bones, rheumatism, bilious diarrhea, dyspepsia, pneumonia, yellow fever,
diphtheria, and more. Ellen, however, often enjoyed access to physicians,
and she liked to follow her comments about illness with information
about doctor's visits and homeopathic remedies.[16]

Women's letters in the Natchez Trace Collection are also good sources
of information on the plantation mistress's role in caring for sick or in-
jured slaves as well as on the health, illness, and medical care of bondswomen. When the Boatners, Fannie Pugh's neighbors, fought a major out-
break of cholera that proved fatal to seventeen of their slaves, Fannie

14. Frances Pugh to Margaret Winchester, November 13, 1852, June 22, 1856, Winchester Family Papers, Box 2E912.

15. Additional collections relating to the Chamberlain and Hyland families are housed
in the Mississippi Department of Archives and History: the Jeremiah Chamberlain Letter,
1851, and the Chamberlain-Hunt Academy Records, 1885–1973. See also Hurley,
"Change, Continuity, and Tradition in the Nineteenth-Century South," for an excellent
analysis of the lives of the women in this family.

16. See, for example, Ellen Hyland's letters to her sister dated August 5, 1859, January
24, July 7, 1860, May 16, 25, 1861, Chamberlain-Hyland-Gould Family Papers, Box 2E508.

reported that the mistress of the plantation was "almost worn down nursing the sick." Fannie feared the disease would come up the bayou and infect the Pugh estate, adding that "it would break us to lose 17 negroes—I feel more sorry for the poor negroes than I do for their owners—for a negro is looked upon here pretty much as they do a mule or a horse." In other letters, Fannie Pugh reported on the sudden death of slaves, testifying to the highly vulnerable position of that population. In one 1852 letter, she described the horrendous injury and death of the child of the slave Venus; the three-year-old was "cut almost in two in a cane carrier." And in another, she blandly noted the news that the slave Fanny had smothered her month-old baby, "who would have been a fine child had it lived." This chilling episode, so reminiscent of Sethe's murder of her daughter in Toni Morrison's novel *Beloved,* perhaps reflects one slave woman's terrible defiance of the system that enslaved her child.[17]

NTC subcollections also give evidence of professional health care for plantation women, both mistress and slave. The NTC Slaves and Slavery Collection includes interesting testimony, perhaps from a doctor or overseer, that describes the death of "Old Mary" from pneumonia, despite therapeutic bleeding and medicine. The Dr. Henry Tennent Papers contain a ledger in which Tennent recorded his visits and treatments to his various patients in the Pine Ridge, Mississippi, area from 1834 to 1847. The ledger carries separate accounts for several women, including Rachel Foster, whom he visited seven times during July 1835, filling a prescription on each visit. Other accounts record Dr. Tennent's trips to area plantations. Several sets of notes catalog his treating of female slaves and his conducting obstetrical consultations.[18]

Information on available professional medical attention is also found in the NTC Legal Records Collection, which contains a list of persons confined in the Paupers' Hospital in Natchez in 1832. This legal record stipulates funds for the hospital's attending physician and provides the names and lengths of stay of patients, some of whom died while under the hospital's care. Several of the indigents were women, including Nancy Pitts

17. Frances Pugh to Margaret Winchester, September 27, 1854, November 13, 1852, February 14, 1854, Winchester Family Papers, Box 2E912.

18. T. Young to M. N. Hulburt, January 19, 1851, Slaves and Slavery Collection, Box 2E773; Day Book, 1834–1847, Henry Tennent Papers, Box 2E607.

(who was treated in the hospital on two separate occasions), Susan Case, and Margaret Watson.[19] Such documents offer a glimpse of a largely inarticulate population for whom few records exist.

Ephemeral materials in NTC add rich detail on the medical care available to some southern women. A receipt for Miss Kate Coulter's dental treatment in 1861, for example, gives very specific information on mid-nineteenth-century dental care. Dr. N. C. Orrick's receipt is a printed form, complete with a diagram of teeth on which a dentist could note problems needing treatment. Dental operations, including the lancing of gums, "natural or mineral teeth set on pivots," "separation of jaw teeth with a file," and "extraordinarily large and complicated Gold plugs," are listed, with prices noted. The receipt indicates that in 1861 the unfortunate Miss Coulter had a tooth extracted while under nitrous oxide, a procedure which cost her three dollars.[20]

The Natchez Trace Collection contains substantial information on slaves and slavery in the Natchez District, an area in which planters and slaves constituted an overwhelming presence. The use of the NTC in researching topics related to slavery is fully described in Randolph Campbell's essay in this book, and therefore warrants only brief mention here. One pertinent topic is the difficult relationship between mistress and slave within the plantation household.

NTC letters from the wives of planters often contain not only revelations about that relationship but also their descriptions of the slave women, helping fill in the stories of this additional group of southern women. Fannie Pugh's letters, for example, supply bits of information here and there on slave women in her charge. Fannie occasionally mentioned her slave Annie, whose blowup with her mistress was described previously. As a slave, Annie had little control over her life, and was destined to be sent to Natchez with Fannie's mother, Frances Sprague, in 1850, possibly because Mr. Pugh, Mrs. Sprague reported, "hates Annie off the earth." In another letter, written in 1858, Fannie described a slave for sale because

19. List of Indigents in Pauper's Hospital, Winchester Papers, Legal Records Collection, Box 2.325 / AA14C.
20. Receipt from Dr. N. C. Orrick, November 24, 1861, Broadside Collection.

her owner "can't prevent her running out through Paincourt at night and having white beaux." Fannie noted that the woman, Lizzy, was about thirty, a "good plain cook, good cake and bread maker, also a beautiful washer and ironer, she likes to cook and wash, is perfectly healthy, has no children and I know her to be a smart likely woman . . . her color is between a mulatto and brown—the price is $1000 cash or $1200 at a longer time—she is cheap for $1000, the way negroes are selling."[21]

Other NTC subcollections also offer information on the lives of female slaves and free black women. The Rowland Chambers Papers, for example, contain an indenture for Maria Conway, a free woman of color living in Madison Parish, Louisiana. In 1859 she bound her two daughters, Harriet, aged six, and Pandian, aged four, until age eighteen to Dr. Chambers, a dentist, who agreed to "instruct them in the duties of House Servants or as seamstresses."[22]

One of the most important NTC subcollections related to slavery is its Slaves and Slavery Collection, an artificial subcollection created around this specific topic to house documents that lacked other evident association. Its contents, especially materials relating to runaway slaves and indentures of free black women, offer evidence of the efforts of southern women to control their lives in the face of severely limited options. One document, for example, records a marriage between slaves who had different owners, while others contain information about free black women like Clarissa Bartlett and Aggy Watts, who bound themselves and / or their children into service for a specified period of time. One of this collection's most poignant documents describes an apparent kidnapping of a free black woman. Written in pencil and barely legible, it states: "Maria Smock born in Fredericksburg, Virginia, daughter of Wm Smock, born about 1807, Mother name Lucy [dark?] woman now free when Maria was born—All came to Lexington K.Y.—when she was going to school in Lexington. Then a man came on horseback—and took her and carried her to Frankfort put her in jail & the next day put her on board of a flat

21. Frances Sprague to Margaret Winchester, December 8, 1850, Winchester Family Papers, Box 2E913; Frances Pugh to Margaret Winchester, June 24, 1858, Winchester Family Papers, Box 2E912.

22. Rowland Chambers Papers, Box 2E554.

boat & boat to New Orleans from thence she was sent up to James . . . on the Coast. She has to this time been sick."[23]

Abundant materials in the NTC on education in the South offer research opportunities for studying the education of daughters of Natchez District families, especially in planter households.[24] Personal letters mention women who took on the task of schooling young children at home. Margaret Sprague Winchester taught her youngsters at her home, the Elms, located near Natchez, purchasing copy books, a geography book, and an atlas for their use. Margaret's aunt, Margaret Louisa Howell, organized a school in her home for her children and apparently several others. In a lengthy letter to her sister Margaret Sprague, Mrs. Howell outlined her rigorous all-day program of instruction that included prayers, readings from the Bible, discussion, dictionary work, geography and astronomy lessons, and spelling. Margaret Howell noted that her pupils varied in their abilities: Hickey had idle habits; little William was better, "though not much." Neither, she noted with pride, could read or spell as well as her daughter Varina.[25]

The NTC's Basil Kiger Papers invite research centering on the many letters reflecting Miss Mary Bell Kiger's years away at school. The Kiger Papers document the lives of the family of planter Basil Gordon Kiger of Vicksburg, owner of Buena Vista Plantation near Brunswick Landing in Warren County, Mississippi. Kiger and his wife, Caroline Isabel Gwin Kiger, had three children: William Gwin, born in 1847; Basil Gordon,

23. Notes documenting consent for the marriage of Gilbert Jones and Ellen Anderson, January 16, 1851, Indenture of Clarissa Bartlett, Vicksburg, December 6, 1837, Indenture of Aggy Watts, West Feliciana Parish, October 9, 1841, undated document, Slaves and Slavery Collection, Box 2E773.

24. For a historical overview of educational facilities available to women in Mississippi, see Trey Berry, "A History of Women's Higher Education in Mississippi, 1819–1882," *Journal of Mississippi History* 53 (November 1991): 303–19. Berry's article includes a list of private female institutions established in Mississippi from 1818 to 1891.

25. Margaret Winchester to Josiah Winchester, February 25, 1854, various receipts, Winchester Family Papers, Box 2E912; Margaret L. Howell to Frances E. Sprague, September 14, 1831, Winchester Family Papers, Box 2E913. The Mississippi Department of Archives and History houses some seventy-five linear feet of papers documenting the Elms and its successive owners and occupants from the 1800s to the 1900s.

born in 1852; and Mary Bell, born in 1856. A significant portion of the Kiger Papers describes the education of the Kiger children as they attended, variously, Oakland College, near Rodney, Mississippi; the University of Virginia; and the Virginia Female Institute, in Staunton. Evidence in the form of a sequence of personal letters written from each of the parents to each of the children, their letters in return, and, often, their letters to one another could serve as the basis for valuable comparative studies based on gender.

The rich correspondence of Mary Bell with her mother, father, and brothers reflects the life, education, and maturation of a sixteen-year-old girl away from home and in school in the early 1870s. Mary Bell's letters detail the curriculum and lifestyle at the Virginia Female Institute, report on schoolmates and describe her board and room (which she and her roommates called the "Vale of Sunshine and Shade"), and outline her courses and extracurricular activities. They even mention pranks the girls played on one another—short-sheeting beds and powdering pillows "so some of the girls woke up this morning with gray hair." In 1873, during her second year at the Virginia Female Institute, Mary Bell sent home a complete daily schedule, which attests to the school's substantive curriculum.

Mon & Wednes	Time	Tues & Thursday
Chronology	9–9$\frac{1}{2}$	Chronology
French	9$\frac{1}{2}$–10	French
Algebra	10–10$\frac{1}{2}$	Algebra
Free	10$\frac{1}{2}$–11	Free
Free	11–11$\frac{1}{2}$	Pars[e]ing
Elocution	11$\frac{1}{2}$–12	Free
Recess	12–12$\frac{1}{2}$	Recess
Literature	12$\frac{1}{2}$–1	Literature
Chemistry	1$\frac{1}{2}$	Chemistry
German	1$\frac{1}{2}$–2	German
French	2–2$\frac{1}{2}$	Free
Sacred Languages	2$\frac{1}{2}$–3	Writing
Dinner	3–3$\frac{1}{2}$	Dinner
Practice	3$\frac{1}{2}$–4	Practice

Mon Wednesday, & Friday Calisthenics in the evening, Tuesday evening skating, Thursday & Saturday evenings dancing.[26]

The several dozen letters between Mrs. Kiger and Mary Bell are quite
detailed, reflecting the difficult separation of this mother and her only
daughter. Mary Bell's letters suggest her initial loneliness as a new student
and her quick integration into her new life. At the beginning of her first
term, Mary Bell pleaded with her mother to "write to me about every person and thing from the family down to the dogs, cats, chickens, and tur-
keys"; by November, she expressed her desire to stay for three school ses-
sions rather than just two. Of special interest are Mrs. Kiger's letters
voicing her hopes as to how schooling would benefit her daughter. The
school's religious instruction was especially important, she noted, as was
its preparation for life's uncertain future—wise counsel from one living in
a city so recently ravaged by war and its aftermath. She cautioned Mary
Bell that the "time might come when you would be thrown entirely upon
your own resources," and added, "if you are well educated you could always take care of your self."[27]

Many smaller subcollections in the NTC contain useful bits of information relating to the formal education of Natchez District women as well
as the educational institutions that served them. The Burling Family Papers, for example, consist almost entirely of the receipts and accounts of
Mrs. Burling, a widow responsible for the education of her daughters Caroline, Eliza, Harriet, and Sophia. Tuition receipts and other accounts indicate that they attended various schools, including the Natchez Academy
and the Jamaica Plain Seminary. One receipt records forty-five dollars in
expenses for instructing "the three Misses Burling" in the art of dancing.
Similarly, the John J. Barrow Papers document the education of Amanda
R. Barrow, Mr. Barrow's sister and ward, at the Patapsco Institute in Maryland during the early 1850s.[28]

26. Mary Bell Kiger to Caroline Kiger, April 19, October 11, November 2, 1873, Kiger
Family Papers, Boxes 2E518 and 2E519.

27. Mary Bell Kiger to Caroline Kiger, September 19, 1872, Kiger Family Papers, Box
2E517; Caroline Kiger to Mary Bell Kiger, November 19, 1872, Kiger Family Papers, Box
2E518.

28. Various receipts, 1817, 1818, 1819, 1821, Burling Family Papers, Box 2E552; various receipts, 1852, 1853, John J. Barrow Papers, Box 2E549.

TERMS OF MADAM FLORIAN'S
SEMINARY FOR YOUNG LADIES:

For board and tuition, including all the useful parts of education, viz.
Reading, Writing, Arithmetic, the French, English and Italian
languages; Geography, History and every kind of needle work,

	Per Quarter	Doll.	80. 00. Cts.
Drawing,	*do.*		15. 00.
Piano Forte,	*do.*		15. 00.
Harp,	*do.*		15 00.
Singing,	*do.*		15. 00.
Dancing,	*do.*		15. 00.

The young ladies are to find their own beds and bedding, towels, sil-
ver fork and spoon, and to pay extra for their washing.

Such ladies as have no instrument of their own, may be accommodated
with the use of Piano Fortes or a Harp at six dollars per quarter, in-
cluding the tuning.

N. B. Every quarter to be paid in advance.

New-Orleans,

Announcement for Madam Florian's Seminary, a school for young ladies located in New Orleans. On the back of the announcement is a tuition bill for Natchez planter Stephen Minor, who sent two of his daughters to this school in 1811; their tuition for one quarter was $232. *From the Minor Family Papers, NTC, the Center for American History, the University of Texas at Austin.*

The Natchez Trace Collection also contains informative circulars and forms issued by schools that served southern women. For example, the Chamberlain-Hyland-Gould Papers contain materials relating to the education of Ellen and William Hyland's daughter Pattie, including her grade report from the Fayette Female College, Fayette, Mississippi, for the period ending June 1867. A letter from the school's principal accompanied the report. It noted that Pattie was commendable in every respect and requested reimbursement for funds advanced her during the term for necessary clothing and dental treatment.[29]

Similar forms for other female educational institutions in the NTC's Ephemera Collection list curricula and expenses and often provide detailed information on a school's mission and facilities. A circular for the Franklin Female College in Holly Springs documents $113 in charges to J. R. Davis for boarding his ward Mary Brown during the 1859 spring school session. A circular for the Lexington Baptist Female College documents that student Bethel Beck was offered courses in painting, drawing, and embroidery in addition to those in the "Collegiate Department." A prospectus for the Mount Vernon Institute in Baltimore, administered by Mrs. Mary J. Jones and her daughter as well as four other instructors, lists courses and expenses and offers references, including satisfied parents from Natchez and Louisiana. And an announcement circular for Trinity School, an Academy for Young Ladies in Pass Christian, Mississippi, under the guidance of Miss S. M. Burgess, offered the services of able professors in French, German, and music. Trinity School pupils, it noted, would be under the constant surveillance of a teacher, "while the Principal will devote herself most assiduously to their moral and intellectual culture." Tuition, with board, washing, and lights, was set at $150 per five-month session; music lessons cost an extra $50.[30]

The centrality of the Civil War to the American experience is reflected in the amount of women's testimony on it in the Natchez Trace Collection. Such materials invite research on the various ways women participated in this shared experience, coped with changed identities brought on by war-

29. T. H. Cleland to William S. Hyland, June 24, 1867, and Printed Report, Fayette Female College, June 21, 1867, Chamberlain-Hyland-Gould Family Papers, Box 2E508.

30. Various announcements, Ephemera Collection.

time upheaval, and reconstructed their lives in the aftermath. Personal letters in the collection contain women's opinions of the war's cause and progress, rumors and facts about battles and troop movements, expressions of anxiety about and reactions to the loss of loved ones and property, tales of deprivation and fear, and evidence of the social transformations brought on by war.[31]

The emotions displayed by Mrs. Frances Sprague were echoed by mothers and sisters in correspondence throughout the NTC: devastation at the loss of a loved one and bitterness at the presence of an occupation army. Anxious about her several sons fighting in the conflict, Mrs. Sprague was especially worried in early 1862 about the fate of son Kempe, who was then held prisoner. That spring she learned of Kempe's death, and in April she reported it to her daughter Margaret: "You will have heard before this of your poor brother Kempe's death and I am alive to tell it. . . . Oh my dear child may God preserve you and my other children to me for the rest of my life." In November 1863 she wrote that "1500 yanks passed my house on Friday. They have been whipped out of the back country. Three of the officers dined with me at their own invitation. I happened to have nine ladies dining with me that day all strong southern women and it would have done your heart good to have heard the conversation. . . . I saw Mrs. McMintz in the city some yank had her for a wife and she has my Emily for a waiting woman. So goes the world now under Yankee rule." By war's end Mrs. Sprague clearly was eager for some semblance of stability and wrote, "I hope and trust God has not so far deserted this country as to have us in the hands of such a set of rogues both black *and* white as this war has turned loose upon us, and it is the duty of all good men to help those in authority to restore good order. . . . if you had gone through half of what I have been through in the last three years you would help all you could to get law and order once more among us."[32]

Dramatic testimony of life during the war is found in the NTC's Crutcher-Shannon Family Papers, a collection of approximately seven

31. For an excellent compilation and analysis of the words of privileged Confederate women and the way the Civil War affected their lives, see Faust, *Mothers of Invention*.

32. Frances Sprague to Margaret Winchester, April 1, 1862, November 22, 1863, August 17, 1865, Winchester Family Papers, Boxes 2E912 and 2E913.

inches of personal and financial records of a Vicksburg family.[33] A principal correspondent in this collection is Emily (Emma) Shannon, daughter of Levina Morris Shannon and Marmaduke Shannon, publisher of the *Vicksburg Daily Whig*. Emily married William O. Crutcher in May 1861, just as the war began. By October, Will had enlisted in the Confederate Army, eventually to become captain of the E Company of the 2nd Mississippi Battalion, known as the King Cotton Guards. In the spring of 1863, an ailing Will left the army, and he and Emily moved to San Antonio, Texas, where they lived for the remainder of the war. Tragedy struck the Shannon and Crutcher families while the young couple was in Texas. Several of Emily's siblings died, and in May 1863 the *Daily Whig* printing office burned down. Less than two years after the war and his subsequent travels to Cuba and Mexico, Captain William O. Crutcher also died, in Vicksburg.

Emily and Will's separation from each other during the first half of the war and the couple's distance from family during the second half resulted in heavy correspondence among family members, including some who remained in Vicksburg during the siege and surrender of that city in 1863. Emily's letters prior to her departure for Texas frequently convey substantial information on the Vicksburg home front, including her work in the city hospital, the work of a women's association to raise money to benefit hospitals, and the war relief activities of the Vicksburg Free Market.

Emily Crutcher's description of the Vicksburg Free Market is vivid and highly informative. According to Emily, her mother-in-law was especially responsible for the market's success: "She just devotes her whole time to others, and runs around seeing butchers and bakers and meal-men and visits all the sick and holds a perfect levee everyday of all the poor people, hearing their sad stories, comforting, encouraging, helping and giving until she certainly deserves to be canonized, for nobody ever more fully earned the name of saint since the Bible days than she has."[34]

A participant in the market's beginnings, Emily wrote letters that supply excellent information on this attempt by women to join together to

33. See also the three cubic feet of Crutcher-Shannon Family Papers, 1826–1929, housed in the Mississippi Department of Archives and History.

34. Emily Crutcher to Will Crutcher, January 21, 1862, Crutcher-Shannon Papers, Box 2E511.

serve their city's needy during a time of crisis. Emily's letters also reveal
how the necessities of war both drove and enabled women to expand their
participation in the public sphere, at least for a time. Her remarks on the
Vicksburg Free Market constitute a virtual history of its origins. The market, she wrote her husband,

> sprang from a little advertisement your mother and Mrs. Howe to-
> gether concocted, and published, asking the planters to assist, in
> taking care of the poor,—and a few bushels of meal and potatoes
> were sent to your mother which she distributed by sending Ella and
> [?] around to the different houses. Then the quantity augmented so
> that Mrs. Howe and little Sister Smith had to assist in giving it out.
> Still increasing, the provisions were left at the store, and Tom and
> Jake distributed according to orders, and then there was a string of
> women here from morning till night after an offer for *"male."* Fi-
> nally your father told the ladies they might have a portion of the
> room under the carriage room, and come to distribute themselves,
> and the Vicksburg free market assumed something of the propor-
> tions it now occupies. Mr. Jacob Peale was appointed by the Board of
> Police, to take care of the soldier's families, but after trying it awhile
> he came to the ladies and told them that it was no use talking—he
> could *not* manage those Irish women, that his means were inade-
> quate, anyhow, and he would turn the whole lot over to them, and
> give them all the assistance in his power. The market is held every
> Tuesday morning. Your mother and I started as soon as breakfast was
> over, for the store, and found Mrs. Howe [and others] waiting in the
> counting room for us—went into the carriage room and took of[f]
> our bonnets, and I my cloak (for I had my furs) while the other la-
> dies had to be encumbered with theirs, for it was very cold. Went
> down stairs, and saw a rope stretched from the door that leads into
> the street, and on the other side of the line, a patient crowd of
> women with baskets and bags, and then I dived into the hogsheads
> of meal and barrels of flour, and scarcely saw anything more till half
> past twelve o'clock when the last one went away satisfied. Some 90
> families went away supplied with meal, flour, beef, peas, potatoes,
> turnips, cabbage, pumpkins, molasses, sugar, salt and soap enough

for a week. Now that is pretty well, to follow from such a small beginning. That is the best situation too, for such an institution, for
the planters come to the store on business, are invited down stairs to
see what is going on, and immediately go home and send in a load
for next week. It seems to please them so much to see the ladies
working with their own hands, and all the gentlemen in town are
becoming interested.[35]

The Natchez Trace Collection contains evidence of the experiences of
several Vicksburg families during the war. Appearing in several subcollections, the Vicksburg letters testify to the interconnectedness of Natchez
District families. Levina Shannon's letters to her sister detail her town's
destruction, the surrender, and the condition of the Confederate troops
and residents. "The yankees turned Dukie [their brother] out of what was
left of our house and installed a lot of free negroes in it. When the yankees
invested the city there was only fifteen days rations in it which was made
to last seven weeks. The soldiers were starving, they eat mules, cats, dogs,
toads, rats, and everything they could get . . . one [soldier] told me that he
has seen rats sell for five dollars a pair." Months later she noted that
"Vicksburg looks like a picture of desolation, nearly every body's fences
are down, the houses look dilapidated, a number have been pulled down
to build fortifications. . . . I scarcely ever go out on the street and when I
do I feel like a stranger." The family's devastation only increased near
war's end, when Dukie was killed while on picket guard near Mobile.[36]

The James J. Cowan Papers contain letters from other Vicksburg
women during the war. This two-inch collection of family correspondence
and financial papers includes many detailed letters to and from Mrs. Maria
Louisa Cowan and her husband James, who served as an artillery commander near Mobile. During the war, Mrs. Cowan and other family members moved out of the center of town to nearby Beech Grove, a move
Maria considered exile, though warranted. Writing to a friend in 1862,
Mrs. Cowan noted,

35. See Emily Crutcher's letters to Will Crutcher dated March 27, April 15, November
18, 1861, January 6, 21, 1862, in the Crutcher-Shannon Family Papers, Box 2E511.
36. Levina Shannon to Emily Crutcher, July 13, November 19, 1863, Marmaduke
(Dukie) Shannon to Emily Crutcher, April 14, 1865, Crutcher-Shannon Family Papers,
Box 2E511.

The Yankees are still shelling town every day and playing the wild with stores and houses but I am thankful to say our house is not struck yet although a good many shells are thrown in the yard and elsewhere near. One went through Dick Buck's parlour and struck the Piano. Some Soldiers are living in our house. The Catholic and Babtist[sic] church are ruined almost ours not hurt they succeeded in hitting the Court house at last. They have dug a Canal and built a railroad across the Point to transport Provisions to New Orleans and avoid our Batteries when the [?] Vicksburg will be cut off from the Miss river. We are putting up more guns above town and have no fears of their ever taking our Batteries. . . . There are sick soldiers at almost every house and the well ones are always coming and going the whole country is full of them.

Nearly two months later Maria wrote Eliza again, expressing her sense of "considerable peril here" and her hope that "we shall be ready for them when they come again."[37]

Letters between husband and wife describe Mrs. Cowan's several relocations of the family during the war as well as James Cowan's war experiences. Mrs. Cowan's letters convey her anguish over the reported assault and capture of Cowan's battery in April, followed by her relief on receiving the news of her husband's survival and parole in May. Letters to Mrs. Cowan from family and friends in Vicksburg and Jackson reported the deaths of friends and fellow citizens. One letter mentions the death of Marmaduke Shannon, brother to Emily Shannon Crutcher.[38]

The NTC contains testimony reflecting southern women's patriotic reactions to the conflict and, as the deprivations of war continued, to the toll that the war inevitably exacted. Irene, sister of Maria Cowan, wrote defiantly from Jackson at the very close of the war that "the '*gig is up*' I suppose, at least on this side of the *Miss River*. How awful! to contemplate— How galling to submit! It makes my heart bleed to think of *Our* Splendid

37. Marie L. Cowan to Eliza T. Mau——ry, July 6, August 29, 1862, James J. Cowan Family Papers, Box 2E555.

38. Irene [?] to Maria Cowan, April 11, 1865, Sergeant Major Lundy, First Mississippi Light Artillery, to Mrs. Cowan, April 21, 1865, Irene to Maria Cowan, April 23, 1865, James J. Cowan to Maria L. Cowan, May 11, 1865, ibid.

boys—who prematurely died and whose lives have been given up in *Vain*—for country. I feel that they *must* be resurrected since their sacrifice of life has availed nothing but *subjugation*. T'were better *borne* if we had gained what they *died* to maintain."[39]

Ellen Hyland, who died in 1863, defined the conflict as God's punishment: "We needed chastisement both as individuals and as a nation for our inordinate pride. . . . May we as Christians and as a nation truly humble ourselves before God and repent of our great sin." Conversely, Cornelia (Nellie) Burt saw all the tragedy of war as the direct result of a "hateful foe," and wondered "how many anathemas are heaped on the heads of all Yankees for our troubles."[40]

Cornelia Burt's family was another directly affected by the war. Her letters and those of her sister in the NTC's Chamberlain-Hyland-Gould Papers reveal her bitterness at its devastating effects. "Death has entered and torn from us our loved ones," she wrote Pattie in 1866, adding, "We have been torn asunder and scourged. We have wandered far and near, have experienced privation, want, and insult from the hand of our enemy." According to Miss Burt, the family left Jackson and moved several times in order to find a "retreat from the Yankees." They settled in Georgia, but fled again in the face of General Sherman's army, shells, and lack of food. One brother died "by the hand of the hated Yankee" and another was lost, later, to sickness.[41]

Although most of the Natchez Trace Collection materials concern privileged southern women, the collection also contains evidence that will support research on southern women whose livelihood depended all or in part on their earnings. In the Winchester Papers, letters to and from Mrs. Frances E. Sprague, widowed while a relatively young woman, make clear her interest in earning money by running a boarding house and contain particulars about that form of employment.[42] Family financial records

39. Irene to Maria Cowan, May 4, 1865, ibid.
40. Ellen Hyland to Mary [?], May 25, 1861, Cornelia (Nellie) Burt to J. C. Hyland, February 22, 1867, Chamberlain-Hyland-Gould Family Papers, Box 2E508.
41. Cornelia Burt to Pattie Hyland, July 22, 1866, ibid.
42. See, for example, Frances Sprague to Margaret Sprague, October 4, 1844, and Eliza Ann Dupuy to Frances Sprague, March 20, 1845, Winchester Family Papers, Box 2E913.

name tradeswomen with whom Margaret Winchester dealt. For example, she regularly purchased goods and services from Natchez tradeswomen such as Mrs. Sarah Jenkins, who sold Margaret milk and sewed for her from around 1864 to 1872.[43] Other records reveal that she bought goods from Rosina Solari, Eliza McDonnell, and Lizzie Fox. Personal letters written by Fannie Pugh also contain scattered bits of information on white women who worked in the household as help or nurses. Additional evidence on working women is found in the scattered but still valuable pieces in hundreds of NTC smaller manuscript collections. One small collection contains a receipt for Fanny Brustic's dressmaking services to Mrs. Eustis in 1839. Another lists tenants living on Compromise plantation. Of the twenty-eight tenants listed in 1882, seven were women.[44]

Letters from teacher and writer Eliza Ann Dupuy in the Winchester Papers also reflect the life of a working woman and underscore the diversity of the southern women's experience revealed in the NTC. A former resident of Natchez and part of that city's literary circle, Miss Dupuy (1814–1880) earned her living as a teacher and author of romantic fiction. Her most successful novel, *The Conspirator*, was first published in 1843 while Dupuy still lived in Natchez. The story of Aaron Burr's efforts to create an empire in the Southwest, by 1868 it had sold more than 25,000 copies. By the time of her death in late 1880, Miss Dupuy had written some fifteen works of fiction, including *The Country Neighborhood* (1855), said to have been based on life in the Natchez area. Her novel *The Planter's Daughter: A Tale of Louisiana* (1857) was described by one contemporary critic as "redolent of murder, madness, tears, robbery, revolvers, corpses, and confusions."[45]

43. See, for example, receipts for August 1, October 31, 1864, February 12, 1865, Winchester Family Papers, Box 2E912.
44. Receipts for Eliza McDonald dated August 15, 1865; for Lizzie Fox, November 28, 1870, and March 18, 1871; for Rosina Solari, February 3, 1868, and April, May, June, 1868; Frances Pugh to Margaret Winchester, March 4, 1853, November 6, 1854, Winchester Family Papers, Box 2E912; Fanny Brustic Receipt, 1839, Box 2E522; Accounts, 1882, Compromise Plantation Records, Box 2E555.
45. Various works will acquaint readers with the type of fiction written by Eliza Dupuy or enjoyed by her readers. See, for example, Nina Baym, *Woman's Fiction: A Guide to Novels by and about Women in America, 1820–1870* (Ithaca: Cornell University Press, 1978); Elizabeth Moss, *Domestic Novelists in the Old South: Defenders of Southern Culture* (Baton Rouge:

Miss Dupuy's letters to her friend Frances Sprague give evidence of the economic realities of a single wage-earning woman in the antebellum South. In them she reports on her efforts to publish her new work of fiction, *The Pirate's Daughter*, acknowledges her impatience with her vexing New York publisher, and asks Frances to use her influence to get Natchez booksellers to buy copies of her latest work. Miss Dupuy's letters describe her practical figuring of her personal finances and her recognition that she must resume teaching in order to earn a living wage. Formerly a governess in the home of Thomas G. Ellis near Natchez, Miss Dupuy was familiar with some of the teaching options available to her and to other women. In letters to Frances Sprague, she weighed those options—teaching at a Free School in Mississippi, as a live-in teacher with a private family, or in a large academy "where teachers are society for each other"—as she considered her future.[46]

The view of teaching as an acceptable profession for southern women, including those widowed by war, is evident in some of the same documents that detail the schooling of daughters of upper-class families. Emily (Emma) Crutcher, a widow by 1866, took up teaching after the Civil War, and the Crutcher-Shannon Family Papers include her grade books from her years as teacher at the Main Street Girls High School in Vicksburg, from 1874 to 1878 and 1887 to 1892. Several subcollections in the NTC also contain information on both educating southern women and female teachers. For example, the Burling Family Papers contain tuition bills from various female teachers for educating the Burling daughters.[47]

Natchez Trace Collection letters and financial records are also rich sources for the study of southern women's participation in the marketplace, both local and distant. Such materials shed light on the women's domestic world through data on their purchase of clothing, furnishings,

Louisiana State University Press, 1992); *Notable American Women, 1607–1950: A Biographical Dictionary* (Cambridge, Mass.: Belknap Press, 1971), 1: 533–34. A collection of Eliza Dupuy's letters is housed at Duke University Library.

46. Eliza Ann Dupuy to Frances Sprague, March 20, June 23, July 19, 1845, July 1845, Winchester Family Papers, Box 2E913.

47. Grade books, Crutcher-Shannon Family Papers, Box 2E533; various receipts, 1817, 1821, Burling Family Papers, Box 2E552.

food, and other consumables and through evidence of direct involvement in the financial management of the domestic sphere. NTC financial records associated with family papers or found in the many NTC ledgers for merchants underscore the regular participation of women in their local marketplace, and letters written by planters' wives and other elites which regularly testify to busy lives and the daily coping with sickness, bad weather, recalcitrant servants, schooling, and gardening also routinely mention the responsibilities of daily marketing and/or property management. The Winchester Papers contain more than twenty inches of household accounts and receipts for Margaret Winchester, whose residence in Natchez gave her ready access to a wide range of merchants, goods, and services. Her household accounts and receipts track her routine purchase of fabric, clothing, sewing notions, food, garden equipment, candles, hats, livestock (including lots of chickens), furniture, medicine, kitchen utensils and equipment of every description, and reading material. In April 1866, for example, Mrs. Winchester (or perhaps her servant) visited one Mr. Walsh for shoe repair on at least five different days. Further, Mrs. Winchester routinely engaged repairmen and seamstresses; in 1872, for example, she spent $29.25 to have seven mattresses made up, the ticking washed, and the "Sopha" repaired.[48]

Mrs. Winchester also occasionally bought goods on credit, and family accounts, receipts, and notes from vendors indicate that at least one, M. E. Dickinson, was forced to press her for overdue payment. On June 28, 1867, Miss Dickinson requested payment on Mrs. Winchester's bill of $18.50 for sewing clothing; her note read, "If you cannot let me have the whole amount will you let me have part?" On several occasions Mrs. Winchester paid off her debts with goods rather than by cash. During the war she bought fabric from Miss A. C. Smith and retired a portion of her debt of $33.50 by $3.50 paid in cash; $7.00 in rice; .50 each for potatoes, beef steak, and tea; and .80 for meal. In March 1866, she paid off a portion of her bill of $42.30 to Miss Smith for sewing services with a combination of cash, one yard of alpaca, and one pound of butter.[49]

48. Various receipts, Winchester Family Papers, Box 2E912.

49. Accounts of Mrs. Winchester with A. C. Smith, 1862–63 and 1865–66, Winchester Family Papers, Box 2E912.

Margaret (Mrs. Josiah) Winchester's bill for the purchase of one bonnet from Natchez milliner Madame Ducie in February, 1861. *From the Winchester Family Papers, NTC, the Center for American History, the University of Texas at Austin.*

The Natchez Trace Collection's numerous store ledgers offer additional evidence of women's participation in the marketplace. The accounts of Jefferson County blacksmiths Thomas Stirling and William Gillaspie record that Elisa Braseal hired them in 1821 to sharpen her shears and repair a steel trap.[50] Similarly, the store ledger for Hinds County dry goods merchant and grocer J. L. McManus lists accounts for female customers, including Sarah Jones, Mrs. Ann Wolf, Mrs. Catherine A. Funchess, Mrs. Virginia Burnett, and Felia Lacey. Mrs. Jones's accounts, for example, document her purchases totaling $23.89 from February through December of 1855. The majority of her purchases during that year were domestic items, including fabric, shoes, spoons, thimble, thread, pins, needles, a comb, one vial of calomel, and one box of "chill & fever pills."

The accounts for Mrs. Burnett suggest her tenuous economic position or at least her lack of ready cash. From September through December of 1854, Mrs. Burnett purchased $27.26 worth of fabric, hardware, and crockery. She paid a portion of her bill in goods in the form of $7.31 worth of beef, bacon, chickens, and sewing work. By January 1855, Mrs. Burnett's bill stood at $19.25, of which she paid $11.00 in cash, then reduced her debt by another $5.00 through labor, thus leaving her with a $3.95 balance on January 15, 1855. Other accounts for women exist in the Natchez Business Store Ledger for the mid-1820s and in the business records of Harrison and Lewis Mercantile in Hinds County, Mississippi.[51]

NTC subcollections also document the activities of single or widowed upper-class southern women who were heads of households and regularly dealt directly with attorneys, bankers, plantation managers, and cotton factors in the management of their affairs. Frances Sprague is one example. Upon the death of her husband in 1838, Mrs. Sprague became responsible for her family's extensive land holdings and personal property, including slaves. Although she received advice and assistance from her late husband's law partner George Winchester and, later, her lawyer son-in-law Josiah Winchester, Frances appears to have involved herself in the

50. Stirling and Gillaspie Blacksmith Records, Box 2E616.
51. J. L. McManus Mercantile Business Records, Box 2E626; Natchez Business Store Ledger, Box 2E630; Harrison and Lewis Mercantile of Hinds County, Mississippi, Boxes 2E584–2E599.

management of these affairs. In the early 1840s, perhaps to acquire ready cash following her husband's death, she sold several slaves and deeded to her sister Elizabeth Kempe hundreds of acres of property as well as a lot in Natchez for the loan of $9,000 over three years. Months before the end of the Civil War she made further arrangements for her property: "I have at last got rid of I hope a great deal of trouble by hiring out this plantation for two years, I am to get 8000 dollars a year without any deduction for bad crops, and it is a good man who has hired on the wagon for two years. . . . I hope I will have a little more peace in 65 than I had in 64, and may God grant the whole country will have too. We must pray all the time for peace to be restored once more to this poor distracted country."[52]

Other women landowners are also represented in NTC subcollections. Nancy Bieller, for example, sent instructions to E. W. Brazelton, her property manager in Rodney, Mississippi, to look out for her interests concerning a possible loan of oxen to a neighbor. She directed him to "be neighborly . . . render and receive favors, but not in such a way as to make any of my beasts or tools unfit for service to the farm." She urged him to "hurry your wood getting—get 3000 cords, if possible, by the 1st Jan'y next. If the taxes are due yet, pay them out of money left with you."[53]

Materials relating to Sarah Billingsley's property document her ownership in 1851 of a plantation in Warren County, Mississippi, some twenty-four slaves, sales of cotton through various factors, and personal possessions in her Vicksburg residence, including a piano, a clock, and a carriage. Other separate small collections of financial records in the NTC document the dealings of Mrs. Elizabeth Burling of Natchez, whose property was managed by Natchez cotton factor James C. Wilkins, and of Mrs. C. G. Covington of New Orleans.[54]

With its abundance of letters written by upper-class women, the Natchez Trace Collection is replete with evidence of privileged women's social

52. Receipts for the sale of slaves, November 26, 1840, April 12, 1841, Frances Sprague deed with George Winchester, July 9, 1841, Winchester Family Papers, Box 2E913; Frances Sprague to Margaret Winchester, January 2, 1865, Winchester Family Papers, Box 2E912.

53. Nancy Bieller to W. E. Brazelton, July 20, 1837, Nancy Bieller Letter, Box 2E551.

54. Various receipts, 1851, Sarah Billingsley Papers, Box 2E551; Elizabeth Burling Papers, Box 2E552; Covington Family Papers, Box 2E555.

lives and thus offers opportunities for research on the character and evolution of their participation in that sphere. "Frolics," visits, and teas are frequently described, as are other, more formal social gatherings. NTC newspapers record local festivities and social events, as do the ephemera found
in the collection. Ephemeral items, including invitations, calling cards,
dance programs, and announcements of lectures, musical events, and boat
excursions, are located both in family papers and as part of the NTC
Broadside and Ephemera collections. Their often formal language, stylized
type, and decorative embellishments reflect social events of elegance and
refinement and give evidence of the content and variety of entertainment
and social engagements available to some southern women.

The NTC's extensive collection of imprints invite research on the
types of leisure reading that upper-class southern women enjoyed. Reading
materials included almanacs, literary, religious, and fashion magazines,
nursery and seed catalogs, newspapers, and popular novels. The availability of regional and nationally published magazines and newspapers, as well
as books, is shown by advertisements of local booksellers and stationers in
the NTC Broadside Collection. Similarly, access to leisure reading is reflected in the many ads published in local and regional newspapers that
form the NTC Newspaper Collection, a collection of more than two hundred newspaper titles that is especially strong in the decades before the
Civil War for titles and issues from Louisiana and Mississippi towns and
cities. The NTC Sheet Music Collection and the NTC Photograph Collection also include examples of music and stereopticon views that entertained many Natchez District families.

Finally, some women's letters in the Natchez Trace Collection give direct
evidence of women's efforts to define and expand their identities in the
face of the social and gender conventions that so shaped their world.
Emily Shannon, for example, chaffed at the enforced idleness caused by a
friend's visit. In her letter to her fiancée in 1861, she noted that she did
not welcome the unexpected and prolonged visit from Miss Annie Coulson: "To my infinite disappointment [she] laid aside her hat and took out
her work to spend the day . . . she repays one five minutes' call from me too
liberally with two whole days." Emily apparently liked Miss Coulson ("she

is very superior to all the rest of the young ladies put together") but admitted she was simply "tired of company."[55]

Emily also was distressed by her peers' lack of physical fitness. Few of the ladies working in the Vicksburg Free Market, she noted, "have strength to stand it—such physical wrecks as the American women are. And especially the married women, for the germs of disease often remain dormant, until they are married, and afterward develop with alarming rapidity." Emily blamed their alarming weakness on "want of exercise and tight lacing" and felt their condition was only "aggravated by the medicine." The root of the problem, according to Emily Crutcher, was heredity, or "weak constitutions," which, however, "would not interfere with a reasonable share of health and strength, were it not for the preposterously false way in which women nowadays live. Their mothers did not feel the effects of this ignorant way of existing because they possessed strong constitutions."[56]

Emily also expressed disbelief at the apparent willingness of some of her contemporaries to limit their own futures through idleness and deliberate ignorance. Frustrated with their "utter waste of time, talents and strength," she especially lamented the "perfect right of ignorance and stupidity into which some of these women are plunged. . . . Living on from one year's end to the next without thinking one thought which would raise them above the level of children or one single hope or aspiration for the future that their *cooks* might not indulge in; and, worse than all, poisoning the lives of others by their indulgence, in that certain resort of vacant mind, gossip and slander, so they go on, from silly, vapid youth, to venomous old age, and dying, leave the world, *worse* than if they had never lived." To attain true happiness, which Emily felt was "the ultimate object of all," she recommended "*full* employment of all the powers of soul, mind, heart and body."[57]

For teacher and author Eliza Ann Dupuy, happiness meant meaningful activity and the "sympathy" of close friendship, a relationship apparently not easily available in her social circle. In her 1845 letter to longtime

55. Emily Crutcher to Will Crutcher, December 23, 1861, Crutcher-Shannon Family Papers, Box 2E511.

56. Emily Crutcher to Will Crutcher, January 6, 1862, ibid.

57. Emily Shannon to Will Crutcher, January 21, 1861, ibid.

friend Frances Sprague, she wrote, "I am tired to death of being of no use
to any body." Bored with reading, sewing, and writing letters, Eliza admitted to Frances that the "leisure that I so eagerly desired has become the
weariness of wearinesses." She even found visiting friends unsatisfying: "I
have to go to houses, whose inhabitants are horribly indifferent to me, and
spend whole evenings in gossip that my soul detests, because the people
are good sort of souls, and seek me so that I must be found—there is nothing to interest me in so stupid a place, that I feel like one living in a wilderness." What she missed, she confided to Frances, was "a single ultimate
friend . . . one to whom I can speak as to myself. This seems a puerile complaint, but those who have lived without sympathy can readily understand
it."[58]

Frances E. Sprague died June 5, 1892, some forty-seven years after she
received Eliza Dupuy's heartfelt letter. Her funeral was held in Natchez,
and friends and acquaintances were invited to a service scheduled for
10:30 A.M. in the city's Presbyterian Church.[59] A widow for more than
fifty-four years, Mrs. Sprague had outlived her daughter Fannie by more
than thirty-two years, her son Kempe by nearly thirty, and her son-in-law,
Josiah Winchester, by five. She had helped raise one daughter's children,
traveled, bought and sold property, and survived a catastrophic war.

Most of what we know about Mrs. Sprague we learn from the Winchester Family Papers, a collection largely composed of documents written by
or to George and Josiah Winchester, the two men with whom she was
linked through her husband's business and a daughter's marriage.[60] NTC
materials offering direct evidence of Mrs. Sprague's life are rich and include legal documents, financial records, ephemera, and, especially, the
personal letters Mrs. Sprague wrote to family and friends and those written to her by the same. Taken together, such materials create more than
this one woman's silhouette; they reveal much of her personal story, often
in her own words. Historians of the South and of woman's history can use
Mrs. Sprague's story, as well as the Natchez Trace Collection's extensive

58. Eliza Ann Dupuy to Frances Sprague, July 1845, Winchester Family Papers, Box
2E913.

59. Funeral card of Frances Sprague, ibid.

60. The Frances Sprague Scrapbook, 1881–1887, is housed in the Mississippi Department of Archives and History.

documentation on other southern women, to help write their individual and collective histories, to build our understanding of the role of women in the nineteenth-century South, and as part of comparative regional studies.

At the conclusion of her 1990 review essay of Elizabeth Fox-Genovese's book *Within the Plantation Household: Black and White Women of the Old South*, Suzanne Lebsock urges those studying southern women's history to "read closely, reframe questions, stake out positions, clarify terms—and head back to the archives."[61] The Natchez Trace Collection offers a productive focus for those who follow Lebsock's final suggestion.

61. Lebsock, "Review Essay: Complicity and Contention," 83.

MORTON ROTHSTEIN

Acquisitive Pursuits in a Slaveholding Society:
Business History in the Natchez Trace Collection

The Natchez Trace Collection contains much detailed information about antebellum business activities and the relationships among its participants in the several counties on both sides of the Mississippi River as well as in Natchez itself. Students of business and economic history will find much of interest in the records of enterprises in the Natchez District from its beginnings as a Spanish and then French outpost.

My own research on the entrepreneurs of the town and its hinterland began more than thirty years ago at—oddly enough—the New York Historical Society. I was studying unprocessed business letters related to that seaport's nineteenth-century grain and flour exports when one of the archivists, impressed by my diligence in searching through such materials, took me into the stacks to show me other unprocessed holdings. (The Society's leaders were at that time more interested in preserving their art collection than examining their manuscript acquisitions.)

Among the largest of their untouched manuscript holdings was the set of Leverich family records, in which letters and ledgers about business activities were thoroughly intermixed with personal correspondence. On sampling the dusty bundles of mail, still tightly folded and tied between thin boards for storage, I became aware that much of the collection had to do with Natchez and its environs, especially its growing and shipping of cotton in the period from the 1820s to 1870s. I also realized that the Stephen Duncan so prominent in these piles of mail was the same business figure whom my Cornell University doctoral mentor Paul W. Gates had previously described as quite possibly the nation's leading cotton planter.

It was surely the cotton boom of the 1810s that drew the oldest two of the four Leverich brothers, after they had served their apprenticeships in New York City mercantile firms, to New Orleans and Natchez in search of business opportunities. In the 1830s they introduced their two younger brothers to Duncan's nieces, sisters recently arrived from Carlisle, Pennsylvania. The two Leveriches married the two Gustine girls and took them back to New York. The recognition of that family connection, a vital though often hidden determinant of business relationships, led me to Carlisle and Philadelphia, where the Library Company and the Pennsylvania Historical Society had several major and a dozen or so minor archival collections related to early Natchez commercial life. Research visits to the eastern cities led to longer efforts in the major repositories of the Carolinas, Georgia, Alabama, Louisiana, and Mississippi.

Years later, after many disruptions in my research plans, probing the Natchez Trace Collection was rather like discovering previously missing pieces of the now-familiar business activities that had occurred in the wealthy and bustling District during the late eighteenth and most of the nineteenth centuries. This collection of collections enables a deeper understanding of how business was conducted, how it evolved, and the strengths and foibles of those involved in it. Natchez itself was a rather small town, little more than a village even by antebellum standards, with fewer than four thousand inhabitants in 1840 and little more than six thousand in 1860. Several dozen of its well-informed residents, however, shrewdly combined ownership and administration of plantations with banking, shipping, and mercantile pursuits. The houses of leading citizens on the outskirts of the town reputedly held more millionaires per capita by the eve of the Civil War than virtually any equivalent town, city, or county in the United States. From their homes and offices in and around Natchez, these people were in touch with major cotton and sugar firms and markets in New Orleans, Philadelphia, and New York. From the territorial period to the Civil War, several planters also corresponded directly with merchants in London and Liverpool. The owners and managers of relatively small shops and such professionals as doctors and lawyers also left intriguing though usually much less voluminous records about their activities. It is no wonder that few if any other parts of the Cotton Kingdom have had as much scholarly attention lavished on them.

For several generations scholars have known about a limited number of letters, account books, wills, and legal documents related to business activities in the town, whose inhabitants by the 1830s were heavily involved in the flush times of the century's greatest expansion in growing cotton for overseas markets. The sources of their livelihood before the improvement of cotton gins had been more diverse; raising livestock had been the chief means of sustenance, supplemented by planting indigo and tobacco and by lumbering. Although the availability of the gin caused them to focus increasingly on cotton, it also took some time for Natchez planters to adopt the varieties of cotton that the gin could handle (introduced in the 1820s by Rush Nutt and his son Haller), and to adjust to the strengths and foibles of the process.

Natchez at this time had a small cluster of modest shops, warehouses, and offices providing services for the town's residents and for the plantations owned by several of them in the sugar-producing districts of Louisiana, in the cotton parishes in the northeastern quadrant of that state, and in the eastern counties of Arkansas. By the 1840s and 1850s, the town's population growth had slowed and it had become primarily an investment and service center for those leading citizens who sought better returns on their accumulated capital, by such means as extending private loans to planters and merchants in nearby newly developing counties and parishes, purchasing public lands in other states in both the North and the South, and investing in real estate, railroad securities, and government bonds in the United Kingdom as well as in the United States.[1]

1. Bennett H. Wall, "Breaking Out: What Is *Not* in Southern History, 1918–1988," *Journal of Southern History* 55 (February 1989): 3–20. I have discussed several of the area's leading businessmen in "The Twilight of the 'Nabobs': Civil War Losses and the End of Natchez, Mississippi, as an Investment Center," in *Cities and Markets: Studies in the Organization of Human Space* (Baltimore: University Press of America, 1997) and in "The Changing Social Networks and Investment Behavior of a Slaveholding Elite in the Antebellum South: Some Natchez 'Nabobs,' 1800–1860," in *Entrepreneurs in Cultural Context*, ed. Sidney M. Greenfield et al. (Albuquerque: New Mexico University Press, 1979). The best work on the town itself is still D. Clayton James, *Antebellum Natchez* (1968; rpr. Baton Rouge:

Now that the Natchez Trace Collection is available, researchers interested in Natchez District business have access to more archives than ever before. The NTC contains many relatively small but choice groups of papers with significant business materials, and at least four exceedingly rich, even daunting, subcollections.

First among the major holdings are the Winchester Papers, which cover the greatest span of time, from the territorial days of the military outpost to 1820, when George Winchester arrived in Natchez from Massachusetts. The extensive Winchester law firm began when Winchester joined Robert H. Adams as junior partner in an established practice; when Adams resigned to serve as a judge, Winchester became the leading partner in the

---

Louisiana State University Press, 1993). Two useful books on the town and its hinterland during and after the Civil War are Ronald F. Davis, *Good and Faithful Labor: From Slavery to Sharecropping in the Natchez District, 1860–1880* (Westport, Conn.: Greenwood Press, 1982), and Michael Wayne, *The Reshaping of Plantation Society: The Natchez District, 1860–1880* (Baton Rouge: Louisiana State University Press, 1983). On the concentration of wealth in the counties and parishes fifty miles up and down the Mississippi River from the town, see Lee Soltow, *Men and Wealth in the United States, 1850–1870* (New Haven, Conn.: Yale University Press, 1975). On the concentration of wealth throughout the South, see James Oakes, *The Ruling Race: A History of American Slaveholders* (New York: Knopf, 1982), and Gavin Wright, " 'Economic Democracy' and the Concentration of Agricultural Wealth in the Cotton South, 1850–1860," *Agricultural History* 44 (January 1970): 63–85. For an anthropological study of the earlier development of an American frontier "business culture," see Michael Zuckerman, "Fate, Flux, and Good Fellowship: An Early Virginia Design for the Dilemma of American Business," in *Business and Its Environment: Essays for Thomas C. Cochran*, ed. Harold I. Sharlin (Westport, Conn.: Greenwood Press, 1983), 161–84. For a brief commentary on the economic opportunities in the lower Mississippi valley (including the older parts of the region before the Cotton Kingdom came into being), and especially cattle herding as a source of income, see John D. W. Guice, "Cattle Raisers of the Old Southwest: A Reinterpretation," *Western Historical Quarterly* 8 (April 1977): 167–87. Two articles that review much of the discussion in a broader context are Rowland Berthoff, "Celtic Mist over the South," *Journal of Southern History* 52 (November 1986): 523–50, and Tamara Miner Haygood, "Cows, Ticks, and Disease: A Medical Interpretation of the Southern Cattle Industry," ibid., 551–64. On the hybridization techniques that Nutt and others used to improve the cotton product, see John H. Moore, "Cotton Breeding in the Old South," *Agricultural History* 30 (July 1956): 93–103, and his excellent study *The Emergence of the Cotton Kingdom in the Old Southwest: Mississippi, 1770–1860* (Baton Rouge: Louisiana State University Press, 1988). There is also a choice group of letters on cotton seed experiments in the Nutt Family Papers at the Huntington Library.

firm. He then took on a succession of junior partners, most notably his nephew Josiah in the 1840s. The firm's records gradually become denser throughout the nineteenth century, representing some of the leading entrepreneurial families in the Natchez area through war and peace. The second major holding for business historians is the large deposit of Bank of the State of Mississippi Records. They cover primarily the period from the bank's founding in 1809 to the 1840s, when its charter was canceled and it went out of business, though not without a trail of litigation that lasted for years. The papers of James C. Wilkins, once perhaps the town's most prominent merchant as well as a banker and planter, and one of its most colorful political and military figures, constitute the third subcollection important for business research. His records show the advantages of having connections in New Orleans, Lexington, Pittsburgh, and other markets for conducting mercantile pursuits. They also indicate the hazards of conducting business while succumbing to a weakness for the bottle. Finally, there are the voluminous papers of the large Archer family, who settled near Port Gibson, about twenty miles north of Natchez, with a paterfamilias who became prominent in both political and commercial circles. It requires some knowledge of the town's and region's history to appreciate these sources fully, since virtually all of them are directly tied to holdings in other university libraries, state archives, and historical societies in many southern states. In addition to these other locations of records pertaining to Natchez business, there are collections in New York City, Boston (especially the Dun & Bradstreet records at the Harvard Business School), Philadelphia, and Baltimore, as well as holdings in Great Britain, that provide special insights into the business that made so many wealthy.[2]

2. Don E. Carleton has described the contents of the collection in *Natchez Before 1830: L. O. Crosby, Jr., Memorial Lectures II*, ed. Noel Polk (Jackson: University Press of Mississippi, 1989), 60–74, a book that also has an essay, "Some Sources of Pre-1830 Natchez History," by Alfred E. Lemmon, that includes many references to the Natchez District. An organization similar to the Historic New Orleans Collection, of which Lemmon is administrator, has been established at Natchez, preserving many of the well-worn materials formerly stored at the county courthouse, as well as materials previously in private hands. Thomas D. Clark and John D. W. Guice, *Frontiers in Conflict: The Old Southwest, 1795–1830* (Albuquerque: University of New Mexico Press, 1989), and William C. Davis, *A Way Through the Wilderness: The Natchez Trace and the Civilization of the Southern Frontier* (New

*   *   *

The Winchester Papers are filled with the routine, the occasionally bi-
zarre, and the often complex business of successful law offices, most of it
involving the transfer of property. In addition to the documentation of
debt collecting and estate handling described by John D. W. Guice in this
volume, there are indentures, drafts of oral arguments for use in court-
rooms and for appeals of lower court decisions, various papers served on
and for clients, accounts of loans, copies of land transfers, and inventories
to legatees and executors of wills, foreclosures, and the like. The early history of the practice included the frequent partnership changes so characteristic of lawyers in that period. The first head of the Winchester firm,
Robert Adams, had come to Natchez from Tennessee at the beginning of
the century and joined the informal group of conservative Federalists who
traded public appointments while they dominated the town's politics.
Adams resigned in the mid-1820s to take a succession of public offices,
and George Winchester was left in full charge as senior partner of the
firm. He had several short-term partners in the 1820s and 1830s, including
J. B. Maxwell and Aylette Buckner. The latter was eager for higher in-

York: Harper-Collins, 1995), provide up-to-date listings of sources and literature for the period through the War of 1812 and into the 1830s. The largest and richest sources, many unexplored for their business-related content, remain the Special Collections at the Louisiana
State University Library, Baton Rouge; the Southern Historical Collection at the University of North Carolina, Chapel Hill; and the Mississippi Department of Archives and History, Jackson. See also Connie G. Griffith, "Collections in the Manuscript Sections of
Howard-Tilton Memorial Library, Tulane University," *Louisiana History* I (fall 1960): 320–
34. For outstanding efforts in placing the "borderlands" literature in the context of recent
Spanish imperial history, see Gerald E. Poyo and Gilberto M. Hinojosa, "Spanish Texas and
Borderlands Historiography in Transition: Implications for United States History," *Journal
of American History* 75 (September 1988): 393–416; William S. Coker, "Research in the
Spanish Borderlands: Mississippi, 1779–1798," and Jack D. L. Holmes, "Research in the
Spanish Borderlands: Louisiana," both in *Latin American Research Review* 7 (summer 1972);
and Peggy K. Liss, *Atlantic Empires: The Network of Trade and Revolution, 1713–1826* (Baltimore: Johns Hopkins University Press, 1983), 33–73, 79–83, 112–25, 160–71, 223–41. Additional leads regarding Natchez's Spanish, French, and British occupations and its territorial periods can be found in Jay Gitlin, "Crossroads on the Chinaberry Coast: Natchez and
the Creole World of the Mississippi Valley," and Light T. Cummins, "An Enduring Community: Anglo-American Settlers at Colonial Natchez and in the Felicianas, 1774–1810,"
both in *Journal of Mississippi History* 55 (1993).

Natchez Feb. 26. 1841

on demand

I hereby promise to pay to George Winchester Esq the sum of Three Thousand Dollars for value received —

Jno. C. Jenkins

This promissory note from Natchez planter John C. Jenkins to Natchez attorney George Winchester, 1841, is one of hundreds of similar notes and receipts in the Winchester Papers documenting the relationships between Natchez planters, attorneys, and bankers. *From the Winchester Family Papers, NTC, the Center for American History, the University of Texas at Austin.*

come and left the practice to join Frederick Stanton, then a relative new-comer to Natchez, in what became one of the town's most successful mercantile enterprises. In the early 1840s, George took in his nephew, Josiah Winchester, as full partner in the firm. Both were from Massachusetts and staunch Whigs, which gained them, too, special entry into the shrinking circle of old-line Federalists, well represented if no longer dominant among the owners of multiple large-scale plantation operations throughout the area. After George died, Josiah took former court clerk Ralph North into the firm, and both kept busy on behalf of several steadfast Unionists in the Natchez District, such as Stephen Duncan, over claims that dragged on into the 1880s. Before the Civil War, both George and Josiah served as state court judges and spent time in Jackson trying cases and discussing opinions rendered by the supreme court of Mississippi. One old settler in Natchez asserted, with some exaggeration, that the town's "Bench and Bar were distinguished for ability and purity; many . . . left national reputations—all of them honorable names to their families and professions."[3]

The District also attracted a considerable number of doctors from northern states, most notably several who had, like Duncan, trained at the University of Pennsylvania under Benjamin Rush. One of the ironies illustrated by the collection is that few, if any, showed much sympathy for Rush's growing antislavery views, turning their energies instead to planting, banking, and other enterprises. Medical training required more for-

3. William Henry Sparks, *The Memories of Fifty Years* (Philadelphia: Claxton, Remsen & Haffelfinger, 1870), 328, 344. He describes Adams as "a man of remarkable ability"; he and another lawyer were "considered the ablest members of the Bar in the State." The basic work on the legal profession in Natchez is William Baskerville Hamilton, *Anglo-American Law on the Frontier: Thomas Rodney & His Territorial Cases* (Durham, N.C.: Duke University Press, 1953). Hamilton has much economic and business material from the town's territorial period in his dissertation, "American Beginnings in the Old Southwest: The Mississippi Phase" (Duke University, 1937). Many cases involving business and banking in the Natchez District can be pursued in the court records at the Mississippi Department of Archives and History, Jackson, and the Louisiana Supreme Court Collection at the University of New Orleans. I am indebted to Marie Windell for access to and help with the latter collection, which is replete with materials on Natchez, such as, for example, notices of Winchester taking on new partners A. G. Metcalfe and Isaac Caldwell from the *Natchez Mississippian and Advertiser*, November 29 and December 27, 1823.

mal study and training than did the law, yet physicians had fewer chances for acquiring either wealth or reputation in an age when doctors often did more harm than good for their patients. Duncan, for one, became so disillusioned with ineffective medical treatments that he gradually shifted from offering standard therapies to homeopathy. A further irony connected to the Winchester collection is the interest that Judge George Winchester had in Varina Howell's progress with her studies as a youngster. A friend of her Whig family and impressed with her ability, Winchester became Varina's tutor and had a great influence on her, inculcating a devotion to Whig party principles and a firm belief that their advocates were both socially and politically much more respectable than Democrats.[4] It was obviously a belief that did not last, since Varina grew up to marry Jefferson Davis and preside over dinners in the capitol of the Confederacy.

Among the most interesting Winchester legal papers are letters concerning the estate of Stephen Minor, the famed "Don Estaban" who had served as executor of the estate left by his father-in-law, Bernard Lintot, until his own death in 1815, after which Minor's wife and son John sent records of the amounts they spent on the estate's expenses while it was being divided. In the same group are two documents from the recently arrived Robert J. Walker, the famous cabinet minister of the 1840s who, along with his brother, had come from Carlisle, as had Duncan. Although cousins of Duncan, they came to disagree sharply with him on political matters. In the 1830s, Walker responded to Kate Minor's request for help in dealing with lawsuits challenging her title to the land on which stood

4. Lucie Robinson Bridgforth, "Medicine in Antebellum Mississippi," *Journal of Mississippi History* 46 (1984), 82–107; William K. Scarborough, "Science on the Plantation," in *Science and Medicine in the Old South*, ed. Ronald L. Numbers and Todd L. Savitt (Baton Rouge: Louisiana State University Press, 1989), 79–106; Harnett T. Kane, *Natchez on the Mississippi* (New York: William Morrow & Co., 1947), 238–40. For a valuable sociological history of medicine in the United States, see Paul Starr, *The Social Transformation of American Medicine* (New York: Basic Books, 1982), 3–78. An equally impressive work is Charles E. Rosenberg, *The Care of Strangers: The Rise of America's Hospital System* (New York: Basic Books, 1987). For a brief discussion of antebellum "professionals" who became notable planter-businessmen in various parts of the South, see Oakes, *The Ruling Race*, 57–65. For a fascinating account of the lives of other women connected to the Winchesters, see Katherine J. Adams's essay in the present volume.

the Minor family home, Concord. A similar situation was that of Ann
Farrar, the daughter of an early settler under the British rule, whose 1826
letter indicates she was a widow determined to hold and use items that she
claimed she owned as part of her recent purchase of town lots in Natchez
from Dr. William N. Mercer, her son-in-law. Convinced that Mercer was
about to move those items to his wife's plantation at Laurel Hill, she had
turned to Winchester for legal protection of the things she particularly
wanted—seeds for putting in a crop of cotton on her plantation and some
bricks she wanted to save for the commercial buildings in town whose
construction she was supervising. This letter, incidentally, is only one example among many in the collection documenting the entrepreneurial
drive and talents of women.[5]

By the 1850s, Josiah Winchester's practice consisted more and more of
providing the proper forms for land purchases and drawing up mortgages,
some of them worrisome because the lawyer had trouble collecting payments or attempting foreclosures on them. As they accumulated wealth, a
few planters were increasingly acting as private bankers, lending funds to
friends, relatives, and neighbors, for which they received a much better return on capital than they could get from other investments while the buy-
ers enjoyed lower interest rates over longer periods of time than were available in local markets. After the Civil War, Winchester testified before the
Southern Claims Commission in support of several claims by his Natchez
area clients, and also undertook other tasks to help with their business
transactions.[6] Stephen Duncan and his two sons and three sons-in-law be-

5. On Stephen Minor's career as assistant to the last Spanish governor and as interim
governor of Natchez before the United States took control of the District, see Jack D. L.
Holmes, *Gayoso: The Life of a Spanish Governor in the Mississippi Valley, 1789–1799* (Baton
Rouge: Louisiana State University Press, 1965), and "Stephen Minor: Natchez Pioneer,"
Journal of Mississippi History 42 (1980): 17–26. There is also a small but choice group of
Minor family papers in the Natchez Trace Collection. On Cartwright as family physician
and "pro-slavery ideologue," see Robert E. May, *John A. Quitman, Old South Crusader*
(Baton Rouge: Louisiana State University Press, 1985), 122, 349, 394. On Anna Farrar, Dr.
Mercer, and other relatives by marriage into the Butler family, see Pierce Butler, *The Un-
hurried Years: Memories of the Old Natchez Region* (Baton Rouge: Louisiana State University
Press, 1948), which gives a rather prettified picture of those relationships.
6. On Winchester's testimony, see Frank L. Klingberg, *The Southern Claims Commission*
(University of California Publications in History, 1955), 110–12, 222–25, and "The Case

came some of Winchester's major clients and called on the attorney for a variety of services in connection with mortgages and debts that many planters in both Mississippi and Louisiana owed the patriarch. Many of the Winchester Papers from the late 1850s to the 1880s concern the business affairs of various Duncan family members as they sought to collect payments on their loans, in order to restore their plantations in the Yazoo region of northern Mississippi as viable enterprises by repairing wartime levee breaks and reconstructing sheds, gins, and other pieces of equipment. Their objective was to increase resale value, and in other ways to liquidate and divide the assets that "Doctor" Duncan had accumulated.

One of the most galling of these debts, and certainly the most difficult to collect, stemmed from a series of loans the senior Duncan had made to Wade Hampton and family of South Carolina in the 1850s.[7] The Hamptons had borrowed the money to buy large tracts of land in the Yazoo

---

of the Minors: A Unionist Family Within the Confederacy," *Journal of Southern History* 13 (February 1947): 27–45. There is much additional information about the law firm's activities during the Civil War in the records of the Commission for Adams County, Mississippi, in the National Archives, RG217. On Duncan's reputation as an entrepreneur, see Sparks, *The Memories of Fifty Years*, which refers to Duncan as "one of the best businessmen in the Union . . . a man of rare sagacity and wonderful energy." The entry on Adams County in the Dun & Company credit books, Baker Library, Harvard University, describes Duncan in March 1857 as "well known . . . in Wall Street," and as one who "deals largely in both domestic & Sterling Exchange for his shipments of cotton and for a few friends." Duncan also financed local enterprises that seemed promising, such as a lumber mill and a cotton gin manufactory, but preferred to remain a silent partner in them. John Hebron Moore, *Andrew Brown and Cypress Lumbering in the Old Southwest* (Baton Rouge: Louisiana State University Press, 1967), 24, 30, 38, 43–50. For an attempt to estimate the extent of losses resulting from the Civil War, see Louis A. Rose, "Capital Losses of Southern Slaveholders Due to Emancipation," *Western Economic Journal* 3 (December 1957): 39–51.

7. On the Hampton connections, see Virginia G. Maynard, *The Venturers: The Hampton, Harrison, and Earle Families of Virginia, South Carolina, and Texas* (Charleston, S.C.: privately printed, 1981), 184–86; Charles E. Cauthen, *Family Letters of the Three Wade Hamptons, 1782–1901* (Durham, S.C.: University of South Carolina Press, 1953), 37–53; and Ronald E. Bridwell, "The South's Wealthiest Planter: Wade Hampton I of South Carolina, 1754–1835" (Ph.D. diss., University of South Carolina, 1980), which relies on the estimate in *Niles' Weekly Register* of 1823 that the senior Wade Hampton was then worth $1.6 million by his eldest daughter's marriage to John J. Pringle, member of a long-established family in that state.

Delta region, near that part of Issaquena County where Duncan himself
had recently carved out six large plantations, one for each of his surviving
children and one for himself. Virtually incessant negotiations during and
after the war about the terms of the mortgages on Hampton lands took up
much of the elder Duncan's time after his departure from Natchez shortly
after the fall of Vicksburg for New York City, where he would, during the
years following the war, conduct business on his way to and from summer
watering places in Saratoga and Newport. (He kept up a heavy output of
letters to Winchester and others denouncing those who had supported secession for ruining the South. His reputation as a shrewd businessman was
exceptional, and some of the investments he handled were drawn from
savings within his own family circle—such as widowed aunts and maiden
sisters in his native Carlisle and in Philadelphia—making the losses at-
tributable to the Civil War all the more vexing.) After his father's death
in 1867, Stephen Duncan, Jr., the only unmarried surviving offspring in
the immediate family, became the reluctant chief negotiator with the
Hampton family and the renegotiator (with Winchester's advice) of loans
to owners of plantations in nearby Concordia and Tensas Parishes. The
later portions of the Winchester collection include letters from former
"servants" who had moved to the North, documents settling suits by creditors of the Bank of the State of Mississippi and successor firms in which
family heads had been active, and, finally, Stephen Duncan, Jr.'s will written at the turn of the century donating the plantation Auburn and its surrounding land to the city of Natchez as a public park.

Earlier business correspondence between Duncan and members of the
Levin Marshall family also appears in the Bank of the State of Mississippi
Records. The bank was founded in 1809 with a twenty-five-year charter,
and its president and board of directors held monopolistic power, exer-
cised by extending credit to "accommodate" entrepreneurs, until the institution's demise in the mid-1830s.[8] Directors were drawn from both the

8. The rules for the territorial government's participation in launching the bank are
laid out in Douglas C. McMurtrie, *The Mississippi Banking Act of 1809* (Chicago: Black Cat
Press, 1936), which includes a facsimile of the 1811 original. For a narrative that contains
a solid discussion of the bank's early history, see Davis, *A Way Through the Wilderness*, 210–
15. Modern works concerning the bank are Robert C. Weems, Jr., "The Bank of Mississippi:

Federalist and Jacksonian leaders in the District, most with prestigious political connections. The first president was Winthrop Sargent, Mississippi's first territorial governor, who had a previous record of difficulty in getting along with settlers as the first governor of the Northwest Territory, and a record that Republicans believed was no better in the Mississippi Territory. Sargent had married a wealthy young widow within a few months of landing at Natchez. After 1801, when President Jefferson appointed someone else to his position, he retired to the large plantation Gloucester, which was part of his Natchez wife's dowry, and ran it successfully. Sargent's successor at the bank was Stephen Minor (grandfather of Levin Marshall), who presided while the directors worked to raise money for a building, a safe, office supplies, and enough subscriptions of stock to meet the requirement of the charter that the bank have a capital of fifty thousand dollars before it could begin making loans. The bank subcollection contains drafts of rules for the board and some fragments of early correspondence. Minor, a much less confrontational person than Sargent, had served as an aide to the last Spanish governor of the Mississippi Territory, and as governor *pro tem* during the last days of Spanish rule, and was also a successful planter. The papers show that he was not only a prominent local citizen, but had business friends in high places in New Orleans.

Minor seems to have been merely a figurehead, for the active supervision of the bank apparently began when the board accepted his resignation and replaced him as president with Samuel Postlethwaite. Born in Carlisle, Pennsylvania, he had become one of Natchez's most prominent merchants. He had obtained business experience and cultivated banking and mercantile connections in both Philadelphia and Lexington, Ken-

---

A Pioneer Bank of the Old Southwest, 1809 1844" (Ph.D. diss., Columbia University, 1951), and "The Makers of the Bank of Mississippi," *Journal of Mississippi History* 15 (1953): 137–54, and Marvin Bentley, "Financial Institutions and Economic Development in Mississippi, 1809 to 1860" (Ph.D. diss., Tulane University, 1969) and "The State Bank of Mississippi, Monopoly Bank on the Frontier (1809–1830)," *Journal of Mississippi History* 40 (1978). These studies are based primarily on the bank's records, especially account books and miscellaneous correspondence, in the Mississippi Department of Archives and History and Louisiana State University holdings. Compared with these repositories, the NTC has fewer account records but richer correspondence, which reveals more about the bank's policy decisions and about its relations with its branch offices in the major towns of the state.

tucky, in the 1790s before moving to Natchez in 1802 and setting up a mercantile business. Postlethwaite demonstrated a variety of talents in civic affairs, made the most of his solid business connections with several Philadelphia merchants, and had courted and married Ann Dunbar, one of "Sir" William Dunbar's daughters, before 1807, when his twenty-one-year-old nephew, Dr. Stephen Duncan, arrived in Natchez to practice medicine.[9] Duncan, too, made a fortunate marriage soon after his arrival and made a good friend in Washington Jackson, a Philadelphia merchant who became a major figure in the cotton trade at New Orleans and Louisville, obtained land on the Mississippi River near the plantation that Duncan was running, and moved much of his merchant shipping business to New York and then to Liverpool, where he spent the rest of his life. Most of the voluminous bank collection consists of letters to and from the two enterprising settlers from Carlisle and the cashiers of the branch banks at Woodville, Port Gibson, and Vicksburg. Postlethwaite died in 1825, but Stephen Duncan, the most actively involved member of the bank's board of directors, had by then taken over many of the president's responsibilities, and struggled to maintain the virtual monopoly that the revised charter of 1809 gave the bank in exchange for designating (and partially financing) it as the state's bank. Duncan was soon elected president and began officially handling the bank's affairs in the mid-1820s, working with Gabriel Tichenor, who remained cashier, a position that put him in charge of day-to-day duties.[10]

9. On Minor, Sargent, and other territorial governors, see Holmes, *Gayoso*, 50–51, 256–59, 268–69, and "Stephen Minor: Natchez Pioneer," 17–26. For a favorable view of Sargent, see Mary Joan Elliott, "Winthrop Sargent and the Administration of the Mississippi Territory, 1798–1801" (Ph.D. diss., University of Southern California, 1970).

10. On Postlethwaite, see his own "Flatboating on the Mississippi: Journal of a Voyage from Louisville to Natchez . . . 1800," *Missouri Historical Society Bulletin* 7 (April 1951): 312–29, and Davis, *A Way Through the Wilderness*, 211–14. Primary sources for the Postlethwaite family include a small collection of family papers in the Natchez Trace Collection, some genealogical information in Natchez's Armstrong Library, and a diary in the Huntington Library, Pasadena, California, which chronicles two trading voyages in 1807 and 1810 led by Postlethwaite for his father-in-law, the destination being saltworks at Natchitoches, Louisiana, that Dunbar had acquired a decade or more prior to the Spanish departure. Salt was often a profitable item, especially before steamboats began coming up the river with cargoes that included "Liverpool salt," as designated in local newspaper advertisements. Duncan withdrew from the practice of medicine soon after his marriage to a

By that time, however, the bank was coming under attack by many of the state's planters; the smaller-scale settlers had been suspicious of the institution from the outset, since it seemed much less liberal in its lending policies than were individual planters and merchants. The antibank sentiment swelled with the Jacksonian movement, and though Duncan ran for and won a seat in a new state constitutional convention, he could do little to protect the bank from those who wished to cancel its charter. Indeed, the legislature began withdrawing its support from the bank, spreading the funds to new banks in the eastern half of the state and granting a charter in 1830 to the Planter's Bank in Natchez, an action some thought was of dubious legality. The only recourse for Duncan and his "sound money" associates was to wind down business in the old bank and transfer funds and loans to a new institution in Natchez, dubbed the Agricultural Bank, for which Duncan also served as president. The giddy pace of founding new banking facilities halted suddenly with the Panic of 1837, made worse in Mississippi (as Duncan had predicted) by the desperate expedient of repudiating the bonds (debts) issued by the previous legislature. The state became notorious in national and international financial centers for decades for that major violation of the rules.[11]

---

daughter of John Ellis, a wealthy landowner and early settler in the District, since the move gave him a plantation on the Homochitto River. His successful management of that enterprise while it was still producing indigo and tobacco (soon replaced with cotton) earned him respect and a reputation for energy and prudence that lasted to his death.

11. Notices in the *Mississippi Republican* from June through December 12, 1820, indicate that Samuel Postlethwaite was listed as chairman of the board of directors of the Natchez Steamship Company, which ran the *Vesuvius* after replacing the boiler with a new one from Philadelphia. Soon afterward, Duncan helped organize and served as president of a "company," or partnership, for buying a new steamship named *Walk on the Water*. There were also notices that year that Washington Jackson was moving to Philadelphia and entering into a mercantile partnership there with his older brother. He often returned on business trips, however, and his plantation on the Mississippi at Jackson Point was still listed on Persac's map in 1858. The Dun & Company papers list Jackson as a solid, respectable merchant, but one who had a "special friend" in Duncan, who was ready to help him financially. Levin Marshall also served as cashier in the Natchez branch of the Bank of the United States and began investing in land and slaves during the boom of the 1830s. See Theodora B. Marshall and Gladys C. Evans, eds., "Plantation Report from the Papers of Levin R. Marshall, of 'Richmond,' Natchez, Mississippi," *Journal of Mississippi History* 3 (1941): 45–55.

Letter informing James C. Wilkins of his appointment as one of the directors of the Bank of the State of Mississippi. *From the James C. Wilkins Papers, NTC, the Center for American History, the University of Texas at Austin.*

*   *   *

One Natchez bank that did rather better than the majority after 1832 was headed by James C. Wilkins, a friend and brother-in-law of Stephen Duncan. Wilkins was the scion of a Pittsburgh family active in frontier trading that had settled in the Pittsburgh area during the American Revolution. He and his older brother Charles—from whom there are many letters in the Wilkins Papers with the salutation "Dear Campbell," his middle name—engaged in separate commercial ventures near the lower Mississippi River at the beginning of the century. These ventures were no doubt helped by the status of the family head, General Wilkins, who had led a military force during the transition from Spanish to American rule at Fort Adams south of Natchez. Several letters from Charles in the period from 1801 to 1807 deal with the problems he encountered as provisioner for the troops on guard at various frontier posts in the area, problems exacerbated by slow payment from the federal government. He eventually returned to Pittsburgh to look after his ailing father and the family's stake in its mercantile enterprises. Another small group of letters is concerned with the death of Wilkins's father about 1810 and disagreements over the claims against the parents' estate that dragged on for more than a decade, especially regarding the efforts of Hyman Gratz of Philadelphia to collect on a debt that Wilkins had taken over. A larger but still rather slim portion deals with Wilkins's speculations in land and slaves, which gave him five or more developed plantations by the 1840s. He had foreclosed on them in his capacity as a private banker. On the operation of these plantations or about his activity in politics, however, there is little more in this collection than is available elsewhere, and the condition of the letters is deplorable, especially since Wilkins's handwriting was rapidly becoming illegible.[12]

12. On these financial travails in Mississippi, the best recent work is Larry Schweikart, *Banking in the American South from the Age of Jackson to Reconstruction* (Baton Rouge: Louisiana State University Press, 1987), 24–27, 52–53, 175–82, 202–205. For a study of a state that handled the banking crisis of the antebellum period quite differently, see George D. Green, *Finance and Economic Development in the Old South: Louisiana Banking, 1804–1861* (Stanford, Calif.: Stanford University Press, 1972). For the points of view of seaboard merchant bankers, see Edwin J. Perkins, *Financing Anglo-American Trade: The House of Brown, 1800–1880* (Cambridge, Mass.: Harvard University Press, 1975), and the fine study of Harold D. Woodman, *King Cotton and His Retainers: Financing & Marketing the Cotton Crop of*

The major interest of business historians in this set of papers is likely to
lie in the unique reports to Wilkins by John Linton, his partner in the
mercantile firm from 1815 to Linton's death in 1834.[13] Linton lived
mostly in New Orleans and wrote long, detailed letters about firm business, commercial news and gossip, and seaports on the eastern board and
in western Europe. Several letters contain references to Vincent Nolte,
the colorful Italian-born merchant-shipper whose exploits as a businessman were recorded in a best-selling book, *Fifty Years in Both Hemispheres,
or Reminiscences of the Life of a Former Merchant,* which became the basis
of *Anthony Adverse,* a romantic novel of the 1930s and a successful Holly-
wood film.[14] Most of the letters gave details of packing and shipping cotton
by Natchez-area planters and merchants while also forwarding news and
gossip from Liverpool brought by visiting merchants. It is evident from
them that disruptions in the market, especially during the great cotton
speculation of 1825, were particularly stressful for both members of the
Natchez-New Orleans firm.[15]

---

the South, 1800–1925 (Lexington: University of Kentucky Press, 1968), both of which have
many references to the Natchez area. For a broader discussion of such banking development, see Richard Sylla, "Small Business in the United States, 1780–1920," in *Small Business in American Life,* ed. Stuart W. Bruchey (New York: Columbia University Press, 1980),
240–62.

13. There is a draft of "Articles of Agreement & Copartnership" between Wilkins and
Linton, dated January 1, 1816, specifying that they would open a counting house in New
Orleans, to which Linton should "repair as soon as convenient" for "doing a Commission."
Each partner put up $5,000 for initial capital. Linton's father, also named John, had such a
business in New Orleans, but was in financial trouble. Collection of his debts with Gratz
was the source of the trouble encountered in Pittsburgh by the younger Linton and his new
partner. The four-page agreement was witnessed by Washington Jackson and John Ker, a
prominent "old Settler" of solid business reputation. See also the letter from Richard Biddle
to Wilkins, September 20, 1819. Both documents are in the Wilkins Papers, in Boxes
2E541 and 2E542, respectively.

14. Nolte's book was translated into English from the German and published by Red-
field, Nassau Street, New York, in 1854. The original was published in 1853, and the author
described himself on the title page as "late of New Orleans," since he had opened an office
there in the 1820s. The book also contains a lively description of General Lafayette's visit
to the United States, and especially to New Orleans and Natchez, during the 1825 panic in
the cotton trade, pages 31–328.

15. There is a description of the 1825 crisis that details the actions of Jeremiah Thompson of New York, the merchant who controlled the largest number of ships and the largest
amount of cotton there in the 1810s and 1820s. As soon as he received the news of the cot-

One notable exchange reveals much about the extent of the interstate market in slaves during the beginning of a recovery in prices of both land and slaves in 1831. Wilkins asked Duncan's opinion of an offer by a local planter to sell him eighteen slaves: ten men from thirteen to thirty-six years old, five women aged twenty-two to forty-five, and three children aged six to ten. The planter wanted $9,450 for the entire lot and Wilkins wanted verification that that was a good price, since Duncan had recently been traveling along the southern seaboard to buy large lots of slaves for his new plantations in the sugar-producing regions of Louisiana. Duncan responded that the "valuation of the negroes was at least 20% too low, if made for cash. If on a credit of 1, 2, and 3 years, 40% too low." He thought that prices on average in Natchez for "prime negro men, acclimated . . . were worth in cash $700 to $750, women of same character $575 to $650, and children in proportion." He was, however, willing to have a dealer "affix the age and the highest amount of cotton picked by each negro—to his or her name. I might value them without seeing them or, if you prefer it, you can select a gentleman and I will ride up on Monday next and value them." He added, "I would be glad to purchase 20 unacclimated Negroes at the valuation put on yours." Six years later Wilkins's investments were clearly doing well, since the Commercial Bank of Rodney reported in 1835 that his account there stood at $212,357, although part of that sum may have been generated by his speculations in Indian lands at Chochuma, Mississippi. There are many such exchanges between planters and bankers in the separate group of miscellaneous letters and documents in the Natchez Trace Collection's Slaves and Slavery Collection.[16]

---

ton shortage, he sent a packet ship to New Orleans with several of his agents, including Nolte, to act for him in buying as much of the commodity as possible. See Robert G. Albion, *The Rise of New York Port (1815–1860)* (New York: Scribners, 1939), 113–21. There is an excellent treatment of changes in "commercial intelligence" in Alan R. Pred, *Urban Growth and the Circulation of Information: The United States System of Cities, 1790–1840* (Cambridge, Mass.: Harvard University Press, 1973), especially 92–93 and 249–54. For a complex overview of global trade in agricultural commodities before shipping costs were reduced, see Terence K. Hopkins and Immanuel Wallerstein, "Commodity Chains: Construct and Research," in *Commodity Chains and Global Capitalism*, ed. Gary Gereffi and Miguel Korzeniewicz (New York: Praeger, 1994), 17–20, 48–50.

16. Wilkins Papers, Boxes 2E546 and 2E547. Such efforts to obtain second opinions about the quality of land, slaves, etc., especially from highly respected relations, were stan-

                        *   *   *

The last large collection, the Archer Family Papers, has been examined
and used carefully by Joan E. Cashin in A *Family Venture: Men and Women
on the Southern Frontier* (Oxford University Press, 1991), an exceptionally
fine work of social history but with relatively little interest in terms of
business. The Archer family's move to Mississippi, detailed by Randolph
Campbell in this volume, took place at roughly the same time as that of
another Virginian, Charles Cocke, who moved with his family to a plantation across the Mississippi River in Louisiana.

   The two families remained in close contact and shared the news they
received from Virginia friends. Archer and Cocke were both well-educated, thoughtful farmers who became involved in many ancillary enterprises in short order. One letter dated April 23, 1839, from a Virginia
friend to Archer discusses the possibilities of building textile mills closer
to sources of supply and of planting mulberry trees for raising imported
silkworms for another try at American silviculture. The friend, however,
could not stir up much enthusiasm. Letters from 1833 until secession indicate a longstanding friendship, perhaps going back as far as their lives in
Virginia, between Archer and William St. John Elliott, one of the more
successful and illustrious figures in Natchez.

   Archer occupied a place not so exalted as Elliott's, but he carried on a
wide correspondence about many family matters, such as the education of
his children and the health of his extended family, and about business
matters that preoccupied his neighboring planters and merchants. They
discussed grievances about merchant's charges, news about the rise and
fall of interest and exchange rates, and experiments in farming and the
improvement of livestock. Archer's hope of emulating the "nabobs" had
led to many frustrations in buying plantations and hiring people to run
them for him—dry years and poor crops, incompetent or unwilling overseers and "stewards," and headaches in shipping what he did produce.[17]

---

dard procedures. For a brief but solid discussion of precautions and business goals in general,
see Mansel G. Blackford, *A History of Small Business in America* (Boston: Twayne Publishers,
1991), 1–26.

   17. A persistent problem for Archer was finding a capable manager, as we would call
the "steward," who could take charge of his plantations. For this business recruitment dilemma, see William K. Scarborough, *The Overseer: Plantation Management in the Old South*
(Baton Rouge: Louisiana State University Press, 1966).

A parallel interest of Archer's, that of making a mark in improving transport, developed by the 1850s. Archer traveled to New York in November 1858 for a meeting of the bankers and directors of the Southern Pacific Railroad Company and reported to his wife his pleasure at the re-election of the current board since they were "men of capital and of business talent." Confidence in the project led to his borrowing a "large sum" for purchasing more stock, over six thousand shares, which he expected to reach a price of one hundred dollars per share within a year or two. With this kind and size of investment and his determination in the backwash of the Panic of 1857 to purchase more slaves, Archer by the time secession was an accomplished fact was surely near his goal of becoming a latter-day nabob. During the Civil War the family letters show little out of the ordinary, although the area around Port Gibson was in Union hands within a year or so of the real fighting. One of Archer's sons mentioned several times that he and his family were managing well on the plantation that the elder had provided, but reported nothing unusual about the course of business except the loss of horses and mules and the high prices of foodstuffs, clothing, and other commodities.

By the latter part of the war Archer, like many other southerners, had fallen on hard times. If he had not yet made it as a businessman, he was hardly alone. The majority of settlers in the Natchez area, and certainly in the less prosperous areas of the lower Mississippi valley, were suffering heavy losses in their efforts to carry on farming and business enterprises, often at hand-to-mouth levels. Many materials in the smaller groups of letters assembled in the remarkable Natchez Trace Collection document the lives of these less fortunate planters, bankers, merchants, and professionals. There are also many obscure stories about able farmers and townspeople.[18] One classic account of a shopkeeper is the famous diary of the

18. For a glimpse into the mundane, hard-working, upright world of middle-level plantation owners, see Mach B. Swearingen, "Thirty Years of a Mississippi Plantation: Charles Whitmore of 'Montpelier,'" *Journal of Southern History* 1 (May 1935): 198–211, for the story of a transplanted upper-middle-class Englishman who quietly and peacefully made a new life for his family. See also the descriptions of many small enterprises in James, *Antebellum Natchez,* 202–42, and Marius M. Carriere, Jr., "Mount Locust Plantation: The Development of Southwest Mississippi During the Frontier Period, 1810–1830," *Journal of Mississippi History* 48 (1986): 187–98.

free black man William Johnson, who owned a barbershop in Natchez from which he earned a reasonably good living and who also made small loans of cash to customers he considered credit worthy.[19] We now need to add their stories to the ones published in scholarly journals and books, so that we might probe further into the beliefs and ideas that in 1861 led a group of rational businessmen to "try" and then execute by hanging a number of local black people.[20] Only then can we possibly shuck off our preconceptions about what it all means.

19. William Ransom Hogan and Edwin Adams Davis, eds., *William Johnson's Natchez: The Ante-bellum Diary of a Free Negro* (Baton Rouge: Louisiana State University Press, 1951). It was reprinted in 1989 with a new introduction. This book imparts a unique view of the smaller businesses in the town.

20. Winthrop D. Jordan, *Tumult and Silence at Second Creek: An Inquiry into a Civil War Slave Conspiracy* (Baton Rouge: Louisiana State University Press, 1993), makes a brilliant beginning.

Shearer Davis Bowman

Reflections of Sectional Conflict in the Natchez Trace Collection

Named for the Amerindian trail and United States frontier road that ran between Nashville, Tennessee, and Natchez, Mississippi, the Natchez Trace Collection is a huge reservoir of largely untapped source material that illuminates the history of the lower Mississippi valley during the nineteenth century. The many constituent subcollections, large and small, focus on the states of Mississippi and Louisiana, and the majority of documents date from the three decades of intense North-South sectional conflict that extended from the Mexican War of 1846–48 to the close of Reconstruction in 1876–77. The state most amply represented in the Natchez Trace Collection is Mississippi, which became the Union's twentieth state in 1817, and which one historian has aptly portrayed as "the most southern of southern states—a prototype where is mixed all the peculiar forces and tensions that have made the American South unique in the nation."[1]

Mississippi's prototypical southernness emerged during the four antebellum decades that opened with the 1819–21 controversy over Missouri's admission to the Union as a slave state. This Missouri controversy was the first serious political manifestation of the sectional dispute over slavery's

---

1. John R. Skates, "Mississippi," in *The Encyclopedia of Southern History*, ed. David C. Roller and Robert W. Twyman (Baton Rouge: Louisiana State University Press, 1979), 825.

westward expansion that would begin to take center stage in U.S. politics during the late 1840s and would culminate in the secession crisis of 1860–61. During the 1820s and the fabled flush times of the 1830s, cotton-fueled prosperity attracted to Mississippi from older states to the north and east what one scholar has termed "a diverse company of proud, predatory, courageous, land-hungry Americans," a number of whom are represented in Natchez Trace subcollections.[2] In the process of realizing their entrepreneurial ambitions, these settlers found the presidential administration of Andrew Jackson a willing accomplice in effecting the final dispossession and trans-Mississippi "removal" of the Native American Chickasaw and Choctaw tribes. (The smaller Natchez tribe had been virtually exterminated by the French during the 1730s.) In the 1850s Mississippi supplanted Alabama as the "Heartland of the Cotton Kingdom," after having become by 1840 one of two states where African American slaves constituted a majority of the population. The other, South Carolina, became, on December 20, 1860, the first state to secede from the Union and the only constituent member of the future Confederacy whose secession convention voted unanimously (169–0) in favor of the separation. Although Mississippi followed the Palmetto State's lead, becoming on January 9, 1861, the second state to quit the Union, its convention vote of 88–15 testified to the endurance of antisecession sentiment in some nonplantation areas located outside of the fertile Delta-Loess soil region abutting the Mississippi River. This Delta-Loess plantation region included the Yazoo Delta above Vicksburg, which had not been heavily settled until the development of a nascent levee system during the 1840s, and the Natchez District, reaching from Vicksburg south to the Louisiana border, which had been home to settlers of British as well as African ancestry since the last third of the eighteenth century.[3]

Most of the Natchez Trace subcollections focus on the environs of Vicksburg and Natchez in southwestern Mississippi, and reveal much

2. Lucie R. Bridgforth, "Natchez Trace," in *Encyclopedia of Southern Culture*, ed. Charles Reagan Wilson and William Ferris (Chapel Hill: University of North Carolina Press, 1989), 387.

3. On the Delta-Loess plantation region, see William K. Scarborough, "Mississippi, Slavery in," in *Dictionary of Afro-American Slavery*, ed. Randall M. Miller and John David Smith (New York: Greenwood Press, 1988), 484–85.

about a fascinating variety of antebellum immigrants who played prominent roles in the state's political, economic, social, and cultural life during
the era of sectional conflict. Much of the archival content serves to illustrate how residents of Mississippi were closely linked by ties of ancestry or
upbringing, education or religion, business or politics, to other parts of the
United States. Hence it is hardly surprising that scholars working with
Natchez Trace subcollections have often found it necessary to consult directly complementary manuscripts housed at other repositories south of
the Mason-Dixon Line. For example, a graduate student at the University
of Texas, John F. Waukechon, became interested in the Charles Backus
Dana Papers (1802, 1820–1881), consisting primarily of family correspondence and draft sermons. He then located another substantial and invaluable cache of Dana papers at the Louisiana State University library in
Baton Rouge. Waukechon's resulting master's thesis tells a remarkable
story of both geographical and religious migration in antebellum
America.[4] Dana (1810–1873), son of a New Hampshire Congregational
minister and graduate of both Dartmouth College and Andover Theological Seminary in Massachusetts, taught school in Baltimore before becoming one of a new (and little-studied) breed of "evangelical" Episcopal
priests in the 1830s. For more than a quarter century he served as rector of
Christ Church in Alexandria, Virginia, counting members of both the
Washington and Lee families among his parishioners. In 1860, he left Virginia to become rector of St. James Parish in Port Gibson, Mississippi (located about halfway between Vicksburg and Natchez), and moved again
after the Civil War to Trinity Church in Natchez.

Another University of Texas graduate student, Philip M. Gavenda, used
the NTC's extensive Richard T. Archer Family Papers (1790–1919) as the
foundation for his study of the politics of Richard Thompson Archer
(1797–1867), which was supplemented by another set of Archer Family
Papers housed in the Virginia Historical Society in Richmond. Scion of a
planter family in Southside Virginia's Amelia County, Archer attended
William and Mary College before joining the multitude of white Virgin-

4. John F. Waukechon, "Charles B. Dana and Virginia Evangelical Episcopalianism:
His Family, Career, and Sermons" (master's thesis, University of Texas at Austin, 1992).

ians who migrated to the Old Southwest during the early nineteenth century in search of fresh opportunities and new wealth. Although he became an unusually wealthy cotton planter and vociferous spokesman for southern rights, Archer never held political office on the state or national level, and scholars have not heretofore had access to a manuscript collection focused on his career in Mississippi. Therefore, Archer has received scant attention from historians of the secession movement. His correspondents, however, included a large number of politically prominent individuals, who seem to have respected him even though they seldom embraced his secessionist, fire-eating extremism. To wit, the future president of the Confederacy, Jefferson Davis, while serving as secretary of war in 1857, informed President Franklin Pierce that "Mr. Archer is an extreme man . . . [with] little attention and no support." Yet Davis also complimented Archer as a man "of high personal respectability, and great tenacity of purpose."[5]

The Richard T. Archer Family Papers constitute an extraordinarily rich mine of information on both plantation slavery and antebellum politics. Readers interested in an informed and detailed discussion of the Archers as a slaveholding family should consult the essay in this volume by Ran-

5. Philip Martin Gavenda, " 'In Defense of the God-Given Right to Own the African': The Politics of Richard T. Archer" (master's report, University of Texas at Austin, 1993); *The Papers of Jefferson Davis: Volume 6, 1856–1860*, ed. Linda Lasswell Crist and Mary Seaton Dix (Baton Rouge: Louisiana State University Press, 1989), 132, as cited in Gavenda, "Politics of Archer," 11. Two other graduate students in history who have made use of the Natchez Trace Collection in master's theses on antebellum Mississippi politics are Alan David Constant, "The 1840 Presidential Election in the Natchez District, Mississippi" (University of Texas at Austin, 1993); and Thomas William Miller, "A New Perspective on Southern Whig Decline: A Comparison of the Mississippi and North Carolina Whig Parties, 1848–1856" (University of Texas at Austin, 1992). Archer is mentioned briefly in Percy Lee Rainwater, *Mississippi: Storm Center of Secession, 1856–1861* (1938; rpr., New York: Da Capo Press, 1989), 40, and in Ollinger Crenshaw, *The Slave States in the Presidential Election of 1860*, Johns Hopkins University Studies in Historical and Political Science, series 63, no. 3 (1945; rpr., Gloucester, Mass.: Peter Smith, 1969), 266. Archer is not mentioned in William L. Barney, *The Secessionist Impulse: Alabama and Mississippi in 1860* (Princeton, N.J.: Princeton University Press, 1974), Eric H. Walther, *The Fire-Eaters* (Baton Rouge: Louisiana State University Press, 1992), or Bradley G. Bond, *Political Culture in the Nineteenth-Century South: Mississippi, 1830–1900* (Baton Rouge: Louisiana State University Press, 1995).

dolph B. Campbell. Campbell points out that in 1860 Richard T. Archer owned five plantations in two counties, Claiborne and Holmes, and at least 432 slaves—all of which testified to more than thirty years of successful entrepreneurial perseverance in a usually favorable economic climate. In another essay in this volume, William G. Shade examines Archer as exemplifying the "bourgeois capitalism" of Natchez nabob planters. As Archer wrote in 1833, "I shall probably be rich. . . . Land rises very fast in value here." In 1856 a Louisiana planter and correspondent aptly characterized Archer as "a business man and what may be termed a good trader." Several years earlier Archer himself had expressed a businesslike view of slaves as "property peculiar in kind and of a magnitude that it is almost the sole basis of Southern prosperity and happiness."[6]

Like most cotton planters, Richard Archer suffered during the depression years that followed the Panic of 1837, for which he, a states' rights Whig since the Nullification controversy earlier in the decade, blamed the Jacksonian Democrats. Prosperity returned in the 1840s, even as sectional debates over the "Texas Question," the Mexican War, and the Mexican cession brought the divisive issue of slavery's westward expansion to the fore in national politics. During this decade the explicit focus of Archer's political concerns shifted from banking reform to protecting the rights of slaveholders. He seems to have sat as a delegate in the Mississippi "southern rights" convention held at Jackson in October of 1849, and he wrote a multitude of letters during the controversies surrounding the Compromise of 1850, sometimes signing anonymous letters to local newspapers "plain planter" or "rustic" despite his cosmopolitan affluence. "I hold the (now obsolete) doctrine that all sovereignty abides in the people of the

6. Richard T. Archer to Stephen Archer, March 18, 1833, Richard T. Archer Family Papers, Box 2E647, as quoted in Gavenda, "Politics of Archer," 8; Downing (in LaFourche Parish) to Archer, November 4, 1856, Richard T. Archer, circa 1850, addressee unknown, Archer Papers, Box 2E647. Like many other wealthy planters, Archer also made nonagricultural investments. On October 9, 1856, he wrote to his wife from New York City that he had been reelected to the board of directors of the Southern Pacific Railroad, in which he owned 5,941 shares. He expected them to be worth $100 each before the end of 1857, and to "provide a good estate for each of our children." Archer Papers, Box 2E646. Archer did not, however, anticipate the Panic of 1857. On May 8, 1858, he wrote to his son Abram, "I expect we will be swindled out of all we have invested in the SPRR Co." Archer Papers, Box 2E647.

several States," he proclaimed. Insistence on state sovereignty was essential to the protection of southern rights; and on the crucial issue of slavery's status in federal territories, both state sovereignty and southern rights
had been violated "by the gordian knot of Congressional intervention,"
first in the Compromise of 1820 and now in the Compromise of 1850.
"When the people of the South are driven by aggression and intolerable
oppression to defend their rights and assert their political equality, I (if I
live so long) shall rejoice to unite with them in resistance and in separation from the Northern States." Archer insisted that "the Constitution
was an experiment" and not intended to be "perpetual." Those who rejected his fire-eating sectionalism Archer labeled "submissionists." Especially deserving of this appellation, he believed, were the "large slaveholders" of Adams County, who "have always been federalists in principle.
And I presume would be monarchists if it were possible to introduce mon-
archy into the country. They would from their great wealth enjoy a distinction under a monarchical government which can never be attained in
a republican government."[7]

After John Brown's abortive raid on the federal arsenal at Harpers Ferry
in 1859 elicited considerable sympathy for Brown in the North, Archer
penned a proslavery call to arms for publication in the *Vicksburg Weekly
Sun*: "The irrepressible conflict has begun, the South is invaded, it is time
for all patriots to be united, to be under military organization, to be ad-
vancing to the conflict determined to live or die in defense of the God
given right to own the African." In a campaign speech delivered at Port
Gibson in August of 1860 on behalf of Southern Democratic nominee
John Breckinridge, Archer insisted that a Lincoln victory in the electoral

7. Richard T. Archer Family Papers, as cited in Gavenda, "Politics of Archer," 50; September 1850 draft of a letter addressed to several men in Natchez and Adams County, 1850
missive on "the Southern construction of the Constitution," "Son of a Rebel of 1776" to
the *Natchez Free Trader*, ca. 1850, Archer Papers, Box 2E647. As William G. Shade ex-
plains in this volume, the category "states' rights Whig" was created by twentieth-century
historians to describe the nullifiers who abandoned the Democratic party temporarily in the
1830s. In his petition to Andrew Johnson for a presidential pardon after the Civil War, Archer stated, "I was educated in the School of State Sovreignty [sic] and the right of secession." Archer Family Papers, Virginia Historical Society, as cited in Gavenda, "Politics of
Archer," 13.

college would make him an executive "usurper" rather than a constitu-tionally legitimate president—hence the southern states would be com-pletely justified in quitting the Union. Like most white southerners on the eve of the Civil War, Archer could not distinguish between the radical, violent, and immediatist abolitionism of John Brown and the moderate, free-soil, and racist antislavery endorsed by Abraham Lincoln, who was committed not to abolition but merely to slavery's geographical contain-ment, which would set the stage for the gradual, long-term emancipation of slaves in conjunction with their colonization outside the United States. Archer believed the Republican presidential candidate "ineligible" to hold office because his party's design was to "violate our [southern] equal rights in the territories," to "incite rebellion in our slave population," and to "destroy the labor system of the slave states," thereby reducing them to "desolution and pauperism." "The normal condition of the negro is slav-ery," declared Archer, and "it is a normal right of the white man to buy him for a possession and an inheritance forever." Because Lincoln's aim was to destroy slavery and the South, "no majority of electoral votes can make him President *de jure* of the United States. He is an enemy, he is therefore an expatriated foreigner for all purposes of the Constitution."[8]

Two of Archer's antebellum correspondents, William L. Sharkey and Jo-seph E. Davis—both of whom exhibited public personas quite different

8. Archer to Editors of the *Sun*, December 8, 1859, Archer Papers, Box 2E647; *Speech of Richard T. Archer, Esq., Delivered on the Tenth Day of August, 1860, at Port Gibson, Missis-sippi* . . . (Port Gibson: J. E. Elliott, 1860), as quoted in Gavenda, "Politics of Archer," 56–57, 18, and in Crenshaw, *Slave States in the Presidential Election of 1860*, 266. The examples of Archer and his more famous fire-eating contemporary, John A. Quitman (1799–1858), indicate that there were notable exceptions to William L. Barney's generalization that "the young slaveholding planters, farmers, and lawyers of the Breckinridge Democrats, the most ambitious and dynamic elements in the South's political economy, were the first to perceive the crisis and they reacted most intensely to it" (*The Secessionist Impulse*, 313). On Quit-man, see the study by Robert E. May, *John A. Quitman, Old South Crusader* (Baton Rouge: Louisiana State University Press, 1985). Barney's emphasis on younger southern males finds recent corroboration in Gary W. Gallagher, *The Confederate War* (Cambridge, Mass.: Har-vard University Press, 1997), 96–105, which treats both secessionist sentiment and Con-federate nationalism among slaveholding military officers who came of age during the 1850s.

from Archer's—are represented by smaller Natchez Trace subcollections. Sharkey (1798–1873), a planter-jurist and prominent "Union Whig," can serve as an excellent historical foil to Archer the secessionist Democrat. As chair of the June 1850 Nashville Convention, Sharkey played an important role in derailing the efforts of fire-eaters to use the convention as a secessionist platform, and in 1865 President Andrew Johnson appointed him provisional governor of Mississippi. According to Eric Foner, Sharkey "epitomized the Whiggish planters and entrepreneurs" who opposed secession and refused to support the Confederacy. Although Sharkey is well known to political historians of the South during the era of sectional conflict, the NTC's William Lewis Sharkey Papers, 1823–1881, constitute his only extant collection of personal papers. A native of east Tennessee's Sumner County who fought at age sixteen with Andrew Jackson in the Battle of New Orleans, Sharkey migrated to the Natchez District after the War of 1812; by 1825, he had settled in Vicksburg, where he practiced law and won a seat in the state legislature. In 1832, he was elected to the Mississippi High Court of Errors and Appeals, moved to Jackson, and was soon chosen chief justice by his colleagues. Sharkey won reelection to the court many times, despite opposition from some fellow Whigs who disliked his support for Henry Clay's nationalist "American System" of federal funding for a national bank, protective tariffs, and internal improvements. In a November 1847 letter, an Adams County voter explained, "I am a Whig, an anti Bank Whig, and deny that there is any necessary connection or affiliation between Whigism and Bankism, or that party politics should have any influence on the election of judicial officers." In 1851, however, Sharkey resigned from the high court and returned to private practice. By this time he had become a substantial landowner and slaveholder, with nearly 700 acres and 28 slaves in Warren County in 1848. By 1850 he also owned 18 slaves and real estate worth $25,000 in Jackson and Hinds County; the real estate apparently included a two-story frame dwelling for himself, his wife Minerva, and their infant daughter Fanny.[9]

9. Eric Foner, *Reconstruction: America's Unfinished Revolution, 1863–1877* (New York: Harper & Row, 1988), 188; S. K. Montgomery, Adams County, Miss., November 5, 1847, to the Honorable William L. Sharkey, Jackson, Receipt for payment of Warren Co. taxes for 1848, Aetna Insurance Company, August 10, 1855, fire insurance policy, Robert H. Archer,

Chief Justice Sharkey became a political figure of regional and national repute when he served first as presiding officer of Mississippi's 1849 southern rights convention and then as president of the Nashville Convention in June 1850. The latter was a sectional gathering of delegates from slaveholding states that convened in response to the Mississippi convention's call for a meeting to promote a unified southern response to antislavery proposals pending in Congress, especially free-soil demands that the Mexican cession be closed to slavery. At the Mississippi convention, Sharkey, much like South Carolinian John C. Calhoun, maintained that he was devoted to both the Union and the ardent defense of southern rights within the Union. The next spring in Nashville, Sharkey's repeated "inconsistencies and vacillations" reflected his growing support for the Compromise of 1850 as offering sufficient protection to southern interests while also preserving the Union against the threat of secessionist radicalism.[10]

In the NTC's Sharkey Papers is a noteworthy letter written to the chief justice as the Nashville Convention was considering a public address that eventually resulted in twenty-eight resolutions. The letter's author was George Winchester (1793–1851), prominent Natchez jurist and states' rights Whig. He and his nephew Josiah are the foci of the largest single Natchez Trace subcollection, the Winchester Family Papers, 1783–1906. That enormous cache of documents contains an abundance of legal and business correspondence with a wide array of Natchez District individuals; elsewhere in this volume, Morton Rothstein utilizes it to examine the Winchesters' business dealings, and William G. Shade analyzes their political activities.

A native of Massachusetts who had attended Yale College in the 1810s and migrated to the Natchez District in the early 1820s, George Winchester served as a justice on the state supreme court from 1826 to 1829 and as

---

Baltimore, to William Sharkey, September 7, 1868, concerning Fanny's attendance at Archer's boarding school, William Lewis Sharkey Papers, all of which are in Box 2E509; Jennings, *The Nashville Convention*, 229. Sharkey makes many appearances in Thelma Jennings, *The Nashville Convention: Southern Movement for Unity, 1848–1851* (Memphis, Tenn.: Memphis State University Press, 1980), and in William C. Harris, *Presidential Reconstruction in Mississippi* (Baton Rouge: Louisiana State University Press, 1967). He is mentioned several times in Bond, *Political Culture in the Nineteenth-Century South*.

10. Jennings, *The Nashville Convention*, 115.

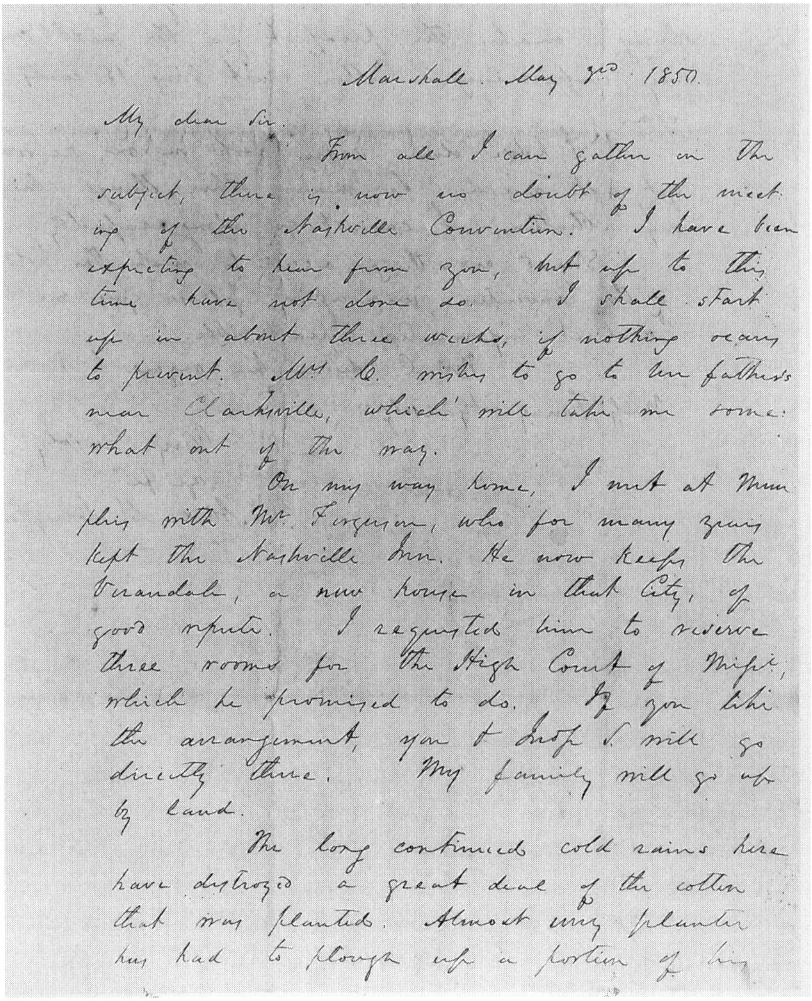
Marshall. May 3rd 1850.

My dear Sir.

From all I can gather on the subject, there is now no doubt of the meeting of the Nashville Convention. I have been expecting to hear from you, but up to this time have not done so. I shall start up in about three weeks, if nothing occurs to prevent. Mrs. C. wishes to go to her father's near Clarksville, which will take me somewhat out of the way.

On my way home, I met at Memphis with Mr. Ferguson, who for many years kept the Nashville Inn. He now keeps the Verandah, a new house in that City, of good repute. I requested him to reserve three rooms for the High Court of Missi., which he promised to do. If you like the arrangement, you & Judge S. will go directly there. My family will go up by land.

The long continued cold rains here have destroyed a great deal of the cotton that was planted. Almost every planter has had to plough up a portion of his

This 1850 letter to Mississippi lawyer, jurist, and Whig political activist William L. Sharkey comments on the forthcoming Nashville Convention, a gathering of delegates from slaveholding states, at which Sharkey presided. *From the William L. Sharkey Papers, NTC, the Center for American History, the University of Texas at Austin.*

JACKSON, MI., JULY 22D, 1844.

DEAR SIR—You are respectfully requested to attend a Mass Meeting of the Whigs of the South, to be held at this place on the 3d of October next.

Very Respectfully,

DAN'L MAYES,
C. R. CLIFTON,
JAS. RUCKS,
W. P. ANDERSON,

DUDLEY S. JENNINGS,
ROBT. HUGHES,
WM. YERGER,
J. M. DUFFIELD.

F. S. HUNT.

Hon. Geo. Winchester

We have expected the attendance of our friends, in the State, without special invitation; but fearing that you might not consider it your duty to come, unless reminded of it. I beg to say, we expect you.

Very respectfully,

Yr. ob'n. s't

C. R. Clifton

Appended to this 1844 invitation is a handwritten note to Natchez attorney and Whig party leader George Winchester urging him to attend the political meeting in Jackson, Mississippi. *From the Winchester Family Papers, NTC, the Center for American History, the University of Texas at Austin.*

a state senator in 1836–37. Like Sharkey and Archer, he was a delegate to the October 1849 Mississippi southern rights convention, and also served with Sharkey on the seven-member committee that had drafted an "Address to the Southern States" calling for the subsequent convention in Nashville.[11] Although Winchester did not attend the Nashville Convention, his mid-1850 letter to Sharkey expressed support for Calhoun's constitutional doctrines and also encouraged Sharkey not to insist on the unconstitutionality of California's admission as a free state, since doing so would detract attention from more fundamental questions about the constitutional prerogatives of slaveholders in the federal territories and the District of Columbia. You should, advised Winchester, "be careful of the California trap. There is rather too much anxiety displayed by some gentlemen to press it into this constitutional controversy between North & South."[12]

Winchester's letter closes by referring Sharkey to a remarkable five-page enclosure, "a short outline upon the subject as an attack by Socialists on inequalities of Capitalists & Labourers. This between ourselves." In this draft outline Winchester seems to reveal the impact of his upbringing and education in Federalist New England by attacking "a set of fanatic Philosophers, who call themselves social Reformers," and who view existing social and political inequalities of all kinds as "sins against God and natural law." Hence they want to abolish all these inequalities "so that all may be restored to that equality and freedom to which they were born." Not surprisingly, "the most dangerous of these social Reformers are those who attack the social, civil & political inequalities of Capitalists and Labourers in the Slave States." A crucial weapon in the abolitionists' ideological and political arsenal, in Winchester's opinion, was an expansive and unconstitutional interpretation of federal power vis-à-vis the states, whose exercise must end in the destruction of "the Union between the Slave & the non Slave States." As a northerner by birth and education, but a southerner by choice and interest, Winchester sought to formulate an antiabolitionist argument that would appeal to citizens in the free states. Once the radical reformers had succeeded in destroying "the do-

11. Ibid., 7. On the states' rights Whigs, see note 9.
12. George Winchester to Sharkey, [1850], Sharkey Papers.

mestic relation of master & slave," he argued, their arguments and efforts "may afterwards be applied to remove further inequalities which exist also in the social rank of Capitalists and Labourers at the North." This new campaign "may raise the slave labourers of the South to an equality of so-cial rank with the free labourers of the North, but it can only do so by de-grading free white labourers to the social [level] of free Black labourers[,] placing the former in a still lower rank relative to the capitalists of the North."[13] Winchester's provocative argument flew directly in the face of the "free soil, free labor, free men" ideology that would come to character-ize the Republican party of William H. Seward and Lincoln in the 1850s. The extent to which Sharkey accepted Winchester's thinking is not as-certainable from documents in the Sharkey subcollection.

The subcollection also sheds light on Sharkey's support for the Ameri-can (or Know-Nothing) party's Philadelphia platform of 1855, and on his outspoken endorsement of the Constitutional Union ticket in the presi-dential election of 1860. Of particular interest is the draft of a campaign address composed in the late summer or fall of 1860 and apparently di-rected to "a conservative element in the North," with the goal of wooing them away from the Republican party and "the poison of fake and ideal philanthropy." Sharkey expressed regret at "the unanimity of the North in 1856" behind the Republican nominee for president, John C. Frémont; but "many no doubt were then ignorant of the extreme doctrines of the Republican party, since more fully developed." The party's "abstract sec-tional sentiment of opposition to slavery" mirrored the sectional fanati-cism of southern Democrats, both serving to destroy the "conservative na-tionality" and "fraternal affection" that should bind northerners and southerners alike as "descendants of our patriotic sires." Sharkey was overly sanguine about the Whiggish Constitutional Union party's strength in the South, which he claimed "presents an unbroken front for Bell and Everett." Even so, "the South cannot elect them" without strong support from northern voters, who should look to Bell and Everett's sup-

13. Ibid. George Winchester seems to have been one of those proslavery intellectuals who were natives of New England, schooled in Federalist "conservative" thinking at col-leges in the Northeast before they took up residence in the South. See Larry E. Tise, *Pro-slavery: A History of the Defense of Slavery in America, 1701–1840* (Athens: University of Georgia Press, 1988).

port for "the principles of protection of domestic manufactures." In short, the North must prove itself "national[,] patriotic and conservative" by rejecting the sectional Republican party in favor of the preserving of the Union.[14]

Further, the NTC's Sharkey Papers contain some documents that enlarge our understanding of his postbellum career and outlook. Representative of his brief service as provisional governor of Mississippi for several months in 1865 is the lengthy draft of a speech to the combined state senate and house, which Sharkey termed "the first constitutional legislative body which has assembled in Mississippi for the last five years." The new governor clearly recognized that the recent "terrible and disastrous war," and the abolition of slavery effected thereby, had brought "an entire change in our domestic relations and our internal condition." In assessing the former slaves' status and likely performance as free laborers, Sharkey expressed views common to secessionist as well as Unionist planters: "Our chief difficulty will be found, it is presumed, in compelling the negro to perform his engagements, and unfortunately his recent course of training received from the freedmen's bureau will operate as a great drawback in this particular. . . . They must be instructed as to the necessity of labor, and in the duty of fidelity to their contracts." The governor noted that the state's "vagrant laws" might require some revision so as to become an effective counterweight to the freedman's "natural propensity for idleness." The legislature's adoption of a revised vagrant act as part and parcel of the state's infamous Black Code of 1865, along with its refusal to ratify the Thirteenth Amendment, aroused new antisouthern sentiment and protest in the North. As a consequence, when newly elected U.S. senators William Sharkey and James Alcorn (also a prominent Whiggish Unionist) arrived in Washington in December of 1865, Congress refused to seat them. Sharkey was still in Washington in January in 1867, when he wrote his niece that he had not yet obtained his seat in the Senate, "nor am I likely to do so." Hence he intended to pursue professional opportunities for financial gain. "I know I am growing old, and cannot work much longer,

14. Draft of 1860 speech, Sharkey Papers. Of related interest is a letter of June 12, 1860, to Sharkey from J. C. McAlpine of Linden, Cass County, Texas, expressing support for Sam Houston "as the only man who can go before the masses with sufficient strength to defeat the -isms of the day" and thereby "preserve the Union."

and the idea of being reduced to poverty in my old age is terrible to me."
An analogous response to the impact of radical Republican Reconstruction, from a lesser political figure in Louisiana's Tensas Parish, appears in the Winchester Papers. In 1868 Judge E. D. Farrar explained to Josiah Winchester: "As I am about to vacate my office under radical rule and am anxious to find some employment more remunerative than my profession promises to afford—I have again thought of seeking an agency for the purchase of lands in this rich alluvial."[15]

The documents of Joseph E. Davis (1784–1870), the subject of a small Natchez Trace subcollection, and the author of some illuminating letters in the Archer Papers, provide another window on the era of sectional conflict. Older brother of and surrogate father to the future president of the Confederacy, Davis was proprietor of Hurricane plantation, located at Davis Bend on the Mississippi River below Vicksburg. Like Archer and Sharkey, Davis had migrated to Mississippi as a young man (from Kentucky rather than Virginia or Tennessee) in order to make his fortune. Investing income from the practice of law in land and slaves, of which he owned 345 in 1860, Davis's upward social mobility exemplified the Old South's version of the American gospel of success. His politics during the 1850s seem to have been more typical of Mississippi's slaveholders than were those of either Archer or Sharkey, for Davis was neither a frankly secessionist Democrat nor a Whiggish Unionist. To be sure, he firmly believed, as did almost all slaveholders, that "any interference with the unqualified property of the Owner in a Slave was an abolition principle," to quote an 1840 letter from Joseph to younger brother Jefferson. From the time of the Mexican War he seems to have expected a dissolution of the Union. "As to the separation of the States," he wrote Archer in June of 1860, "I think it is a question of time. I have not changed my opinion for twelve years but have seldom expressed it as it was evident the South was

15. Draft of 1865 speech to the Mississippi senate and house of representatives, Sharkey to "My Dear Pattie," January 25, 1867, Sharkey Papers; E. D. Farrar to Josiah Winchester, May 1, 1868, Winchester Family Papers, Box 2E907. As Neil R. McMillen emphasizes, Sharkey as provisional governor firmly opposed any extension of the suffrage to former slaves, "even if limited to the most educated and propertied blacks." *Dark Journey: Black Mississippians in the Age of Jim Crow* (Urbana: University of Illinois Press, 1989), 36.

unprepared." In mid-November, after Lincoln's election, Davis wrote again to Archer: "The election of Lincoln I suppose did not surprise you, & I hope that there is soul enough in the South to turn it to good account."[16]

Despite his unexceptional politics, Joseph Davis was an atypical Mississippi planter in that he does not appear to have shared in the racist disdain for and fear of black African Americans that characterized the great majority of white southerners. For this reason, in conjunction with an idealism apparently encouraged by chance encounters in the mid-1820s with English utopians Robert Owen and Fanny Wright, he succeeded, perhaps more nearly than any other planter of his day, at approximating the idealized proslavery image of the benevolent, fatherly master. Joseph based his system of slave management on the principle that "people worked best when treated well and given incentives than when driven by the fear of punishment."[17] He set up a system of self-government among his slaves that was not well received among his neighbors. A court was held every Sunday in a small building called the Hall of Justice, where a slave jury heard complaints of slave misconduct, including complaints from frustrated white overseers, and testimony from the accused in their own defense. In marked contrast to the fate of slaves elsewhere, no slave at Davis Bend was ever punished except after conviction by a jury of his peers. Joseph Davis sat as judge, but he seems to have seldom intervened in the proceedings, save on occasion to lessen the severity of a sentence.

The most remarkable slave at Davis Bend was Ben Montgomery, whose life and extraordinary relationship with Joseph Davis were brought to light

16. *The Papers of Jefferson Davis: Volume 1, 1808–1840*, ed. Haskell M. Monroe, Jr., and James T. McIntosh (Baton Rouge: Louisiana State University Press, 1971), 464–65; Joseph Davis to Archer, June 13, November 13, 1860, Archer Papers, Box 2E653. The Joseph E. Davis Papers, 1824–1880, Box 2E556, is one of many small, discrete collections that span the period 1790–1900. See Janet Sharp Hermann, *Joseph E. Davis, Pioneer Patriarch* (Jackson: University Press of Mississippi, 1990), esp. p. x. Hermann consulted the NTC's Joseph E. Davis Papers for this biography, but she did not make use of the valuable letters from Davis in the Richard T. Archer Family Papers.

17. Hermann, *Joseph E. Davis*, 54. My accounts of Davis's idealism and system of slave self-government are drawn from Hermann's biography. For a discussion of the idealized paternalistic image of the "prebourgeois" benevolent master and its apparent inaccuracy when applied to most planters, see William G. Shade's essay in this volume.

in Janet Hermann's prize-winning book *The Pursuit of a Dream* (1981). Although Montgomery, like Richard Archer, had moved from Virginia to Mississippi, he had not migrated of his own volition; he was one of some three hundred thousand slaves to leave the Old Dominion between 1830 and 1860, either in company with emigrating masters or as part of the interstate slave trade that supplied manual labor to the expansive Cotton Kingdom. When Joseph Davis purchased Montgomery in Natchez in 1836, Ben was seventeen years old and could read and write, evidently having learned from a white child in Virginia. Joseph Davis, quickly realizing that this young slave had unusual talents and determination, gave him free access to the large library at Hurricane and encouraged him to explore his wide-ranging interests in things literary, mechanical, and mercantile. Montgomery opened his own retail store on the plantation in 1842, managed to establish his own line of credit with New Orleans merchants, and in time became the de facto business manager at both Hurricane and Jefferson Davis's adjacent plantation, Brierfield, whose title was in Joseph's name. After the Civil War, Joseph and Ben joined forces to wrest control of both plantations back from the U.S. government and the Freedmen's Bureau, and in early 1867 Davis sold them to Montgomery and his sons for $300,000, to be paid with 6 percent interest in annual payments of $18,000. In the NTC's Joseph Davis Papers is a remarkable letter written in July 1866 by Montgomery at Hurricane to Davis in Vicksburg. After a salutation of "Kind Sir" and a brief report on the status of the plantation and its inhabitants, the letter closes with the phrase "Your obedient servant," poignant and powerful words when addressed by an ex-slave to his former master. When Joseph died four years later at the age of eighty-five, he was buried at Hurricane in a brick tomb built by Ben Montgomery. Seven years later, in 1877, Ben himself died at age fifty-eight. His sons soon lost the Davis Bend lands, in part because falling prices and natural disasters had made it impossible for them to meet the annual debt payments for several years, and in part because of white conservatives and their self-styled political "redemption" of Mississippi from Radical Reconstruction and black Republican rule in the mid-1870s.[18] In 1878, Jefferson

18. For a detailed political account of Republican Reconstruction and "redemption" in Mississippi, see William C. Harris, *The Day of the Carpetbagger: Republican Reconstruction in Mississippi* (Baton Rouge: Louisiana State University Press, 1979).

Davis succeeded before the state's post-Reconstruction courts in getting Joseph's will overturned.

The Natchez Trace Collection is notable for the number of subcollections that, like the Davis, Winchester, Sharkey, and Archer papers, open windows on the postbellum experiences of families and individuals who had been well established before the Civil War. Manuscripts of this kind are fine grist for the scholarly mills of historians interested in addressing long-standing and complex questions about the relative degrees of change and continuity between the antebellum and postbellum South. The John Carmichael Jenkins Family Papers, 1836–1900, offer new information about the children of a Pennsylvanian who had settled in Adams County during the flush times of the 1830s. Dr. John C. Jenkins (1809–55) has long been familiar to historians of the Old South, thanks to an 1841–55 diary in the possession of the Department of Archives and Manuscripts of the Louisiana State University at Baton Rouge. A native of Lancaster County and the son of a wealthy ironmaster and U.S. congressman, Jenkins graduated from Dickinson College in 1828 and then earned a medical degree from the University of Pennsylvania Medical School in 1833. The newly minted M.D. moved to Wilkinson County during the prosperous mid-1830s in order to take over the medical practice of his uncle, Dr. John Flood Carmichael. When the year 1837 brought death to both the uncle and the flush times, young Dr. Jenkins took over two large and heavily indebted plantations. In 1839 he married Annis Dunbar, the eldest daughter of prominent Natchez area planter-physician Dr. William Dunbar, and the couple soon moved their residence to Elgin plantation, about six miles south of Natchez. By the time Dr. and Mrs. Jenkins both died of yellow fever in 1855, he was the financially successful and agronomically sophisticated owner of several plantations and hundreds of slaves. Cotton, of course, was the mainspring of his wealth;[19] but he had turned his experi-

19. The diary—what the doctor himself called a "Memorandum Book"—became the basis for Albert Garrel Seal's "John Carmichael Jenkins, Scientific Planter of the Natchez District," *Journal of Mississippi History* 1 (January 1939): 14–28. Seal's article informs the more romantic account in Harnett T. Kane, *Natchez on the Mississippi* (New York: William Morrow & Co., 1947), 52–59. According to Seal, 27, n. 123, succession papers in the records of Adams County place the value of the doctor's estate at $181,000 to $200,000. This

mental mind and enormous energy to improving and diversifying his agricultural operations and to broadcasting his innovations in newspapers
and periodicals.

Although the doctor does not seem to have sought political office, he
joined the sectional fray over slavery as a Whiggish Unionist with an
anonymous 1851 proslavery pamphlet entitled "Three Letters, by 'Conestoga,' to a Friend in Lancaster County, Pennsylvania, upon Slavery and
the Fugitive Slave Law."[20] "Look at the vast structure of wealth and power
which has been reared upon the foundation of slave labor in this country,"
declared Dr. Jenkins, who also insisted that "the negro race have proved to
be happier, and in every respect better off as slaves, than when thrown
upon their own resources." This combination of economic prosperity and
Negro improvement had to be part of God's plan, he wrote, for "slavery
was established by divine authority, and among God's own chosen people,
the Hebrews." Moreover, "all our great denominations of Christian sects
agree that slavery was clearly sanctioned by both the Old and New Testa-
ments."

The Jenkins Family Papers add less to our knowledge of the doctor himself than do the papers of George and Josiah Winchester, who served as
the family's attorneys. Both subcollections, however, include superb letters written after the Civil War by and to three of their four children:
Alice D., John F., and William Dunbar.[21] Alice or "Allie," the eldest,

---

figure seems modest in view of some entries that his executors apparently made in Jenkins's
account book shortly after his death. Those entries identify 139 slaves at Tarbert Plantation
in Wilkinson County and estimate their value (as of November 1855) at almost $89,000.
Eighty-seven slaves at the Stock Farm (located primarily in Wilkinson County, but which
also included land across the Mississippi in Louisiana's West Feliciana Parish) are valued at
over $47,000. Moreover, the Jenkins's residence, Elgin plantation, included 117 slaves; al-
though their total monetary value is not recorded, it had to exceed $60,000. John C. Jen-
kins Family Papers, 1840–1900, LSU Southern Historical Manuscripts (microfiche).

20. John Carmichael Jenkins, *Three Letters by "Conestoga," to a Friend in Lancaster
County, Pennsylvania, upon Slavery and the Fugitive Law, November, 1851* (Lancaster, Pa.:
Geo. Sanderson, 1851). Albert Garrel Seal edited these letters as "Letters from the South:
A Mississippian's Defense of Slavery," *Journal of Mississippi History* 2 (1940): 212–31. Seal
seems to have been unaware that they had previously been published as a pamphlet.

21. A fourth child, younger daughter Mary D., married U.S. Army officer Lewis M.
Johnson in the spring of 1865, and they moved north to New York City within a few years.

studied piano in New Orleans, tried her hand at teaching music in Natchez, and became determined to recoup some of the family's wartime financial losses (preeminently the uncompensated emancipation of some 350 slaves) by pursuing a cotton claim under the terms of the Captured and Abandoned Property Act of 1863. (In 1879 the Supreme Court agreed with the U.S. Court of Claims that the Treasury Department must reimburse the Jenkins family for cotton confiscated by U.S. military forces in 1863.)[22] Dunbar, or "Dunnie," the younger son, studied civil engineering abroad in Brussels and Paris. His older brother, John, having served the Confederacy as a teenaged private in the Army of Tennessee, attended Washington College in Lexington, Virginia—"its foundation laid by Washington," explained John, "and new luster being added to its reputation by [Robert E.] Lee," who instituted the nation's first system of elective courses during his tenure as president. In September 1866 John reported that he was "totally unaccustomed to mountain walking," but "after the monotonous red hills of Miss[issippi], this scenery is actually refreshing." Later that fall he lamented, "I have been somewhat unwell owing to a violent cold contracted by imprudence and I have not prosecuted my studies with that vigor which I should have done." Despite this illness, he found the cool climate of the valley between the Blue Ridge and the Allegheny Mountains much preferable to the semitropical weather of the Delta back home. "Fresh air from the mountains braces and invigorates a person and I have felt new life since I have been here: my two mile walk every day is not as much to me as two hundred yards in Miss[issippi] would be." He was amazed at the absence of serious "sickness" in the Lexington area, and "in College there is little or none at all, except when the lessons get too hard, then 'all the ills that flesh is heir to' prevail and are sent in as excuses for absences." (The phenomenon of students succumbing to sudden illnesses at exam time remains familiar to many professors today.) John F. Jenkins himself proved a diligent and accomplished student. Periodic grade re-

The Jenkins family story is sketched in *Biographical and Historical Memoirs of Mississippi* (Chicago: Goodspeed Publishing Co., 1891), 1020–21.

22. On Alice's dogged pursuit of the family claim, and attorney Josiah Winchester's involvement in the suit, see Elizabeth Lee Thompson, "The Effects of a Reconstructed Federal Judiciary: Counselors and Claimants under the Captured and Abandoned Property Act of 1863" (master's report, University of Texas at Austin, 1998).

Washington College,

LEXINGTON, VIRGINIA.

Report for the Half Session ending 8ᵗʰ February, 1868.

Mr. J. F. Jenkins

This Report presents the average standing of the Student for the entire Half Session, combined with the result of the Examination, which is held at the end of each term. Students who obtain a grade of 30 on Examination, and of 50 on Combined Mark, are considered as having passed; those who obtain 60 on Examination, and 80 on Combined Mark, are considered distinguished.

Demerit Marks are given for unexcused absences and other violations of College order—for absence, 10; for tardiness, from 3 to 5. An aggregate of 100 demerit during the Half Session subjects the Student to dismissal, at the discretion of the Faculty.

DEPARTMENTS.	Classes Attended.	Average Mark.	Exam'n Mark.	Comb'd Mark.	Grade in Class.	Whole No. in Class.	ABSENCES. Excus'd	ABSENCES. Unex'd	Demerit	REMARKS.
LATIN.	Senior	88.5	64	76.25		52				
GREEK.	Intermediate	88.75	63	75.87	11	36	3	1	10	
ENGLISH.										
MODERN LANGUAGES.	Jun. French	93	69	81	11	50	4			Distinguished
MORAL PHILOSOPHY.										
MATHEMATICS.	Intermediate	94	43	68.5	6	27	1	1	10	
APPLIED MATHEMATICS.										
NAT'L PHILOSOPHY.										
CHEMISTRY.	Junior	85.7	52	68.9	29	74				
HISTORY AND LITERATURE.										
DECLAMATION AND COMPOSITION.										
								20	Total	

R. E. Lee, President.

This 1868 grade report for John F. Jenkins, son of Mississippi planter John Carmichael Jenkins, attests to his diligence as a student. The younger Jenkins attended Washington College in Lexington, Virginia, following his service as a private in the Army of Tennessee. College president Robert E. Lee signed the report. *From the John C. Jenkins Family Papers, NTC, the Center for American History, the University of Texas at Austin.*

ports, signed by "R E Lee, President," show that he ranked among the top quarter of students in most of his classes, and his performances in Latin and French earned "Distinguished" marks. He was financially dependent on funds forwarded from Mississippi, and the administrator of his father's estate received just the sort of entreaty which is familiar to many parents today. "Can you send me any money? . . . I am entirely out." The estate's administrator was Natchez judge Josiah Winchester (d. 1888), who had assumed the role of Jenkins family attorney after the death of his uncle George in 1851, and who, like William Sharkey, had abjured secession and the Confederacy.[23]

Just as additional correspondence with and about the Jenkins family is scattered throughout the NTC's Winchester Family Papers, so also is correspondence concerning other well-known Mississippi families, including that of magnate Stephen Duncan (1787–1863). Like Dr. John Carmichael Jenkins, Duncan was a Pennsylvania native, graduate of Dickinson College, and medical doctor; but his move to the Natchez District in 1808 preceded the arrival of the younger Dr. Jenkins by almost three decades. Duncan became a founder and president of the Bank of the State of Mississippi, headquartered in Natchez, and therefore makes frequent appearances in yet another large Natchez Trace subcollection, the Bank of the State of Mississippi Records.[24]

A major source of Jenkins family income was the Adams County plantation Elgin, on which Dr. Jenkins had worked over one hundred slaves. While John attended Washington College, the plantation was leased in 1867 for $400 (plus $250 for repair of the cotton gin) to a local retailer and family friend, Alex H. Carradine, who functioned as both furnishing

23. John F. Jenkins to Judge Josiah Winchester, September 24, 1866, Winchester Family Papers, Box 2E908; John F. Jenkins to Judge Josiah Winchester, December 2, 1866, December 18, 1867, five Washington College grade reports, from April 28, 1867, to October 31, 1868, John Carmichael Jenkins Papers, Box 2E510. Box 2E907 of the Winchester Family Papers contains letters to Josiah from Stephen Duncan, Jr., and Wade Hampton, Jr., concerning the estate of Stephen Duncan, Sr.

24. A valuable study is Martha Jane Lee Brazy, "The World a Slaveholder Made: Stephen Duncan and Plantation Society" (master's thesis, University of Wisconsin–Milwaukee, 1987). Brazy was not able to consult the Natchez Trace Collection, but relied heavily on Duncan papers in the Louisiana and Lower Mississippi Valley Collections at the Louisiana State University Libraries in Baton Rouge.

merchant and estate manager in dealings with the former slaves. "I did not send the accounts of the Freedmen," wrote Carradine to Jenkins in early 1867; "you could never understand them in the world, and it is impossible to explain them by letter." In 1867 Carradine seems to have achieved greater success at drawing a profit from his mercantile business than at making Elgin a profitable agricultural operation. According to a December letter from Jenkins to Winchester, Carradine "failed last year in his crop and had not been able to pay me anything on the rent." Yet on the same day Carradine informed Jenkins, "The Negroes came out in my debt this year over a thousand dollars, cotton is 14³/₄ [cents per pound] today in N.O. [New Orleans] a nice state of affairs." Elgin was still under Carradine's management in 1870, by which time John F. Jenkins had returned to Mississippi from Virginia and taken up residence at another family plantation, Tarbert. Younger brother Dunbar, after his European studies, also graduated from Washington College and returned to the Magnolia State, where he helped manage the family properties and eventually became chief engineer for the New Orleans and Northwestern Railroad. The tensions and conflicts that Dunbar experienced in learning to operate plantations with free rather than enslaved labor are evident in a letter written to Alice in February of 1876: "The negroes have gone back into such a state of barbarism that I have to teach them as wild animals & have given orders to my watchman to shoot them down if they attempt to come near the house at night again." It is hardly surprising that he and his brother considered the possibility of securing alternative labor through the German Emigrant Aid Society of Chicago.[25]

Another Natchez Trace subcollection, the Basil Kiger Papers, 1841–1885, focuses on an affluent but heretofore little known Warren County family

25. John F. Jenkins to "Dear Judge," April 28, 1867, Winchester Papers, Box 2E907; John F. Jenkins to "Dear Judge," February 6, 1867, Alex Carradine to John F. Jenkins, April 1867, John F. Jenkins to Josiah Winchester, December 18, 1867, Alex Carradine to John F. Jenkins, December 18, 1867, Jenkins Papers, Box 2E510; W. D. Jenkins to Alice Jenkins, February 29, 1876, Winchester Papers, Box 2E908. John wrote to Dunbar that he and four or five other "of the most respectable planters of the neighborhood contemplated getting 20 or 30 families by December." John F. Jenkins to W. D. Jenkins, October 21, 1874, Winchester Papers, Box 2E908.

with a variety of familial and business connections in Virginia, Tennessee, Louisiana, Texas, and California. Virginia native Basil Gordon Kiger, apparently after service as a colonel in the Mexican War, established himself and his family at Buena Vista cotton plantation, near Brunswick Landing, upriver from Vicksburg in northwestern Warren County. His wife, Carrie (b. 1827), was another native Virginian; their three children, sons Willie and Basil, Jr., and daughter Mary, were born between 1847 and 1856. By 1852 Kiger employed an overseer to supervise the labor of thirty-one hands, who raised some 220 bales of cotton for shipment downriver on steamboats, to which Kiger also sold wood as fuel for their engines. The slaves who picked cotton in late 1852 included some he had purchased in Richmond that September. "My new negroes are improving wonderfully, and I am delighted with my purchase," he wrote in late October to Carrie, who had remained with her family in the Old Dominion after Kiger had returned with his purchases to Mississippi. "You know it is against my principle to sell but were I disposed to do so an offer of $10,000 would not buy them tomorrow. . . . it does my heart good to see them cheerful and happy." Because he intended to clear another hundred acres for cultivation, "I need about 8 more negroes and unless they are unreasonably high, I shall buy them in New Orleans this winter." In the spring of 1853, when Kiger anticipated "the very best crop of cotton that I have ever seen," he also expressed anxiety "about the health of my unacclimated negroes." Kiger's slave force continued to grow in size, until by 1860 Kiger had seventy-six hands working in the fields, as recorded in his copy of Thomas Affleck's widely used and frequently reprinted *Cotton Plantation and Account Book*. Affleck's volume includes a two-page section entitled "The Duties of an Overseer." It seems that the proprietor of Buena Vista took seriously Affleck's admonition here that "*a fine crop* consists, first, in an increase in the number, and a marked increase in the condition and value of the negroes."[26]

26. Buena Vista Plantation Record and Account Book, 1849–57, and Plantation Book, 1852–56, Basil Gordon Kiger to Carrie Kiger, October 29, 1852, May 29, June 5, 1853, "The Buena Vista Cotton Plantation and Account Book No. 3, Suitable for a Force of 40 Hands or Under. By Thomas Affleck. Eighth Edition" (which contains entries for 1860), Basil Kiger Papers, Boxes 2E516 and 2E522. Christopher Morris makes occasional use of this collection in *Becoming Southern: The Evolution of a Way of Life, Warren County and*

With an overseer in charge of the profitable plantation's day-to-day operations, Kiger could partake in genteel rural pastimes and also maintain a two-story brick residence on Washington Street in Vicksburg. In October 1852 he wrote from Buena Vista to his wife in Virginia, "I find more pleasure up here than I do in town. I go fishing and hunting nearly every day. The fish in Steele's Bayou bite beautifully," and he had shot "a fine fat buck." The year 1852 was also a presidential election year, and just before election day Kiger observed from Vicksburg that some persons "have been indulging to such excess as to make it dangerous." Kiger himself campaigned fervently for Whig nominee General Winfield Scott, commander of the U.S. troops at Veracruz and Mexico City during the Mexican War. "I go to Vicksburg on the [steamboat] Saxon in the morning with a view to devote four days to my Country & Party," Basil wrote Carrie in October. "I enter into the contest with my usual soul & spirit. I feel in the first place that we are already defeated. Scott in my opinion has not the ghost of a chance." Although Scott carried Whiggish Vicksburg, Kiger correctly predicted that Democratic nominee Franklin Pierce would defeat "the brave old hero of a thousand fights" on the state and national levels.[27] Pierce's victory, however, did not disappoint Kiger's Democratic in-laws, especially his wife's uncle Dr. William McKendree Gwin (1805–1885), a widely traveled land speculator, railroad promoter, duelist, and United States senator from California, who tried to orchestrate a partnership of investors (including Basil Kiger) to purchase a hundred thousand acres in

---

Vicksburg, Mississippi, 1770–1860 (New York: Oxford University Press, 1995). On Affleck, a native of Scotland who settled first in Mississippi and then in Texas, see William K. Scarborough, *The Overseer: Plantation Management in the Old South* (Baton Rouge: Louisiana State University Press, 1966), 70–71, and Robert W. Williams, "Affleck, Thomas Dunbar," in *Encyclopedia of Southern History*, 6–7. For an examination of Mary Bell Kiger's life as revealed in her letters, see Katherine J. Adams's essay in this volume.

27. Basil G. Kiger to Carrie Kiger, October 29, November 3, 1852, Kiger Papers, Box 2E516. At the time, Carrie's sister Betty was engaged to marry her cousin Ned from Tennessee, whom the Whiggish Basil denigrated as "one of these inept slow motioned know nothing Tennesseans and up to this time I have seen nothing else from that state." Carrie's "Uncle Aleck" M. Gwin agreed that Ned "is a regular grunter. I don't like him much." This family hostility may explain why the engagement was broken off in the spring of 1853. Basil G. Kiger to Carrie Kiger, September 4, 1852, Aleck Gwin to Carrie Kiger, December 14, 1852, ibid.

east Texas.[28] Carrie Kiger visited Dr. Gwin and his wife ("Aunt Mary") in Washington after the 1852 election, and reported to her husband that President-elect Pierce was "a real Gen. Jackson sort of man" and "intends to have his own way in every thing." She believed it "certain that the Dr. will have a great influence with the new administration."[29]

Carrie's other uncle, Aleck M. Gwin, bought a cotton plantation near Brunswick Landing. In late October 1852 he wrote to Carrie, then in Virginia: "We have no news in our neighborhood as usual—of all the dull places in the world, this is perhaps, the dullest. Even politics has no effect on us. Every body is busy getting out their crops, and I am in high glee at the price we are getting and the prospect of even higher prices. My crop will put me clear out of debt, and I could almost say I was a happy man, if it was not for fears of losing my place—but 'sufficient unto the day, is the evil therof' is one of the wise sayings from the Bible that should always be remembered." Less than two months later Uncle Aleck sold out for six thousand dollars and moved to Lafourche Parish in southern Louisiana, where his sister Catherine and her husband owned Terrebone sugar plantation. Aleck Gwin remained there through the Civil War, and wrote "My Dear good Niece" a remarkable letter in mid-March of 1865, by which time most of Louisiana had long since fallen under Union control. After describing his brother-in-law as "the old patriarch" who "can curse the Yankees with a vehemence that would make your hair stand on end," Aleck gave vivid testimony to the self-assertive independence being shown by freedmen and freedwomen on the one hand, and on the other the resentful frustration with which many slaveholding families responded to the end of black bondage:

> In the way of cropping but little is doing in this country. Free labor is not remunerative. Niggers won't work without the fear of a cow hide behind them. The crop of last year amounted to a little over $2,000

28. The earliest reference to this scheme appears to come in a June 5, 1853, letter from Basil Kiger at home to Carrie Kiger in Virginia, Kiger Papers, Box 2E516.
29. Carrie Kiger to Basil Kiger, late 1852, ibid. On the failure of Senator Gwin's ambitious bill for a transcontinental railroad with many terminals north and south, see David M. Potter, *The Impending Crisis, 1848–1861*, ed. Don E. Fehrenbacher (New York: Harper & Row, 1976), 149–50.

worth of syrup—no sugar. We made corn and meat enough to do the place. At the end of the year [1864] every negro gave notice of their intention to leave, and we were all heartile glad of it. We now have three negroes in the field and all the house servants are white. What a blessing it is to have no lazy trifling free negroes in your sight. They are very nice when in their proper place, which is in the field with a strong man with a willing mind and keen cowhide behind them. Trifling as they are I am sorry for the poor wretches, wandering from place to place seeking employment and finding none. We have a white girl as a nurse, and rather a hard case, but she is creole and knows no better.[30]

A letter in the Winchester Family Papers illustrates the dilemma of an overseer dealing with black laborers no longer afraid to voice their expectations and demands. Josiah Winchester in Natchez, as administrator of Dr. John Carmichael Jenkins's estate after the latter's death in 1855, received a letter dated January 6, 1864, from H. C. Wright, the marginally literate overseer of a Jenkins family plantation. Wright was anxious to know if the judge wished him "to remain on the place" in the new year. If so, "you had better come down [and] see the negroas for they say they will not work unless you come and mak them promis or mak some provions [i.e., provisions] for them in the way of clothing & shoes[.] thay have all redy quit[.] my cook came up and told me that she would not do eny mor for us[.] it is with dificult I can get eny thing don at tall . . . there must be a chang for the better or I cant stay on the [place] much longer . . . the negaroas say that you or the Jinkens children must come down and mak them some promis to mak all work a lik or thay quit[.] the talk among them is all to have sepert paches [i.e., separate patches] among themselves."[31]

30. Aleck Gwin to Carrie Kiger, October 23, 1852, March 12, 1865, Basil Kiger to Carrie Kiger, December 11, 1852, Kiger Papers, Box 2E516.

31. H. C. Wright to "Dear Judge Winchester," January 6, 1864, Winchester Family Papers, Box 2E906. On the Civil War's impact upon master-slave relations, see especially Armistead Louis Robinson, "Day of Jubilo: Civil War and the Demise of Slavery in the Mississippi Valley" (Ph.D. diss., University of Rochester, 1976), Leon F. Litwack, *Been in the Storm So Long: The Aftermath of Slavery* (New York: Random House, Knopf, & Vintage Books, 1979), and Ira Berlin et al., *Slaves No More: Three Essays on Emancipation and the Civil War* (Cambridge, Eng.: Cambridge University Press, 1992).

No doubt such experiences encouraged Josiah Winchester to consider new sources of more subservient laborers who would make possible the reestablishment of profitable cotton plantations in the lower Mississippi valley. Winchester seems to have shared the mixture of resentment and confidence expressed by a Louisiana correspondent in May of 1868, after congressional Republicans had imposed military government and black manhood suffrage on the white South: "Notwithstanding evil legislation[,] notwithstanding the malignant spirit which animates our enemies and prompts them to every species of injustice and oppression against our people—the soil still remains and the climate continues to shed its benign influence—The recent rise in the price of the great staple and the fears expressed of the capacity of the east to supply it in sufficient quantities convinces me that the great cotton region of the Southern States will yet be looked to to supply the large portion of the raw material." The major obstacle to such optimistic entrepreneurialism was a suitable source of docile labor, particularly in the atmosphere being generated by Radical Reconstruction. During the early 1870s Josiah Winchester took the lead in attempting to orchestrate the importation of hundreds of Chinese men under contract to provide plantation labor for five years. A copy of a December 20, 1872, letter from New York, signed by Winchester and a partner and addressed to Charles C. Hill in Shanghai, stipulates that "500 Chinese" were to be shipped by the Pacific Mail Steamship Company from Chungking, Shanghai, and Yokohama to Key West, Florida. "We look upon this as the opening hedge, to a large & profitable business, & in all our operations we agree to share equally with yourself that is one third to each of us." An ultimate destination for these imported workers is not identified in the 1872 letter, but one is suggested in the draft version of an 1874 arrangement between Winchester and several unidentified "planters" in the vicinity of Kingston, in northwestern Louisiana's De Soto Parish. The arrangement called for procuring "Five Hundred able, quiet, & industrious Chinese Laborers from China" to provide five years of "honest & faithful labor" on several plantations, each of which was to cultivate "10 acres of cotton to 5 acres of corn." According to the agreement, "the net profits arising from the sale of the products of the plantations respectively" were "to be divided annually between the planters and J. Winchester, as may be determined." Although the fate of this particular scheme remains unclear, the planters' panacea of imported foreign labor proved transitory and illusory. Provisional Mississippi governor William Sharkey had predicted as much in his 1865 address to the state legislature. Commenting upon the "doubtful experiment of foreign laborers," Sharkey stated that it was better to "retain" blacks, "as they are here and acquainted with our system of production."[32]

During the late 1860s, Basil Kiger had a generally positive and profitable experience with free black labor on his Buena Vista plantation. In March 1868 Mrs. Kiger wrote to elder son Willie, then a student at nearby Oakland College,[33] that her husband "is more sanguine this year about planting than he has ever been if we can only escape an overflow."[34] High cotton prices that year, along with freedom from flooding, seem to have rebounded to the benefit of both landowners and laborers. In October 1868, Basil, Jr., also at Oakland College, learned from his mother about a recent meeting of local planters. "They have all broken their agreement and come to the terms the negroes offered to pick cotton. Four bits a hundred [lbs] and furnish their rations. And even at those rates it is difficult to

32. E. D. Farrar to Josiah Winchester, May 1, 1868, Copy of December 20, 1872, letter from J. Winchester and a partner [name not clearly decipherable] to Charles C. Hill, Esq., Shanghai, China, "A Plan for working Cotton Plantations in the neighborhood of Kingston with Chinese Labor for the year 1874 & for four years subsequent thereafter," four pages, Winchester Family Papers, Boxes 2E907 and 2E909; Draft of 1865 speech to the Mississippi senate and house of representatives, Sharkey Papers, Box 2E509. No doubt the lure of imported Chinese labor for southern planters was encouraged by railroad corporations' profitable use of indentured Chinese workers during the 1860s and 1870s on the western reaches of the new transcontinental lines.

33. The early history of Oakland College, located at Rodney, Mississippi, and founded about 1830, is illuminated in the NTC's Chamberlain-Hyland-Gould Family Papers, 1805–1886; Jeremiah Chamberlain (1795–1851) served as the Presbyterian college's first president. The antebellum affairs of another small Mississippi school—Jefferson College, which opened at Washington in 1811—are the focus of much of the Natchez Trace Collection's B. L. C. Wailes Papers, 1811–1860. Wailes (1797–1862), another Whiggish Unionist, albeit far more apolitical than William Sharkey, served as the college's treasurer. He is the subject of a classic biography by Charles S. Sydnor, *A Gentleman of the Old Natchez Region: Benjamin L. C. Wailes* (Durham, N.C.: Duke University Press, 1938).

34. Mrs. Kiger to Willie, March 1, 1868, Kiger Papers, Box 2E516. In the fall of 1868, Willie transferred to the University of Virginia. Much like John F. Jenkins in Lexington at Washington College, Willie Kiger in Charlottesville lauded an "invigorating climate safe from the many diseases that rage so on the banks of the 'father of waters.' " Willie to Mrs. Kiger, November 1, 1868, ibid.

get hands." Nonetheless, a few months later she observed that "people are crazy about planting cotton again, and of course hands are greatly in demand, on almost their own terms either for wages or share in the crop." In 1868 Basil Kiger paid a half share to his hands, who worked in squads and raised about 260 bales on the place. "Your Pa had no trouble at all getting the negroes to remain," reported Mrs. Kiger in February 1869. "They are so well pleased with their success last year they are willing to try it again."[35] And Basil Kiger's half of the 1868 crop was enough to encourage him to plant again in 1869. That fall Mrs. Kiger wrote Willie that his father "has never had any difficulties in obtaining all the hands he needed"; and the principal reason for this success is suggested in subsequent letters from the 1869 picking season. Mrs. Kiger informed Willie that an election was to take place at the end of November, and that "the negroes en masse will vote the Radical ticket." Despite the Kiger family's decidedly anti-Republican, "Conservative" sympathies,[36] "Your Pa has never said a word to one of them about politics," Mrs. Kiger told Basil, Jr. "I shall be very clear of attempting to influence any of them myself. My utter failure with Horace at the other election rather disgusted me." It is tempting, albeit ahistorical, to wish that more planters had followed Basil Kiger's example and refrained from attempting to influence or intimidate their freedmen in the exercise of the franchise. The principal reason for the ability of many planters and freedmen to cooperate economically during the late 1860s, however, was a favorable cotton market; and it is more than historical coincidence that the Democratic "redemption" of Mississippi from Radical Republican Reconstruction in 1875 coincided with a serious depression sparked by the Panic of 1873. As Peter Kolchin has ob-

35. Mrs. Kiger to Basil, Jr., October 1868, February 7, February 14, 1869, Kiger Papers, Box 2E516. In a letter dated January 24, 1869, son Willie explained to his mother, "It makes no difference what contract a planter makes with his hands, if he furnishes them with supplies on credit & they fail to make a crop he loses all by it; since they have nothing that he could take by way of payment."

36. Mrs. Kiger to Willie, November 4, 28, 1869, Kiger Papers, Box 2E517. The second letter also notes that "there is much apathy among the Conservatives." The family's "Conservative," anti-Republican political stance is evident in a November 8, 1868, letter to his mother from Basil, Jr., at Oakland College. He described himself as "low spirited about the political. I have just received full returns from the election which show that Grant is elected by an overwhelming majority in nearly all the states. Pa must be very low spirited. I never saw a bluer set of people in my life than there is here." Kiger Papers, Box 2E516.

served, it is an "unfortunate historical accident that emancipation preceded the onset of a generation-long period of agricultural deflation and
depression that engulfed the Western world."[37]

The Natchez Trace Collection is replete with manuscripts that en-
hance our knowledge and understanding of southern society and politics
during the era of sectional conflict extending from the 1840s to the 1870s.
Although these manuscripts illuminate the world of the mid-nineteenth-
century South predominantly from the perspective of elite individuals and
families, scholars focusing on the Magnolia State and the lower Mississippi valley will find the collection indispensable on a variety of topics. To
wit, the Jenkins Family Papers, together with documents on that family's
affairs in the Winchester Family Papers and a complementary Jenkins collection at the Louisiana State University, offer testimony on myriad facets
of life in nineteenth-century Mississippi, from agriculture and slavery to
higher education and gender roles. Historians of slavery and antebellum
politics will, as several essays in this volume attest, be drawn to the Archer
Family Papers, while the William Lewis Sharkey as well as the Basil Kiger
Papers exhibit Whiggish foils to the fire-eating Richard Archer. Several
subcollections will appeal strongly to historians interested in the manifold
impact of war and emancipation on the experiences, attitudes, and behav-
iors of former slaves and slaveholders. Particularly valuable here are the
Jenkins, Kiger, and Winchester papers, which reveal much about the dis-
puted Reconstruction-era evolution of relations between black and white
Mississippians on the plantations and at the polls. The voluminous Winchester Family Papers are especially notable because George and Josiah
Winchester, transplanted New Englanders, had diverse legal and financial
dealings with many notable individuals and families over many decades
before and after the Civil War. This subcollection, together with the Bank
of the State of Mississippi Records, should prove essential reading for
scholars investigating southern economic and business history.

37. Mrs. Kiger to Basil, Jr., November 28, 1869, Box 2E517, Kiger Papers; Peter Kolchin, "Commentary" on Steven Hahn, "Emancipation and the Development of Capitalist
Agriculture," in *What Made the South Different?* ed. Kees Gispen (Jackson: University Press
of Mississippi, 1990), 95. Eric Foner, *Reconstruction*, 419–20, quotes Mrs. Kiger in a letter of
November 4, 1869, to Basil, Jr., as saying, "Give us five million of Chinese laborers in the
valley of the Mississippi, and we can furnish the world with cotton and teach the negro his
proper place." I have, however, been unable to find this quotation.

WILLIAM G. SHADE

In Re Those "Prebourgeois" Planters:
The Political Economy of Flush Times in Mississippi

Antebellum historians face a vexing problem. Their field of study is filtered by their knowledge of the American Civil War, with the effect of looking into the larger lens of a telescope. Postwar conceptions of sectionalism, generated by the racist Redeemers of the New South and the northern Radical Republicans, who appeared on the stump with bloody shirt in hand, distort our vision of the political development of those states that joined the Confederacy in 1861. It requires an impressive act of will to resist the teleological temptation to read the future apocalypse into the early history of the southern states and thus seek that which set them apart in their origins. This has led to a lively debate in the field concerning how different the antebellum North and South were from each other.[1]

Mississippi seems to be a particularly fruitful laboratory for examining the distinctiveness of the Old South. In the 1850s the state was the "storm center of secession"; more recently the Yazoo Delta has been described as the "most southern place on earth." Plantations there and in the Natchez District were among the largest in the country and their owners among the richest farmers in the world. In 1861, Mississippi's young slaveholders salivated over the promise of secession, and its leading planter-politician

---

1. For a recent example of this debate, see Kees Gispen, ed., *What Made the South Different?* (Jackson: University Press of Mississippi, 1990).

became president of the Confederate States of America. Here if anywhere, except possibly the miasmic lowlands of South Carolina, one should encounter the "prebourgeois" planters who resisted the seductions of nineteenth-century capitalism and impressed upon the society their paternalistic ideology.[2]

Yet the twentieth-century image of benighted Mississippi, the darkest and most remote corner of the southern swamp, the furthest outpost from the metropole both psychologically and physically, allows one to forget how recent in the antebellum period had been the arrival of Anglo-Americans in the region and the degree to which the early settlers were driven by the most commonplace bourgeois sin—greed. As John D. W. Guice details in his essay in this volume, Mississippi in the 1820s and 1830s was a speculator's paradise, the frontier with all its redemptive and mercenary promise.

Mississippi had become a state in 1817, at which time four-fifths of its territory was in the hands of the Choctaw and Chickasaw Indians. The census of 1820 records only 42,000 whites, and their settlement was limited to the southwestern corner of the state, known as the Natchez Dis-

2. Percy Lee Rainwater, *Mississippi: Storm Center of Secession, 1856–1861* (1938; reprint, New York: DeCapo Press, 1989); James C. Cobb, *"The Most Southern Place on Earth": The Mississippi Delta and the Roots of Regional Identity* (New York: Oxford University Press, 1991). See also William C. Davis, *Jefferson Davis: The Man and His Hour* (New York: Harper Collins, 1991), and Bradley G. Bond, *Political Culture in the Nineteenth-Century South: Mississippi, 1830–1900* (Baton Rouge: Louisiana State University Press, 1995). The thesis that the South was prebourgeois and paternalistic is articulated in the works of Eugene Genovese: *The Political Economy of Slavery: Studies in the Economy and Society of the Slave South* (New York: Pantheon, 1965); *The World the Slaveholders Made: Two Essays in Interpretation* (New York: Pantheon, 1969); *Roll, Jordan, Roll: The World the Slaves Made* (New York: Pantheon, 1974); and, with Elizabeth Fox-Genovese, *Fruits of Merchant Capital: Slavery and Bourgeois Property in the Rise and Expansion of Capitalism* (New York: Oxford University Press, 1983). Critics include James Oakes, *The Ruling Race: A History of American Slaveholders* (New York: Knopf, 1982); Laurence Shore, *Southern Capitalists: The Ideological Leadership of an Elite, 1832–1885* (Chapel Hill: University of North Carolina Press, 1986); George M. Frederickson, *The Arrogance of Race: Historical Perspectives on Slavery, Racism, and Social Equality* (Hartford, Conn.: Wesleyan University Press, 1988); and Robert William Fogel, *Without Consent or Contract: The Rise and Fall of American Slavery* (New York: W. W. Norton, 1989). Oakes retreats somewhat from his previous position in *Slavery and Freedom: An Interpretation of the Old South* (New York: Knopf, 1990).

trict. The opening of the Indian lands coincided with the economic boom of the late 1820s and 1830s. By 1850 the total population had jumped to 600,000. Over half were slaves; like South Carolina and Louisiana, Mississippi had a black majority. Among the whites there were 23,000 slaveholders, and nearly 60 percent of those owned over five bondsmen. The census of 1850 enumerated 15,110 cotton plantations.[3]

In 1820 practically the entire non-Indian population had been born outside the boundaries of the state, and it included a significant northern element. Twenty years later, migrants still made up nearly 90 percent of the white population, but only a handful had been born in the North and this group had dwindled in significance. The recently opened northern and eastern portions of the state were peopled by men who had moved in from slave states. Over half the heads of households in 1850 had migrated from the Upper South, especially North Carolina, Tennessee, and Virginia, and a third were from the Lower South.

Owing to the rate of population growth, the political life of Mississippi during these years was exceptionally volatile. Early on, Andrew Jackson swept the state. In 1832 the Old Hero was the only presidential candidate and fewer than one-third of the state's white adult males bothered to vote, although Mississippi's original constitution was one of the most liberal in the country and essentially provided for universal white male suffrage. Four years later nearly two-thirds voted when Democrat Martin Van

3. J. D. B. De Bow, ed., *Statistical View of the United States . . . Being a Compendium of the Seventh Census* (Washington, D.C.: U.S. Printing Office, 1954). On Mississippi's social and economic development, see Herbert Weaver, *Mississippi Farmers, 1850–1860* (Nashville: Vanderbilt University Press, 1945); Charles C. Bolton, *Poor Whites of the Antebellum South: Tenants and Laborers in Central North Carolina and Northeast Mississippi* (Durham: Duke University Press, 1994); John Hebron Moore, *The Emergence of the Cotton Kingdom in the Old Southwest: Mississippi, 1770–1860* (Baton Rouge: Louisiana State University Press, 1988); William K. Scarborough, "Heartland of the Cotton Kingdom," in *A History of Mississippi*, ed. Richard Aubrey McLemore, vol. 1 (Hattiesburg: University & College Press of Mississippi, 1973), 310–51; and Christopher Morris, *Becoming Southern: The Evolution of a Way of Life, Warren County and Vicksburg, Mississippi, 1770–1860* (New York: Oxford University Press, 1995). On the Indians, see Mary Elizabeth Young, *Redskins, Ruffleshirts, and Rednecks: Indian Allotments in Alabama and Mississippi, 1830–1860* (Norman: University of Oklahoma Press, 1962); and Arthur H. DeRosier, Jr., *The Removal of the Choctaw Indians* (Knoxville: University of Tennessee Press, 1970).

Buren won by a whisker over Hugh Lawson White. In the election of 1840, however, with nearly 90 percent of the eligible voters going to the polls, the state went Whig by a convincing margin. Four years after that, although the distribution of the vote remained about the same and turnout dipped only slightly, Democrat James K. Polk rode the popular issue of Texas annexation to victory.

The early political development of the state can be broken into two phases, each associated with distinctive economic conditions. From statehood until the mid-1830s, Mississippi went through a period of personal politics, with low turnouts and little in the way of party competition; in fact, parties in a modern sense hardly existed. Then the state moved into a period characterized by close party competition and extremely high turnouts. During these years the policy orientation and rhetorical arguments put forth by Mississippi's Whigs and Democrats closely resembled those of their fellow partisans throughout the country.[4]

While one might look to fictional characters like William Faulkner's Thomas Sutpen to gain an understanding of the *mentalité* of men living on the southwestern frontier at this time, it is best to begin with Joseph Baldwin's contemporary account of his personal experiences, *The Flush Times of Alabama and Mississippi,* which portrays a scene of comic capitalism:

> What country could boast more largely of its crimes? What more splendid rôle of felonies! What more terrific murders! What more gorgeous bank robberies! What more magnificent operations in the

---

4. For an account of the general development of Mississippi politics at the time, see Edwin A. Miles, *Jacksonian Democracy in Mississippi* (Chapel Hill: University of North Carolina Press, 1960); Richard P. McCormick, "New Perspectives on Jacksonian Politics," *American Historical Review* 65 (January 1960): 288–301, and *The Second American Party System* (Chapel Hill: University of North Carolina Press, 1966), 295–303; David Nathaniel Young, "The Mississippi Whigs, 1834–1860" (Ph.D. diss., University of Alabama, 1968); James Roger Sharp, *The Jacksonians Versus the Banks* (New York: Columbia University Press, 1971), 55–109; Porter L. Fortune, Jr., "The Formative Period," and John Edmund Gonzales, "Flush Times, Depression, War, and Compromise," in *A History of Mississippi,* ed. McLemore, vol. 1, 251–309; Melvin Philip Lucas, "The Development of the Second Party System in Mississippi, 1817–1846" (Ph.D. diss., Cornell University, 1983), and " 'To Carry Out Great Fundamental Principles': The Antebellum Southern Political Culture," *Journal of Mississippi History* 52 (February 1990): 1–22.

land offices! Such . . . levies of blackmail, individual and corporate! Such superb forays on the treasuries, State and National! . . . Such august defalcations! Such flourishes of rhetoric on ledgers auspicious of gold that had departed for ever from the vault. And in INDIAN affairs!—the very mention is suggestive of the poetry of theft—the romance of a wild and weird larceny . . . Swindling Indians by the nation! Stealing their land by the township![5]

Often the arguments asserting southern distinctiveness and the pre-bourgeois nature of planter perspectives involve theoretical reconstruction of what the effects of slaveholding *must have been*—a matter debated at the time by both proslavery and antislavery writers. Manuscript resources such as those in the Natchez Trace Collection enable us to examine the question of southern distinctiveness by highlighting the similarities in outlook of those who moved to Mississippi and their kinfolk who remained in Massachusetts, Pennsylvania, or Virginia. Among the NTC holdings are the papers of three men who represent the outlook of the state's leading planters during the period of economic expansion and political development before the debates over political economy were totally consumed by the issues related to the South's peculiar institution.[6]

One portion of the extensive James Campbell Wilkins Papers deals with political activities of the 1820s and 1830s. These letters illustrate the politics of the flush times and reveal the close similarity between what was happening on the southwestern frontier and in both Frederick Jackson Turner's Old Northwest and the more settled eastern regions of the nation. There is relatively little evidence here of planter paternalism or even the aristocratic Republicanism that still could be found among conservative Virginians. Wilkins was a successful planter, merchant, and banker located primarily in Natchez, although he had extensive holdings of slaves and land throughout Mississippi, Louisiana, Arkansas, and Texas. He was

5. Joseph G. Baldwin, *The Flush Times of Alabama and Mississippi* (1853; rpr., New York: Hill and Wang, 1957), 173–74.

6. On slavery and secession in Mississippi, see William L. Barney, *The Secessionist Impulse: Alabama and Mississippi in 1860* (Princeton, N.J.: Princeton University Press, 1974); and Winthrop Jordan, *Tumult and Silence at Second Creek: An Inquiry into a Civil War Slave Conspiracy* (Baton Rouge: Louisiana State University Press, 1993).

a land speculator of gargantuan proportions, involved in various schemes that transcended Mississippi's factional and partisan boundaries. Like nearly all of the new state's politicians, Wilkins was born outside the state. And like such luminaries as Robert John Walker and Franklin Plummer, he was a northerner, sent from his native Pennsylvania in 1805 to handle his family's affairs in the territory.[7]

Wilkins's family possessed extensive business interests and widespread political connections. His uncle, Judge William Wilkins, who remained in Pittsburgh, was elected senator from Pennsylvania, appointed minister to Russia by Andrew Jackson, and chosen secretary of war by John Tyler. James's brother Ross Wilkins moved to Michigan, where he gained prominence as a United States district judge. Wilkins was related by marriage to the Dallas family and to Robert John Walker, in addition to his connection to the latter by the fact that Walker's mentor was Judge Wilkins. Moreover, the family business was certainly in part politics, although members ended up in different parties by the 1840s.

After arriving in Mississippi Territory, James Wilkins married twice, in both cases to a woman whose family was politically and economically powerful in the Old Natchez region. He succeeded as a cotton planter and factor, a financier, and a land speculator, becoming a central figure in the local social and economic elite; some of his business dealings and relationships, as revealed in the NTC, are detailed by Morton Rothstein elsewhere in this volume. In politics, Wilkins was affiliated with a clique of Adams County lawyers, planters, and merchants who were termed by their enemies the "Natchez Junto."[8]

While some historians have followed the later writings of Democrats

7. James Campbell Wilkins Papers, 1801–52 and undated. Other holdings in the NTC containing information about the Whigs and Mississippi politics from 1817 to 1852 are the Charles Backus Dana Papers, 1802, 1820–81; Basil Kiger Papers, 1820, 1841–85; William Lewis Sharkey Papers, 1823–81; Bank of the State of Mississippi Records, 1804–46; and Benjamin Leonard Covington Wailes Papers, 1811–60. Wilkins first married Charlotte Bingaman, the sister of Adam Bingaman, a leader of the pro-Adams forces and later the Whigs. After Charlotte died, Wilkins married Catherine L. Minor, the daughter of a Pennsylvanian who had served as the last Spanish governor of the Natchez District. See the Minor Family Papers in the Natchez Trace Collection.

8. See J. F. H. Claiborne, *Mississippi as a Province, Territory, and State* (Baton Rouge: Louisiana State University Press, 1964); and D. Clayton James, *Antebellum Natchez* (Baton Rouge: Louisiana State University Press, 1968).

like John F. H. Claiborne to construct a two-party picture contrasting these "wealthy Federalists" with their backwoods Republican opponents, such stereotypes simply do not conform to reality. Wilkins had been a supporter of the Madison administration when he served in the territorial legislature and was also an early supporter of Andrew Jackson, his former commander at the Battle of New Orleans. He chaired the state convention in 1828 that chose the Jackson electors for Mississippi.

Wilkins subsequently broke with the Old Hero over financial policy, but in 1830 he believed that in running for Congress he showed his "determination to create no schism here in the ranks of that party, which elevated to the Presidency our present beloved chief magistrate." His views expressed Jacksonian orthodoxy: "a wise and liberal policy adopted on the subject of public lands & a spot which he and his children after him might call their own placed within the reach of every citizen. Placing the agricultural interest on which all others depend in the front rank . . . permitted to develop its treasures unshackled by onerous restrictions." He thought Mississippi should "encourage the emigration of a virtuous and patriotic yeomanry and above all maintain the state sovereignty inviolate & and thereby perpetuate the union of the states." But as a candidate for office, he wrote to another very wealthy man, with only a slight sense of false modesty, *"I am in the hands of the people."*[9]

During the course of the canvass, Wilkins received letters from his supporters, including Governor Brandon, suggesting a campaign strategy that clearly reflected some of the rules of the new democratic politics. He must get out to meet the people across the state, yet still expect his opponent to portray him as an aristocrat. "They will represent you to the people as a man of domineering wealth a member of the Natchez Aristocracy and will not hesitate to call you a Federalist of the old school and some who call themselves of the Jackson party, will take exception to your attention to Mr. Clay whilst at Natchez." The governor suggested Wilkins counter such rumors by conducting a general tour of the state. As a practical matter, he urged Wilkins to "dispense with your servant in your route" and pointed out which counties would be most profitable to visit.[10]

9. James C. Wilkins to the Committee of Gentlemen of Wilkinson Co., May 1, 1830, Wilkins Papers, Box 2E546.
10. G. C. Brandon to James Wilkins, May 20, 1830, ibid.

Another correspondent repeated the call for a tour of the state, but he added that in the eastern and northern regions the "all controlling issue is internal improvements." These new settlers actively sought connections to the market and embraced the politics of development. The correspondent did argue, however, that "it should not be done by federal government." At the same time he reminded Wilkins of the most pressing issue facing these states at the time—"half of our public lands in the hands of the general government." Clearly an advocate of the cession of the Indian lands to Mississippi, he suggested that Wilkins address the matter in a fashion that would sustain the rights of the states.[11]

Arthur Fox warned Wilkins that the popular candidate from the piney woods region, Franklin Plummer, "takes everything before him like a tornado" and that the regional prejudices of the southeastern portion of the state were being used against him. "You must come out among us." "You have old friends everywhere," he said, urging Wilkins to get out and meet the people, "and be prepared to address them in short, *pointed,* speeches . . . [presented in a] plain unequivocal manner." John Hutchinson's advice was even more direct: "The People generally are intelligent, they can judge a man with good sense." Since the Mississippi weather was hot, "you must keep cool, you must drink but little." He warned the candidate that he would be fatigued from riding and the "change of water, the excitement all will prostrate you." He also warned Wilkins that his opponents would call him "a *federalist* believing what that party did in 98–1802" and connect him to the activities of Aaron Burr in 1806. "Campbell [a leading editor] you are aware is smart and *I* believe equally unprincipled." Hutchinson went on to admonish Wilkins that his success "depends on [him]-self."[12]

11. D. W. Wright to James Wilkins, May 23, 1830, ibid. On land speculation, see Franklin L. Riley, "Choctaw Land Claims," *Publications of the Mississippi Historical Society* 8 (1904): 345–95; and James W. Silver, "Land Speculation Profits in the Chickasaw Cession," *Journal of Southern History* 10 (February 1944): 84–92.

12. Arthur Fox to James Wilkins, June 1, 1830, John Hutchinson to Wilkins, June 6, 1830, C. W. Conner to Wilkins, June 14, 1830, and James R. Marsh to Wilkins, June 5, 1830, Wilkins Papers, Box 2E546. See Edwin A. Miles, "Franklin E. Plummer: Piney Woods Spokesman of the Jacksonian Era," *Journal of Mississippi History* 16 (January 1954): 1–34.

Letter to James C. Wilkins reporting county election results indicating Wilkins's loss locally in his 1830 race for Congress. Wilkins ran on a platform that included "obedience to the will of the people, a strict construction of the Constitution of the United States, the inviolable sovereignty of the states, and a settled determined opposition to the present tariff." *From the James C. Wilkins Papers, NTC, the Center for American History, the University of Texas at Austin.*

In early August, correspondents began to report that Wilkins had lost the election to Plummer. Having left town for a time during the canvas, D. W. Wright blamed it upon his own failure to do more. Only "if the People could have been informed correctly," the vote would have been in Wilkins's favor.[13]

All of the candidates in Mississippi had social position and some connection to power. Everyone who was anyone knew someone. Plummer, from an old New England family, was as well connected as the Pennsylvanian Wilkins, if personally less wealthy and from a poorer region. More important, with the passing of one year, these opponents would become political allies aligned against Wilkins's business associate, friend, and kinsman, Robert John Walker.[14]

Although Plummer was able to portray himself as the candidate of the people and attack Wilkins as an aristocrat, he won by a plurality in a five-candidate race in which his four opponents, including Wilkins, were legitimate Jacksonians. In 1831, when Junto member Robert Adams died, Wilkins was the first choice for U.S. senator, but he declined the appointment. At the time, Walker supported Wilkins, and the two politicians merely represented the interests of different regions of the state rather than economic strata or classes however defined.[15]

But over the next two years, Jackson's opposition to the Bank of the United States split his supporters in Mississippi and led to the eventual formation of the Whig party as a coalition of various anti-Jackson elements. Wilkins drifted into the new coalition and made his second run for Congress as a candidate of the "People's Party." In this effort, ironically, he joined with Plummer in a coalition against the regular Jacksonians— sometimes called by their opponents the "Regency"—whose foremost wire-puller and senatorial candidate was Robert John Walker.[16]

13. L. R. Marshall to James Wilkins, August 4, 1830, D. W. Wright to Wilkins, August 5, 1830, Wilkins Papers, Box 2E546.

14. See James A. Shenton, *Robert John Walker: A Politician from Jackson to Lincoln* (New York: Columbia University Press, 1961).

15. M. D. Patton to James Wilkins, November 4, 1830, Wilkins Papers, Box 2E546.

16. Samuel M. Puckett to James Wilkins, May 24, 1835, G. R. Fall to Wilkins, May 25, July 5, 1835, C. Lynch to Wilkins, June 29, 1835, A. L. Bingaman to Wilkins, July 24, 1835, ibid.

Accounts of cotton sales in Liverpool, May 1824, as reported to Natchez cotton planter, merchant, cotton factor, financier, and banker James Campbell Wilkins. *From the James C. Wilkins Papers, NTC, the Center for American History, the University of Texas at Austin.*

During the 1830s Wilkins was probably the most visible and politically active banker in the state. He served as an officer of both the State Bank (the Bank of the State of Mississippi) and the "rival" Planters Bank.[17] At the same time, he served on the board of the Natchez branch of the Second Bank of the United States and was involved financially with its president, Nicholas Biddle. In 1838, he acted as the agent for the sale of stock for the newly chartered Union Bank.

Wilkins's primary source of income, however, was not these positions but his extensive holdings of land and slaves. During the depression that followed the Panic of 1837, when he became overextended and owed nearly $150,000 in debts, Wilkins was forced to seek the financial aid of his wife's brother, William J. Minor, to whom he deeded 840 acres of Adams County land and half the earnings of the 5,000-acre Coles Creek plantation that was worked by 167 slaves. Nonetheless, he was still exceedingly rich, and emerged from the depression sufficiently well off to become a millionaire in the course of the next decade.

Wilkins gives the lie to those who would find something inimical among cotton planting and banking, town life, or a commitment to the latest technological improvements. He also advocated education, temperance—although he entertained with a good deal of alcohol—and colonization. His brother Ross, a Methodist minister, was even more radical on the issue of alcohol and a racial egalitarian. In the Michigan constitutional convention, the northern brother insisted publicly that Negroes were men and thus "created free and equal." He would strike the word *white* from the new document: "Paper is white and snow is white, yet how many men [are] white as paper or snow?"[18]

17. On banking, see Charles Hillman Brough, "The History of Banking in Mississippi," *Publications of the Mississippi Historical Society* 3 (1900): 317–40; Robert C. Weems, Jr., "Mississippi's First Banking System," *Journal of Mississippi History* 29 (November 1967): 386–405; and Larry Schweikart, *Banking in the American South from the Age of Jackson to Reconstruction* (Baton Rouge: Louisiana State University Press, 1987).

18. Ronald P. Formisano, *Birth of Mass Political Parties: Michigan, 1827–1861* (Princeton: Princeton University Press, 1971), 92. On the bourgeois nature of southern temperance, see Ian R. Tyrrell, "Drink and Temperance in the Antebellum South: An Overview and an Interpretation," *Journal of Southern History* 48 (November 1982): 485–510, and Douglas Wiley Carlson, "Temperance Reform in the Cotton Kingdom" (Ph.D. diss., University of Illinois, 1982); on colonization in Mississippi, see Charles S. Sydnor,

One cannot read even a faint glimmer of prebourgeois, romantic sensibility into the quintessentially bourgeois lifestyle of this Natchez nabob. His correspondents came from all over the country and they were constantly on the go—George Santayana's Americans jumping off one train and onto another—taking care of their business, political, and family affairs. Among the bales of canceled checks is a receipt from the National Hotel in Washington for "Col. Wilkins, Lady, two Child, 2 servants." The cost of their three-day stay was $24.58.

The multiple candidacies and the intrastate sectionalism of the 1830 congressional election typified the general condition of party development throughout the country. While partisan institutions were slightly less developed in the western states than in the older polities along the East Coast, the central years of the 1830s were a time of sifting, which would eventually result in the formation of two distinct parties. Wilkins and other Jackson supporters disagreed with the Old Hero's veto of the recharter of the bank and his subsequent withdrawal of the government deposits. Some, like John Quitman, broke with Jackson over nullification, but others, such as the voluble senator George Poindexter, bore personal animosity toward the president. One might say that Jackson broke with him. These various positions were by no means mutually exclusive, and in the short run they formed the basis for the anti-Jackson alliance that underlay the appearance of the Mississippi Whig party.[19]

The activity of Wilkins in his second attempt to gain a congressional seat reveals rather clearly the limited development in 1834 and 1835 of this heterogeneous coalition that is often depicted prematurely as more cohesive than it actually was. On the Democratic side of the ledger, Walker emerged as Jackson's most powerful supporter and the rising star of the Mississippi Democracy. While he represented the developing periphery, he was a living caricature of "economic man" calling for a land policy for the yeoman farmer—the "settlers and cultivators"—while consolidating his fortune through speculations in Choctaw lands (following the

Slavery in Mississippi (1933; rpr., Baton Rouge: Louisiana State University Press, 1966): 203–38.

19. See Edwin A. Miles, "Andrew Jackson and Senator George Poindexter," *Journal of Southern History* 24 (February 1958): 51–66, and Robert E. May, *John A. Quitman, Old South Crusader* (Baton Rouge: Louisiana State University Press, 1985), 29–75.

Treaty of Dancing Rabbit Creek) and extending his interest in Texas lands like many of his constituents.

In this clear jockeying for personal favor that bore few traces of ideological content or class conflict, Walker not only trampled on "Old Poins," but pushed aside as well young Franklin Plummer, "the spokesman of the piney woods." Walker became the first senatorial candidate endorsed by a state convention, part of a Jacksonian slate that included the incumbent, Hiram Runnels, as the gubernatorial candidate, and J. F. H. Claiborne and Daniel W. Wright for Congress.[20] The choices indicated the unsettled state of partisan affiliation. In 1830 Wright had strongly supported Wilkins against the "demagogue" Plummer. After the convention, Wright declined the nomination and was replaced by Benjamin W. Edwards—a friend, former backer, and business associate of Wilkins.

Plummer, clearly hurt by the Regency's choice of Walker, now joined forces with the "Opposition," and together they came forward with a "People's Ticket" that included Charles Lynch for governor and David Dickson and Wilkins as congressional candidates. The bank was a dead issue; the coalition focused on Van Buren's presidential aspirations and "party dictation," attacking the management by convention as only a new form of caucus rule. While anti–Van Buren sentiment in the South has been generally interpreted as a sectional response to the nomination of a northerner, a majority of the Mississippi aspirants in this election had been born and raised in the North as well. Van Buren fought, particularly in Mississippi, to parry the charge that he was soft on abolitionism, but he could not escape the appeal to anti-party tradition of eighteenth-century republicanism. His opponents emphasized Van Buren's reputation as a partisan politician and the supposed corruptions of New York politics, even down to labeling his supporters "the Regency."

Again Wilkins's correspondents treated the creation of candidates as if they emerged magically from popular consideration: "It is now time for the people to look around & fix for the unions offices to be filled at the next regular election. The friends of F. E. Plummer have determined to run him for the office of United States Senator—and they likewise are determined not to support the candidates of the late Van Buren conven-

20. B. W. Edwards to James Wilkins, November 25, 1830, Wilkins Papers, Box 2E546.

tion." "You should allow your name to be put forward as the people's candidate for congress in conjunction with David Dickson's . . . opposed to *party dictation* + *caucus management*—we know that you not only avow but practice the principles of the genuine republican school." This would cause "most of Plummer's friends" who had not previously voted for Wilkins to turn to him.[21]

Self-appointed advisers such as G. R. Fall, the editor of the *Jackson Mississippian*, who regarded Wilkins as the candidate of the "democracy," urged him to lay his claims before the people. In Carroll County, he was told, "many of the earnest friends of the administration" would vote for him, believing his talents "would give character abroad." Included among his supporters were "Col. R. M. Williams and Governor Runnels." Further, "the River counties will go for you" and in the north the opposition will be kept down "by Wright and various other individuals." In this connection, he mentioned support for Wilkins from Gwin and D. W. Dickson, "now a resident of the northern part of the state."[22]

In a later letter, Fall (pushing Wilkins to run for senator) insisted that Walker "seem[ed] to be entirely indifferent" and was losing support. Then the editor illustrated precisely the personal nature of Mississippi politics at the time: "You can beat Plummer in the event that it becomes expedient to drop Walker. Men who know Plummer best have no confidence in him. They know he would sell his interest in the blood of his Redeemer to accomplish his purposes and will vote against him unhesitatingly. Hinds has the entire confidence of the Jackson party, he is one of nature's noblemen, 'had he lived' to use your language 'in the days of Roman chivalry a monument would have been erected to his memory,' but when pressured he wants talents."[23]

21. Samuel M. Puckett to James Wilkins, May 24, 1835, N. B. Hamm [?] to Wilkins, September 29, 1835, ibid.

22. G. R. Fall to James Wilkins, May 25, 1835, ibid. Charles Lynch wrote Wilkins on June 29, 1835, as a banker, encouraging Wilkins to give a loan to the editor of the *Clinton Gazette*, who might help the candidates, assuring him that he (Lynch) would "see that the payment is promptly met." Wilkins Papers, Box 2E546. He wanted it done through the bank rather than from friends. The convention was a day or so later.

23. G. R. Fall to James Wilkins, July 5, 1835, Wilkins Papers, Box 2E546. He was leaving from Nashville and going to New York and did not mention or seem to know about the convention.

Intrastate sectionalism continued to define political conflict both between and within the supposed parties. While other writers begged the
candidate to come personally to their section of the state, the nature of
the new politics and the attitudes of these supposedly prebourgeois planters toward Wilkins's position as a wealthy man and banker was most
clearly revealed in a letter written on July 24. The author, the editor of the
Clinton Gazette, made no reference to the significance of the day, but
rather informed Wilkins that Plummer was trying to interfere with his
loan and reminded the banker that if he had favors to give he should "confer them on your friends."[24]

Plummer, however, wrote Wilkins, his former opponent, now benefac-
tor and colleague: "There has been a rupture between Runnels + myself
which has caused considerable excitement among our friends" involving
economic problems and loans coming due. The "spokesman of the piney
woods" needed cash and asked the banker to extend a loan of $500 since
he had left a note for $1,200 "as collateral security."[25] Plummer reminded
Wilkins that he had written a favorable sketch of him for the *Clinton Gazette.* In this correspondence, these strange bedfellows seem to have been
on rather auspicious terms. At the same time, Wilkins continued to be
friendly with Duncan Walker, Robert's brother. Surely this whole circle
can best be described in Richard Hofstadter's terms as "men on the
make"—economically and politically.[26]

As if to prove this point, fellow candidate D. W. Dickson wrote from
Nashville as he was returning to Mississippi from Pittsburgh, where he had
gone to "transact some business." First he reported: "Negroes are very
high now, and I learn that the crops will be very short in Mississippi." He

24. Owen Stuart to James Wilkins, July 15, 1835, George W. Grant to Wilkins, July 24,
1835, ibid.

25. Plummer wrote two letters to Wilkins that seem to be in conflict: July 13 and July
27, 1835.

26. F. E. Plummer to James Wilkins, July 13, 27, 1835, Duncan Walker to Wilkins, August 19, 1835, Wilkins Papers, Box 2E546. In *The American Political Tradition* (New York:
Knopf, 1948), 45–67, Richard Hofstadter put forth the classic version of the "entrepreneurial" interpretation of Jacksonian Democracy. Perhaps he erred only in associating the
Whigs with "old money." In Mississippi in 1835 there was no "old money"; the entrenched
aristocracy of Natchez was quite nouveau and rough-and-tumble.

could do quite well, but the traders "demand *cash*. I think it best under the circumstances to delay for a few months . . . the execution of our plan." Dickson then turned to politics: "I have urged it upon all of our *true friends* to run you disconnected from individuals and parties" and to emphasize character and "service to the state in peace + war." He also noted that he would be supporting Hugh Lawson White in the presidential election and implied that he thought that Wilkins would as well.[27]

Yet another plea for Wilkins to "come up among the people" in order to parry opponents' charges that he is one of the "Natchez Aristocracy" revealed the deep rift between the people in the northern part of the state and the old settlers in the southwestern corner. "You have many substantial friends here, but the common people have very little acquaintance with you, and with them it is a matter of some importance to see a man before they will vote for him. Intercourse among the people is especially necessary to your success."[28]

The same writer feared that the circular for Wilkins and Dickson published in Jackson had hurt Wilkins in his area. "I should like to see a circular under your own signature—Let it be strong and pithy and then start out yourself among the people and you need not fear opposition." Lynch, he assured Wilkins, was gaining ground, but Plummer, according to another correspondent, was suffering from his opponents' attacks "in this section of the State." Still another northern Mississippi writer admonished, "Local considerations will induce most of us to support one of the candidates of the opposition, and I believe that were you among us for a week, you would secure and equal support to anyone."[29]

While localism and personal politics were always present, most of the correspondents portrayed the contest as one between the "People's advocates"—Wilkins, Lynch, and Plummer—and the "Caucus ticket" that they associated with party management and support for Van Buren and New York–style politics. "The days of Van Burenism, I hope, in Missis-

27. D. W. Dickson to James Wilkins, September 19, 1835, Wilkins Papers, Box 2E546.
28. Thomas Coffee to James Wilkins, August 22, 1835, ibid.
29. Ibid.; Charles C. Mayson to James Wilkins, August 27, 1835, J. M. Setler to Wilkins, September 10, 1835, Wilkins Papers, Box 2E546. Clearly, these men would have agreed with Tip O'Neill that "all politics is local."

sippi, are numbered; for surely the South can never prove so recreant to her interests as to cooperate in electing a man to the Presidency who has invariably been opposed to her, and who would be among the first, did the occasion offer to aim a deadly blow at the prosperity, nay, at her political existence."[30]

As the campaign in Mississippi proceeded, the presidential election of 1836 increasingly intruded in the form of growing anti–Van Buren feelings and a positive reception of Judge White. The question of Van Buren's connection with the opponents of slavery was being fought out primarily in Virginia and Mississippi. The vice-president had explained his position to the Jacksonian land office appointee, Samuel Gwin, in a letter that was subsequently circulated in pamphlet form throughout the South. Wilkins received a letter from Holmes County in the Delta confirming that "Van Buren has of late (whether justly or not) become so identified with *abolition* that no man who is known to be in his favor can be elected in this country."[31] It is also clear that the nullifiers were supporting Wilkins.

The same letter, however, pleaded with Wilkins to come to Holmes County to assure the people that he opposed the *"caucus ticket."* Two rather odd letters from Anthony Campbell give some sense of how confused—at least to the modern mind— relationships among the Mississippi elite were at the time. Campbell was a member of the political clan connected to both the Richmond Junto and the Nashville Junto and a "whole hog" Jackson man. He had produced the president's letter endorsing Walker, but he had been a Wilkins supporter in 1830 and the two were still on friendly terms.

Campbell wrote to assure Wilkins that Mississippi's leading nullifier, John A. Quitman, was also Wilkins's friend. He reported that Adams County and Natchez had never seen "as much moral and political duplicity" and that on the last day of the election there was chaos. "This depravity seems mostly confined to men who dress well, talk correct english with high pretensions to honor, learning and intelligence." He thought the

30. J. M. Settler to Wilkins, September 10, 1835, Wilkins Papers, Box 2E546. This is the earliest reference to "the South" in the collections discussed in this essay.

31. N. B. Hamm [?] to James Wilkins, September 29, 1835, ibid.

"lower orders" showed a good deal more integrity than their self-proclaimed "betters."[32]

As seen through the Wilkins Papers, southwestern politics in the 1820s and 1830s seems much more closely aligned with those interpretations of history that find a consensus on liberal capitalism than those emphasizing economic or class conflict in either a Beardian or a Marxist mode. Politics was personal rather than partisan or ideological, with the developing party organizations being simply elite electoral machines à la Richard P. McCormick and Maurice Duverger. The very fact that Wilkins was a banker and a large planter attacked by his similarly wealthy opponents as a "Federalist" and an "aristocrat" makes clear how widespread the commitment to seeking the good will and votes of the "common man" had become. The electoral provisions of the Mississippi constitution that Wilkins had helped write were relatively liberal.[33] The turnout in the election of 1828 equaled the national average, and in 1836 nearly two-thirds of the white adult males went to the polls. As elsewhere, interest in state and congressional elections exceeded that in presidential elections.

By the mid-1830s these shifting factional permutations had foundations in policy positions taken by the Jackson administration, but personal politics and the politics of place still predominated. Partisan identification was weak and the various layers of the political system were poorly integrated. Intrastate localism characterized the electoral response of most Mississippians. While this had economic overtones in terms of the mean size of land holdings and slave holdings, it was hardly a conflict between classes or economic outlooks, but rather a matter of the area's stage of economic evolution. The planters' holdings in the newly opened Indian lands were smaller than those in the older portion of the state, but larger on average than in most of the Upper South.

Certainly Mississippi presents a classic case of politically and economically ambitious men attacking the so-called "aristocrats"—who were be-

32. There are two undated letters from A. Campbell to James Wilkins filed in the collection with the letters from 1835.

33. Mississippi's constitutional provisions are discussed by Winbourne Magruder Drake in "Mississippi's First Constitutional Convention," *Journal of Mississippi History* 18 (April 1956): 79–110 and in "The Mississippi Constitutional Convention of 1832," *Journal of Southern History* 23 (August 1957): 354–70.

coming very rich indeed—in an effort to obtain their own piece of the pie. The older and more entrenched interests (that were, in fact, not even a generation old) clashed with those who were pouring into the areas of the north and east that had been predominately Indian country until the expulsion of the Choctaws and Chickasaws after the 1830 Treaty of Dancing Rabbit Creek.[34]

The development of the Second Party System proceeded slowly. There were differences between the level of institutionalization in Wilkins's second run for Congress in 1835 and in his first attempt six years earlier. There were four candidates competing for two seats (after the census of 1830, Mississippi gained a second representative) rather than five running for one. These men ran on tickets associated with candidates for governor and the U.S. Senate seat. These tickets were the product of party conventions. The Whigs on the "People's Ticket" appealed to residual antipartyism while their Jacksonian opponents accepted the new doctrine of party loyalty. Ironically, they suffered both from incomplete organization and from their association with the ultimate party politician, Martin Van Buren.

At the state level there were not any economic issues, at least until the Panic of 1837, which ushered in a new phase in the politics of the state and the nation. In relation to the question of the contrasts between the North and the South, one must conclude that there were very few differences. The question of slavery—given the rise of the abolitionists in the North, the 1835 slave revolt panic in Mississippi, and the conscious attempt to whip up anti-abolitionist sentiments against Van Buren that precipitated the New Yorker's pamphlet-length letter to Gwin—plays a surprisingly small role in the Wilkins Papers. It was not a matter of conflict between the Whigs and the Democrats in state politics at the time. Although Van Buren's victory was a narrow one—a majority of 500 votes out of 20,000 cast—nearly two-thirds of the state's white adult males voted.

The late 1820s and early 1830s brought a shift away from the clearly pre-party politics of local cliques. The importance of the Natchez Junto

34. See Arthur A. De Rosier, Jr., *The Removal of the Choctaw Indians* (Knoxville: University of Tennessee Press, 1970).

composed of rising entrepreneurs joined by ties of kinship and economic interest waned, and somewhat more organized factions emerged that were primarily coalitions of elite circles adhering to prominent individuals whose following was geographically circumscribed and primarily defined by the patterns of migration into the state, but who maintained connections with individuals and groups beyond Mississippi's boundaries. In this phase elections for the presidency and Congress took on new meaning. The vast majority of Mississippians in one way or another had supported Jackson in 1828 and 1832 "due to his high military reputation, his known hostility to european meddling in cis-Atlantic, his public land policy, and his attitude on the Indian question."[35] Nearly all the aspirants for office associated themselves with the Old Hero.

But in Jackson's second term this façade crumbled, and there was a kaleidoscopic reshuffling of the coalition's elements. In particular, the nullifiers joined with the opposition to the Jacksonians, who were being more tightly organized by the group called the Regency. The coalition of the States' Rights party that arose during the nullification crisis and the Whigs who had, with the majority of Mississippians, opposed nullification was inherently unstable. By the end of the decade, Quitman, referring to himself as "a true Democrat and Nullifier," led most of his followers—that is, most of the Calhounites—back into the Democratic fold.[36]

After 1837, because of both the gag rule debate and the economic panic of that year, the Whig and Democratic parties emerged in their most mature institutional form, penetrating throughout the state, organizing both the voters and the legislators, and offering the voters clear choices on public policy. In this, Mississippi's party system reflected the national pattern, and perhaps more surprisingly, the state's Whigs and Democrats adhered to the same principles and supported the same policies as Whigs and Democrats throughout the country. In the state legislature, Mississippi Democrats became increasingly anti-bank and embraced hard

35. James E. Winston, "The Mississippi Whigs and the Tariff," *Mississippi Valley Historical Review* 22 (March 1936): 506.

36. Cleo Hearon, "Nullification in Mississippi," *Publications of the Mississippi Historical Society* 12 (1912): 37–71; May, *John A. Quitman*, 59–69, 92–98.

money while the Whigs temporized and drew the line at the repudiation of the state debt and the destruction of the credit system.[37]

The Mississippi Whigs generally supported their congressional leader Henry Clay against President John Tyler in the early 1840s and even accepted a tariff that supplied "incidental protection." Mississippi Whig leaders despised Polk, in part for casting the tie-breaking vote against seating their candidates in 1838 when the future president was the Democratic Speaker of the House, and most agreed with Seargent Prentiss that annexation was "a mere party question worked up for the Presidential election and the Democratic charge that Clay was a traitor to the interests of the South is as insulting as it is false."[38]

Even Judge George Winchester, who had advocated nullification in 1833 and Texas independence in 1835, took a moderate position on the tariff in 1844 and preferred Clay to Polk. Throughout the campaign the judge was called upon to defend Whig principles publicly.[39] A slightly different perspective on the Mississippi Whigs (from that shown in the Wilkins collection) can be gleaned from the Winchester Papers, one of the largest single holdings in the Natchez Trace Collection. One of the major benefits of a collection such as this is that it enables the researcher to ex-

37. Sharp, *The Jacksonians Versus the Banks,* 51–122; Herbert Ershkowitz and William G. Shade, "Consensus or Conflict? Political Behavior in the State Legislatures During the Jacksonian Era," *Journal of American History* 56 (December 1971): 591–621; Lucas, "The Second Party System in Mississippi," 503–681.

38. George L. Prentiss, ed., *A Memoir of S. S. Prentiss,* vol. 2 (New York: Charles Scribner's Sons, 1879), 342–53; Winston, "The Mississippi Whigs and the Tariff," 510–13; Letter to Editor of the *Mississippi Whig,* quoted in Prentiss, *Memoir,* vol. 2, 315–6. On the campaign, see James E. Walmsley, "The Presidential Campaign of 1844 in Mississippi," *Publications of the Mississippi Historical Society* 6 (1906): 179–97; and Dallas C. Dickey, *Seargent S. Prentiss: Whig Orator of the Old South* (Baton Rouge: Louisiana State University Press, 1946), 229–66.

39. H. F. Lincrall [?] et al. to George Winchester, July 19, 1844, P. N. Lucas et al. to Winchester, July 20, 1844, C. R. Clifton to Winchester, July 22, 1844, George H. Wilcox et al. to Winchester, October 1, 1844, and W. S. Cassedy et al. to Winchester, October 11, 1844, all in the Winchester Family Papers, Box 2E906.

amine slight variations and idiosyncrasies within the *mentalité* of different planters in almost precisely the same social and geographical context.

A northerner like Wilkins, George Winchester had read law in Massachusetts with Joseph Story before moving in 1820 to Natchez, where he quickly became a leading member of society. A jurist and anti-Jackson political activist, Winchester served first as a judge in the criminal court of Adams County and then as a justice in the state supreme court. He ran unsuccessfully for governor in 1829 against Gerard C. Brandon.[40]

In 1833 Winchester supported the nullifiers, and two years later he chaired a meeting advocating Texas independence. In the mid-1830s he served as a state senator and was considered one of the leaders of the Whig party, a friend of John Quitman and Joseph Davis (the brother of Jefferson Davis).[41] In 1844 he was returned to the legislature as a Whig, but he was defeated as a candidate for the United States Senate in 1846 and again in 1847. The following year he was active in the Adams County "Rough and Ready Club" formed to promote General Zachary Taylor. At the time, he denied he was a Whig and in fact deemed the Whigs little better than "the locofocos." He declared that he belonged "to the no party, to the Country, to the great mass of the people" who supported Taylor. His increasing devotion to the cause of southern rights culminated in his selection as a delegate from Mississippi to the Nashville Convention in 1850. His ingenious letter to Sharkey addressing the issues of that convention, which Winchester apparently did not actually attend, is examined in fascinating detail by Shearer Davis Bowman earlier in this volume.

40. There is a biographical sketch of Winchester in *The Papers of Jefferson Davis: Volume 2, June 1841–July 1846*, ed. James T. McIntosh (Baton Rouge: Louisiana State University Press, 1974), 122–24. A lifelong friend of the Howell family, he was Varina Howell's tutor before she married Davis. There are numerous references to the judge in *The Papers of Jefferson Davis*. On Brandon, see Claude E. Fike, "The Administrations of Governor Gerard Chittoque Brandon, 1825–1832," *Journal of Mississippi History* 75 (August 1973): 247–65. As with Wilkins, Winchester's business and legal dealings are examined in detail in Morton Rothstein's essay in this volume. There is a small collection of Brandon papers in the NTC.

41. Hearon, "Nullification in Mississippi," 55–59; James E. Winston, "Mississippi and the Independence of Texas," *Southwestern Historical Quarterly* 21 (July 1917): 36–60; Janet Sharp Hermann, *Joseph E. Davis: Planter Patriarch* (Jackson: University Press of Mississippi, 1990).

Although most of the extreme advocates of states' rights became Democrats before the Hard Cider and Coonskin campaign of 1840, Judge Winchester remained in the Whig party and moderated his position to fit the
national Whig stance, not only on money and banking, but also on the
tariff. In 1844 he was an active participant in the campaign to elect Henry
Clay, and defended the Whig cause at mass meetings throughout the
state. Seeking "the best talent of the State of the Whig party to take up
the gage," the Meadville Whigs invited him, confident that he would lend
his "powerful aid in elucidating the great principles of our party." This
and similar requests for the judge to speak reflected the view that the election represented an opportunity for the people to weigh "the principles
which now agitate the country."[42]

This transplanted Yankee, a moderate in the Whig camp of the early
and mid-1840s, became by the end of the decade a champion of southern
rights, but his correspondence with northern friends reveals the limited
extent of southern sectionalism before the opening of the territorial question during the Mexican War.[43] In a letter from Salem, Massachusetts, discussing business and politics, J. G. Waters calmly analyzed the conflict
that had arisen between President Tyler and the congressional Whigs led
by Clay. "What strange events have occurred since Harrisons [sic] death,"
he wrote his Mississippi friend. "What think you of the appeal of the ex-
Secretaries. I think the general opinion is settling down here, rather
against their secession from the Cabinet on the grounds of its being a too
hasty movement. I think there was some want of tact in the leaders of the
party in Congress urging the passage of the Bank bill in such a head long
manner after the peculiar notions of Tyler had become known to them.
. . . Clay seemed bent upon the plan that the extra session must dispose
of it."[44]

42. Committee of Invitation of Meadville to George Winchester, October 17, 1844,
Winchester Papers, Box 2E906.

43. On the emergence of the proslavery argument in Mississippi, see Sydnor, *Slavery in
Mississippi*, 241–48, and Cleo Hearon, "Mississippi and the Compromise of 1850," *Publications of the Mississippi Historical Society* 14 (1914), 7–45.

44. J. C. Waters to George Winchester, October 1, 1841, Winchester Papers, Box
2E904. The conflict between the congressional Whigs and Tyler is covered in George Raw-
lings Poage, *Henry Clay and the Whig Party* (Chapel Hill: University of North Carolina
Press, 1936); Norma Lois Peterson, *The Presidencies of William Henry Harrison & John Tyler*

Waters thought that Clay had overreached his grasp and been poorly advised on party tactics, although he went to lengths to praise the Whig leader. His greatest concern, which he assumed he shared with Winchester, was the effect this rupture would have on the party. Now that they had power, the Whigs needed to continue "to be governed by principle." Clearly, these conservatives, who were old friends, understood and agreed upon the content of those principles although one lived in Massachusetts and the other in Mississippi.

Another letter written two years later follows a similar line, referring intimately to local politicos and national and international events. Of course, there were always the pressing questions of business and economic conditions. " '*The times,*' so called," Waters wrote in March 1843, "were never so dull since I can remember. As to law business, it is altogether a thing that was . . . I can assure you that there are not four lawyers at our Bar now realizing a support from their business. As for myself I must candidly admit that I feel poor having suffered very much from losses in trade . . . and in stocks in which my little property was invested. I held several shares in that damnable (excuse me) institution that seems to me was the box of Pandora to us all, the U.S. Bank. Of course all I owned there turned out moonshine. Then there were other Banks about here in whose stock I am unfortunately a great loser. But no mind . . . By the bye if you could remit to me the balance of that account it would help very much."[45]

Waters then turned to politics, noting that their "mutual friend," Massachusetts congressman Leverett Saltonstall, was retiring after three terms in the House, "leaving the race course for Mr. [Daniel P.] King of Danvers whom you know and [Democrat Robert] Rantoul of Beverly who is notorious enough to have come within your notice I dare say." He then assured Judge Winchester that he could not predict the result, because of the "many heterogeneous subjects involved in the canvas." Perhaps his most interesting observation is this: "There is a small party of abolitionists here which can throw their weight into any scale to defeat a choice and they

---

(Lawrence: University of Kansas Press, 1989); and Robert V. Remini, *Henry Clay: Statesman for the Union* (New York: W. W. Norton, 1991).

45. J. G. Waters to George Winchester, March 28, 1843, Winchester Papers, Box 2E904.

have practiced this for along while. King [the Whig] is abolition enough to secure some votes, but will not show radicalism sufficient to satisfy the radicals of that party."[46]

Judge Winchester held a more important place in the Mississippi Whig party than did Wilkins. Although he seems not to have been in the inner circle of leaders, he knew everyone who was. Winchester's papers include a jesting plea from one of his "Real friends" urging him to decline the appointment to the state supreme court, condolences over his friend Wilkins's loss of the Senate seat in 1833, and interesting 1830s letters from John Quitman, Joseph E. Davis, and Seargent Prentiss. Yet even the letters written in the 1840s display an extremely low level of North-South rancor, a uniform national party culture or at least a uniform set of experiences with the new positive perception of parties, and an ease of discussion of even so sensitive a subject as abolitionism.[47]

In one fascinating letter, the judge's nephew (and clerk) Josiah wrote from Southboro, Massachusetts, describing his trip north to visit the family. He had traveled up the Mississippi River, across Illinois, and to New England "by way of the Lakes." The route was "well worth taking for once in a mans [sic] life to see the variety, beauty and sublimity of the scenes. Nothing can surpass the richness and the beauty of the Prairie scenery through Illinois."[48]

The subject of this long letter then shifted to the state of the family, noting that "Grandsire" was "fast declining under the weight of years"— "his memory is mostly gone"—but that the family in Salem "were all living and enjoying themselves there pretty much in the same way as you probably found them and left them in 1839. Full of abolitionism—full of temperance—full of religious disputes—Animal magnetism and a thou-

46. J. G. Waters to George Winchester, October 1, 1841, March 28, 1843, ibid. On Massachusetts politics at the time, see Ronald P. Formisano, *The Transformation of Political Culture: Massachusetts Parties, 1790s to 1840s* (New York, 1982).

47. William M. Green to George Winchester, February 15, 1827, John Quitman to Winchester, October 9, 1832, Joseph E. Davis to Winchester, May 29, 1834, Seargent S. Prentiss to Winchester, November 22, 1836, Winchester Papers, Box 2E903.

48. Josiah Winchester to George Winchester, August 7, 1841, Winchester Papers, Box 2E904.

sand other topics of warm discussion." The younger Winchester then described at length a demonstration of hypnotism that had turned him from
a skeptic to a believer in "this doctrine of Clairvoyance."[49]

Clearly the young man neither faced the stony hostility of Puritan New
England nor expressed a hint of southern parochialism. At Congressman
King's house, he met "Mr. and Mrs. Emerson. . . . I promised Mr. E I would
spend several days with him." Finally, he assured his uncle that he had
spoken with a Marblehead fisherman who was putting up for the judge
"two half barrels—and I intend one for Miss Sprague—of tongues . . . and
one of fins." He would court the young lady with the delicacies of northern waters.[50]

A nonpolitical letter from one of the judge's Massachusetts friends reveals a primary reason for so many northerners ending up in Mississippi
and also the transsectional nature of the business and communications
networks that spanned the young republic: "It is one of the most valued
privileges of our long intimacy that permits me to transfer a portion of my
claim on your attention, to my young friend and relative F. Chever Esq. of
this City + an esteemed member of the Bar whose feeble health has com-
pelled him to seek at the South a more genial climate to enable him to
pursue his professional studies."[51]

Winchester, of course, had northern connections with men other than
those he had known in his youth, and his business records include a good
deal of correspondence with northern firms. On one occasion he became
involved in a lucrative divorce case with Horace Binney, the wealthy Philadelphia lawyer who was a close friend and business associate of national
bank president Nicholas Biddle.[52]

Scholars who insist on sharp cultural conflict between the North and
the South generally portray a South secluded from the social, economic,
and intellectual currents of the nineteenth century; a population with little contact or intercourse with the world outside; and a premodern elite

49. Ibid.
50. Ibid.
51. J. G. Waters to George Winchester, October 15, 1843, Winchester Papers, Box
2E904.
52. George Winchester to Horace Binney, March 8, 1836, Winchester Papers, Box
2E903.

isolated on their plantations surrounded by their brooding black bonds-men and separated from their fellow whites except for visits that were so random and infrequent as to be occasions for celebration. In contrast to this cramped vision, it is difficult to imagine any group of Americans more cosmopolitan in their tastes and connections than these Natchez na-bobs.[53]

The Archer Family Papers add a further dimension to an understanding of the Mississippi planters, since Richard Thompson Archer received most of his correspondence not from northerners, but from friends and kinsmen from the Upper South. These papers in the NTC contain extensive manu-script letters—essays, in fact—to local editors dealing with political sub-jects and expressing the proslavery ideology in a form not found in the published anthologies on the subject. The most interesting letters relating to national politics came from his Virginia cousin William Segar Archer, who was first a congressional supporter of Jackson in the early 1830s and then, a decade later, a Whig senator. At the time of the annexation of Texas, he was chairman of the Senate Foreign Relations Committee.[54]

Archer's correspondence and his letters to his wife that are included in the collection are dominated by business matters, especially prices of slaves, land, and cotton. He was immensely wealthy and, like the textbook Whig, could often be found in markets near bales of cotton, attended by his most trusted slaves. He and his correspondents were prosperous plant-

53. There is an oddity in this collection that merits notice. By their nature such files of letters are mostly incoming, that is, addressed to the individual. Here, the only male-female correspondence is from men. Women were known to travel a good bit in the Old South, but in this subcollection as well as the others in the NTC it is the men on the road who wrote home regularly discussing business with their wives. Cf. Elizabeth Fox-Genovese, *Within the Plantation Household: Black and White Women in the Old South* (Chapel Hill: University of North Carolina Press, 1988).

54. Richard Thompson Archer Family Papers, 1790–1919. These include a sketch of Richard Thompson Archer and an inventory by Sara Clark. On Senator Archer and his po-litical activity, see Mary Newton Stanard, "William Segar Archer," in *Dictionary of Ameri-can Biography*, ed. Allen Johnson, vol. 1 (New York: Charles Scribner's Sons, 1928), 342–43; Frederick Merk, *Slavery and the Annexation of Texas* (New York: Knopf, 1972); and William G. Shade, *Democratizing the Old Dominion: Virginia and the Second Party System, 1824–1861* (Charlottesville: University Press of Virginia, 1997).

ers and slaveholders and about as materialistic and bourgeois as any set of nineteenth-century Americans could have been. Since this includes his wealthy First Families of Virginia kin, the circle might be regarded by those asserting the prebourgeois nature of planter *mentalité* as the exceptions giving voice to a redoubt of capitalist sentiment. In addition to the Virginian Archer's cousin the senator, his family included the reformer John Hartwell Cocke, a close friend and neighbor of Jefferson's, and Branch T. Archer, the Texas Republic hero. After Archer's college days as a classmate of Thomas Roderick Dew and subsequent move to Mississippi to make his fortune, he commented to his brother Stephen that the value of land "rises very fast here."[55] Although he endured several setbacks following the Panic of 1837 that led him to curse the bankers who had made his fortune possible, Archer eventually owned three hundred slaves on his various holdings in five Mississippi counties and had extensive speculations elsewhere. Randolph Campbell's essay in this volume details the plantation holdings that made Archer a millionaire, one of the richest men in the United States.

Politically, Archer turned against Jackson on the question of nullification. He even tried to raise a volunteer force of four hundred men to aid the South Carolinians, and raged against the Jacksonians' economic policies that he blamed for his financial problems in the late 1830s. But after supporting Harrison, he rejected Clay on Texas annexation and voted for Polk. By 1850 he was an opponent of compromise, a secessionist, and as one of the state's largest slaveholders, a fervent defender of the positive good of the peculiar institution.[56] Bowman again offers an absorbing illustration of Archer's ardent secessionism as exemplified in various writings in the Archer Papers.

Differing from most former Whigs and from his fellow grandees in the Natchez District in his fire-eating southern-nationalist extremism, Archer once described John Bell, the ex-Whig and the Constitutional Unionist

55. R. T. Archer to Stephen Archer, March 18, September 2, 1833, Richard Thompson Archer Family Papers, Box 2E646.

56. Philip Martin Gavenda's " 'In Defense of the God-Given Right to Own the African': The Politics of Richard T. Archer" (master's thesis, University of Texas at Austin, 1993) is a helpful discussion of Archer's views based primarily on the Archer Papers in the NTC.

candidate in 1860, as a "political Judas Iscariot."[57] Archer was that variety of southern oppositionist who joined with the Whigs and voted for Harrison in 1840, but who never internalized the emerging political culture of partisanship and consequently was never a "Whig" in the modern sense of party identification. He tried to remain a classical republican in politics while accepting liberal individualism as the basis of his political economy and personal outlook.

Archer's response to economic questions needs to be understood to clarify a certain confusion in the historical literature. It will not do to assume that those who supported the South Carolina nullifiers also opposed the credit system and banks or, even more startlingly, that they necessarily rejected all tariffs. Archer, like Calhoun and McDuffie, supported the Bank of the United States against Jackson's assault. On the state level Archer believed that if the banking system were "rightly conducted it confers many benefits and facilities on society with detriment to no one."[58]

Exhibiting the attitude of many Whigs across the country during the depression of the late 1830s and early 1840s, Archer responded angrily when his ox was gored and attacked "the greedy selfish men" who ran state banks. He was not unusual in meeting his own economic reverses with emotional outrage while at the same time accepting the Whig's commitment to the credit system. The tariff is a somewhat more complicated matter, since protection of domestic products ostensibly was the issue that generated the nullification crisis. Yet Archer insisted that he "was not opposed to a tariff which by compromise carried consent of the whole of the states."[59] Here too his personal economic interest dictated his interpretation of the issue. Increasingly, his view on the matter became tied to sectionalism and ultimately to the protection of slavery. His arguments were never very subtle.

---

57. Richard T. Archer, *Speech of Richard Archer, Esq., Delivered on the Tenth Day of August, 1860 at Port Gibson, Miss. . . .* (Port Gibson: J. E. Elliott, 1860), 14. A copy of this printed speech is in the Library of Congress.

58. See the Richard T. Archer letters in "On Banks," Box 2E647. See also Ch. Cocke to Richard T. Archer, November 18, 1839, A. Halsey to Archer, June 5, 1843, James P. Cocke to Archer, August 17, 1846, and S. S. Prentiss to Archer, April 3, 1847, Archer Papers, Boxes 2E646 and 2E653.

59. "Comments on Dr. S. A. Cartwright's address."

Archer had been a Jacksonian until he read the "Proclamation to the People of South Carolina." Like southerners from Richmond to Baton Rouge, he recoiled in disbelief since it followed so closely on the heels of Jackson's annual message, which had adhered strictly to "the doctrines of '98." Unlike most, Archer was not merely offended by the president's constitutional ignorance, but was ready to do battle. The question was not an abstract one of constitutional rights or the right of minorities—which southern scholars have loved to pose—but the simple matter of his personal right to own slaves. His rights were absolute and God-given, and if the Constitution could not be read to guarantee them, then he wished to get rid of it. Hardly a conservative paternalist, this was a man whose very world revolved around property rights—his property rights to "niggers" destined by God to work for him and his fellow planters.[60]

While he later described himself as a "Whig" in the 1830s, Archer, along with most nullifiers, was much too independent to espouse partisan affiliation. He could embrace Harrison, but never liked Clay. Thus in 1844 he openly attacked the Kentuckian and voted for Polk. One of Archer's public letters that year lampooned Clay's second Alabama letter (sent to the *Tuscumbria North Alabamian*) in which the Kentuckian tried to explain his position on annexation to the generally pro-Texas planters. Many Mississippians must have agreed with Archer that Texas annexation was the "most important measure which ever came to the consideration of the National Government."[61]

Archer's interest in slavery was clearly reflected in his tendency to view annexation as a necessary step in the maintenance of the peculiar institution. Unlike Walker, who concocted an argument tying annexation to the

60. His most lengthy statements are in Archer, *Speech . . . August, 1860;* and "Comments on Dr. S. A. Cartwright's address." Cartwright was a New Orleans physician and a proponent of scientific racism. Also see Samuel A. Cartwright, "Slavery in the Light of Ethnology," in E. N. Elliott, *Cotton Is King, and Pro-Slavery Arguments* (Augusta, Ga.: Prichard, Abbott and Loomis, 1860), 690–728. The undated items in the Archer Papers are identified by folder and box number.

61. "Mr. Clays letter published in the Tuscumbria North Alabamian. Amplified and corrected by R T Archer," Folder 5, Box 2E647; R. T. Archer to "Mr. Clay [1844]," printed broadside in the Virginia Historical Society, Archer Papers, Box 2E646.

economic interests of the country, Archer wrote more directly: "Slavery like free labor requires space. If too much crowded either will become too dense for good wages, and ultimately in the progress of population will be stifled and become extinct. Slave labor may also become extinct by the inevitable laws of population, if so confined in territory that it cannot form new states by which to strengthen and defend itself against the antagonistic power of antislavery." He worried that "the slave states may now be said to be enclosed in the folds of the great political Boa anti-slavery." Should slavery become cooped up, Archer in an allusion to the Haitian rebellion hinted at the ultimate possibility of the horrors of "St. Doming."[62]

Archer's obsession with Clay allowed him to believe the rather common idea circulating among southern Democrats that Clay was an abolitionist. "Every true southerner" knew Clay to be "a *cooperator with the Abolitionists and they cannot deny* that he is so regarded by themselves and that they are so well satisfied with him as to oppose Birney lest he may take votes from Mr. Clay." In his parody letter, Archer had Clay claim that he had been "able to do more for abolition of slavery than any living man." Only "party servility reconciles all contradictions and antipathies and supports its voting even if the country is to be ruined."[63]

Fundamentally hostile to parties, Archer in 1848 found appealing the "no party" candidacy of Louisiana planter and war hero Zachary Taylor. But this did not bring him back into the Whig party. By this time Archer related all matters to the touchstone of sectional interest and the protection of slavery. Archer approved of Taylor the slaveholder because he disapproved of Van Buren the "party-man," whom he had never trusted and who was running as a free-soiler. He did not think the other northerner, Democratic candidate Lewis Cass, had a chance to win.[64]

62. "Mr. Clays letter . . . Amplified and corrected." For his fellow Mississippian Robert John Walker's argument, see Frederick Merk, *Fruits of Propaganda in the Tyler Administration* (Cambridge, Mass.: Harvard University Press, 1971).

63. "To the Editor of the Port Gibson Correspondent," Folder 6, Box 2E647; "Mr. Clays letter . . . Amplified and corrected"; Archer to "Mr. Clay [1844]," Archer Papers, Box 2E646. On Clay's position on slavery and his troubles in 1844, see Remini, *Henry Clay,* 642–67.

64. "To the Editor of the Port Gibson Herald [1848]," Folder 6, Box 2E647. Cf. William W. Freehling, *The Reinterpretation of American History: Slavery and the Civil War* (New York:

Speaking primarily to Mississippi Democrats, Archer called upon them and southerners generally to split their tickets and vote for General Taylor and the Kentucky congressman and war hero William O. Butler, who was the Democratic convention's vice-presidential choice. In doing so, they would at least ensure "the election of the man whom 99 of every 100 Southern Democrats prefer to Cass for the vice presidency." Archer believed that free soil was "a Democratic movement" that split the party. Thus he asked Mississippi Democrats: "Will you still vote for Cass though hopeless of his election? Have you no choice between Taylor and Van Buren?"[65]

While there are no letters describing what horror Archer must have felt at Taylor's subsequent actions as president, events brought many southerners into line with Archer's position and the movement for southern rights pressed by Calhoun. The convention held in Jackson in October 1849 marked the only time in his life that Archer was a participant in a public meeting. In all of this Archer is almost a perfect Calhounite although there are no Calhoun letters in this collection and no Archer letters in the published Calhoun papers.[66]

Archer's antipartyism emerged most clearly in his discussion of the reasons "why the cause of Southern Rights does not progress," the subject of

Oxford University Press, 1994), 82–104, and Michael F. Holt, *Political Parties and American Political Development from the Age of Jackson to the Age of Lincoln* (Baton Rouge: Louisiana State University Press, 1992), 192–236.

65. "To the Democrats of Mississippi," Folder 6, Box 2E647. He publicly wrote Jefferson Davis that although he was "a *no party man*" and had little confidence in Millard Fillmore, he would vote for Taylor. *Port Gibson Herald and Correspondent*, October 27, 1848, quoted in *The Papers of Jefferson Davis: Volume 3, July 1846–December 1848*, ed. James T. McIntosh (Baton Rouge: Louisiana State University Press, 1981), 388–89.

66. Hearon, "Mississippi and the Compromise of 1850," 63; Thelma Jennings, *The Nashville Convention: A Southern Movement for Unity* (Memphis: Memphis State University Press, 1980), 27; "The Friends of Southern Rights," Folder 6, Box 2E647. See J. Franklin Jameson, "Correspondence of John C. Calhoun," in *Annual Report of the American Historical Association for the Year 1899*, vol. 2 (Washington, D.C., 1900), 11–1218, and Chauncey S. Boucher and Robert P. Brooks, "Correspondence Addressed to John C. Calhoun, 1837–1849," in *Annual Report of the American Historical Association for the Year 1929* (Washington, D.C., 1930), 125–533, 551–70; and Robert C. Meriwether et al., *The Papers of John C. Calhoun* (Columbia, S.C.: University of South Carolina Press, 1959–   ).

another long, undated letter to an unspecified editor. After noting the general "apathy of its friends" and the tendency of the movement to be "associated with prosperous and wealthy gentlemen" and disdained by the mechanics and the majority of Mississippians, he became particularly agitated that "old party and personal jealousies have influence on many, who probably are not sensible that they have not utterly repudiated these very trivial biases." He preferred "the manly, direct, and confident inflexibility of conscious rectitude" to prudence and fear of going too far in the protection of southern rights.[67]

Such arguments make it clear why Archer conceived of himself as a true republican and a "Son of a Rebel of 1776," who attacked as "submissionists" the wealthy Whig planters of Adams County, whom he described as the descendants of Tories who fled Virginia and South Carolina after the Revolution.[68] In an ironic fashion, he associated true republicanism with Virginia of the Great Generation and the Principles of '98 and with South Carolina of the era of nullification. The southern cause for Archer was the cause of traditional republicanism.

At the time of the Nashville Convention, Archer did get involved in a controversy that marked him as something of a reactionary when he opposed the election of a candidate for the convention on the grounds that the man in question was poor. When publicly charged with class bias, he defended himself by claiming the problem to be not that the candidate was "poor," but that he owned no slaves. "I do not object to Mr. Wilson but that in a question of property peculiar in kind and of a magnitude that it is almost the sole basis of Southern wealth prosperity and happiness, which great question . . . that he has no community of interest with those he represents."[69]

His discussion of the issue, reminiscent of the Virginia conservatives of 1829 who insisted that their property be represented since it was taxed, underscores the manner in which southern planters habitually pressed their property rights in terms of hard cash. Mississippi, he argued had, "slave property . . . worth $5,600,000 and real estate to the value of nearly

67. "Messrs Editors," Folder 6, Box 2E647.
68. "To the Editor of the Free Trader," Folder 5, ibid.
69. "To the Editor of the Free Trader," Folder 6, ibid.

$2,000,000." The security of that property was "indispensable to civil liberty . . . those who defend their 'own rights' are defending 'the rights of all.' "[70]

From these letters and speeches, Archer emerges as both an elite republican and a liberal individualist who is nothing less than a full-blown bourgeois capitalist. He was FFV transported to the heart of the Cotton Kingdom. By every statistical criterion, Archer was a classic planter conservative who was committed to strict construction and states' rights or what he called "the Southern construction of the Constitution." He typified the body of ideas that are usually called Calhounite and moved about the underbrush of the antebellum political world along a trail forged by the South Carolinian—himself a Scotch-Irish, backcountry parvenu. Perhaps Archer was even more extreme than Calhoun. By 1850, he believed, "It is easier to make a new Union than patch up this."[71]

Archer was flamboyant and eccentric, an independent in his political views, although they closely resembled those of the extreme secessionist wing of the Mississippi Democracy as articulated by Albert Gallatin Brown, whom historians have usually understood as representing a distinctly different backcountry political culture. Archer embraced the Nashville Convention, opposed the Compromise of 1850, and called on his state to prepare for war a full decade before the apocalypse finally did descend and sweep away his world.[72]

Unlike Wilkins, Dick Archer was not a banker and did not particularly

70. Dickson D. Bruce, Jr., *The Rhetoric of Conservatism: The Virginia Convention of 1829–30 and the Conservative Tradition in the South* (San Marcos, Calif.: Huntington Library, 1982); William W. Freehling, *The Road to Disunion, Volume I: Secessionists at Bay, 1776–1854* (New York: Oxford University Press, 1990), 162–96; "W. S. Wilson," Folder 6, Box 2E647. Archer went on to say in his letter to the *Free Trader* that by defending his own rights he was defending the rights of the common man: "Your rights are my rights." Recalling that this was a man who had nearly three hundred slaves and was a millionaire by the time of the Civil War reminds one of Charles E. Wilson's comment, when he was Eisenhower's secretary of defense, "What's good for the country is good for General Motors."

71. "Messrs Editors." William G. Archer to Richard Archer, March 28, 1848, Archer Papers, Box 2E646, is a classic capitalist statement, discussing the markets in money, land, and "negroes," and constantly speaking of profits and risks.

72. See James Byrne Ranck, *Albert Gallatin Brown: Radical Southern Nationalist* (New York: D. Appleton Century, 1937).

like bankers. Nor was he a lawyer like Judge Winchester. But he was certainly a capitalist, an agricultural businessman whose correspondence is dominated by concern for the markets—in land, in cotton, in seed, and, of course, in "negroes"—and speculative schemes in Texas and California in partnership with men of his own kind using borrowed capital secured at the lowest price in the money markets of the world. Although he was a planter devoted to agriculture, Archer, ever seeking the main chance, thought there was gold in Texas and contemplated the use of slaves in the California mines.[73]

His extensive correspondence with his cousin William Segar Archer, the conservative Whig senator from Virginia, includes, as one would expect, some political material, but is dominated by business matters.[74] The letters from 1848 and 1849 are surprisingly apolitical and focus on money grabbing in a bull market. An earlier twenty-page letter from the senator—who was chairman of the Senate Foreign Relations Committee, then considering the joint resolution on annexing Texas—has only one page on politics.

Archer, then, was simply a man who went to Mississippi to get rich in land speculation and the growing of cotton for the insatiable international market and who did fabulously well.[75] Like Wilkins and Winchester, he was both a classic capitalist and a sophisticate who traveled widely and had correspondents throughout the country. He was as cosmopolitan as the less wealthy factory owners of the North, and closely resembled them in bourgeois tastes and lifestyle, even though he was sure that he was their superior.

Like those northern capitalists, Archer was fascinated by technology that would make him richer and more efficient, and was constantly embroiled in legal matters that had a whiff of honor about them but were basically business deals. Business matters—the prices and markets of the world—fill his correspondence both with his mother and his wife when he

73. Practically every letter in Boxes 2E646 and 2E653 speaks to these matters.

74. The William Segar Archer letters are in Box 2E653.

75. Gaylord Warren Harris, "Agricultural Statistics of Claiborne County, 1850 and 1860," *Journal of Mississippi History* 15 (October 1953), 235, 237, lists him with nearly $400,000 property and 138 slaves, but he was much richer than that and held probably 300 slaves.

was traveling (as he did nearly every year) and with his family in Virginia when he was at home minding the affairs of his many Mississippi investments. In our time, he would have logged a lot of frequent-flyer miles. It is hard to imagine a New England entrepreneur so consumed by his ledgers.

If Archer's prime invective in 1860 was reserved for his fellow southern Whig, John Bell, he also attacked the other ex-Whig in the election, Abraham Lincoln, the man he had proclaimed "ineligible" for the office, "an expatriated foreigner" who would be a "Monarch, Emperor, Autocrat or Sultan." Archer was never a "modern Whig" or "Democratic Whig" as the terms were used in the 1840s, although he does fit into the category of "states' rights Whig" created by twentieth-century historians to describe the nullifiers, Calhounites, and anti-Jackson men who played a significant role in the 1830s in southern politics before they returned to the Democratic party to take it over.[76]

Even among such independent individuals as the states' rights Whigs, Dick Archer was a loose cannon. Jefferson Davis had been correct when he advised Franklin Pierce that Archer was an individual of "high personal respectability and great tenacity of purpose," but to whom "little attention" was paid and who had virtually "no support."[77] Archer's brutally bourgeois approach to trading in human beings and exploiting the land cannot be easily dismissed by southern romantics (real or "convinced") as "paternalism." While he undoubtedly believed in his moral superiority over both the nonslaveholders in Mississippi and the Boston shopkeepers, this feeling grew out of his masterful ability to profit from his God-given "natural right" to his "slave property."

Archer did not strive for any sense of scholarly detachment in his defense of slavery and his rights as a slaveowner. He clearly believed that the American Revolution entailed little more than the sanctification of his and other slaveholders' property rights. The entire proslavery argument for Archer rested on the sanctity of private property and essentially liberal Lockean rationalizations of that right. In Archer's writings it had the fa-

76. Archer, *Speech of Richard Archer . . . 1860*, 13.

77. To Franklin Pierce, July 23, 1857, in *The Papers of Jefferson Davis: Volume 6, 1856–1860*, ed. Linda Lasswell Crist and Mary Seaton Dix (Baton Rouge: Louisiana State University Press, 1989), 132.

miliar whine about personal "rights" that has come to dominate our society.

In his longest public commentary on slavery, the speech in which he
insisted that God had given the white man a natural right "to buy him
[the Negro] for possession and inheritance forever," Archer specifically
denied the relevance of fellow Mississippian Henry Hughes's paternalistic
argument. "There can be no abolition of slavery; no warranteeism
[Hughes's term] . . . God commands me to buy him; and to buy, presup-
poses property in him." He believed that the right to this property was "superior to civil law" and "inalienable from the race of the white man."[78]

Archer never made any attempt to justify his offbeat racist antinomian-
ism by rational argument. Blacks were "creatures" to be treated humanely,
but not fully human beings. They were property judged in terms of their
value in the marketplace. As Philip Gavenda has pointed out, none of Archer's letters to his wife, mother, or other family members, include the
usual slaveholder's solicitations to his slaves. Archer's views were as bold a
statement of the conception of slaves as chattel to be bought and sold as
one might find, and especially fascinating in light of the fact that he was
the nephew of John Hartwell Cocke, the Virginia reformer, who had freed
his slaves on his death.[79]

These three Mississippi slaveholders bring to life our view of the South in
the Age of Jackson and contribute significantly to the discussion of southern distinctiveness. The Natchez Trace Collection provides a marvelous
source for the enhancement of our understanding of the complexity and

78. Archer, *Speech of Richard Archer . . . 1860*, 6. On Hughes, see Douglas Ambrose,
Henry Hughes and Proslavery Thought in the Old South (Baton Rouge: Louisiana State University Press, 1997); Drew Gilpin Faust, ed., *The Ideology of Slavery: Proslavery Thought in the
Antebellum South, 1830–1860* (Baton Rouge: Louisiana State University Press, 1981),
239–71; William Sumner Jenkins, *Proslavery Thought in the Old South* (Chapel Hill: University of North Carolina Press, 1935); Bertram Wyatt-Brown, *Yankee Saints and Southern Sin-
ners* (Baton Rouge: Louisiana State University Press, 1985), 172–82.

79. R. T. Archer to William S. Archer, February 11, 1840, Archer Papers, Box 2E646.
On Cocke, see Clement Eaton, *The Mind of the Old South* (Baton Rouge: Louisiana State
University Press, 1964), 3–20. The "Dear Mamma" letters and those to his wife in Box
2E646 are devoted to business, but do not contain tender references to either blacks or
whites.

humanity (or inhumanity) of those planters whose papers fell into the hands of one very eccentric collector. It seems that these men saw themselves as citizens of the larger world, rather than simply "southerners." They were not even particularly vocal defenders of slavery until pushed in that direction by threats to their livelihood and prosperity. Sometime before 1850, a defensive posture on the issue appeared where it had not existed openly before, and these three men, to varying degrees, came to see themselves as embattled on the question of their slave property. Like their neighbors in Louisiana, Alabama, and Georgia, these Mississippi planters regarded their republican liberty as endangered by the abolitionists' assault on their most basic rights.

APPENDIX

Selected Subcollections of the Natchez Trace Collection

For purposes of arrangement and access, the Natchez Trace Collection has been organized into subcollections, the larger or more significant of which are listed below. The Natchez Trace Collection also contains more than two thousand small manuscript collections. Inventories for all subcollections are housed in the Center for American History's James Stephen Hogg Reading Room. Bibliographic records for individual NTC subcollections, books, and newspapers are entered on an ongoing basis into OCLC, an on-line computer library database that is accessible over the Internet. Future plans call for inventories to NTC subcollections to appear on the Center's website.

Adair Versus Wilkinson Case Records. 1809–1820. 50 items.
Legal documents concerning Adair's cases against General James Wilkinson, heard in Adams County, Mississippi Territory. Adair charged Wilkinson with false imprisonment after he was attacked in 1807 and shipped to Fort McHenry to serve time on suspicion of conspiracy with Aaron Burr in Louisiana.

Robert H. Adams Papers. 1820–1834. 1 ft., 3 in.
Correspondence, legal papers, financial records, and literary productions documenting the career and life of attorney Robert H. Adams, one-time law partner with Sturges Sprague. Personal papers include letters from his wife Julia and the 1825 visit of General Lafayette to New Orleans and Natchez.

Amos Alexander Papers. 1817–1822. 51 items.
Accounts and receipts concerning the purchase of food, livestock, services, dry goods, and tools in Natchez by Alexander and his family.

Richard Thompson Archer Family Papers. 1790–1919. 5 ft., 4 in.
Correspondence, financial records, and legal documents to and from Archer, a Virginia native, prominent Mississippi planter, and ardent secessionist, and his relatives, friends, and business associates. Papers concern plantation life and economy, agricultural affairs, social life and customs, education, medical practices, household affairs, and slaves and slavery in Mississippi and Virginia.

William L. Balfour Papers. 1841–1863. 4 in.

Financial records relating to the management of the William L. Balfour (1802–1857) estate in Mississippi by Horace G. Blackman.

Bank of the State of Mississippi Records. 1804–1846. 16 ft.

Papers documenting the Bank of the State of Mississippi, with headquarters in Natchez, as well as the economic development of the lower Mississippi River valley in the early nineteenth century. Contains letterpress copy books, loan records, bank share certificates, powers of attorney, promissory notes, letters of credit, cash draft receipts, abstracts of funds, personal accounts, and correspondence with bank officers and with other banks, including the branch of the Second Bank of the United States located in New Orleans.

Barnes-Willis Family Papers. 1783–1840. 1 ft., 11 in.

Papers relating to business affairs, travels, administration of estates, cotton, slaves, and family life of bank director Abram Barnes (1785–1830) of Port Gibson, Mississippi; sheriff William Willis (d. ca. 1821) of Concordia Parish, Louisiana; merchant and attorney John B. Willis of Port Gibson and Washington, Mississippi, and other Barnes-Willis family members.

James N. Brown Papers. 1855–1879. 5 in.

Records relating to the disposition of the estate of Brown (1807–1859?), a wealthy sugar planter from Iberville Parish, Louisiana, by his son-in-law, including records of Brown's plantations Manchac (Iberville Parish), Oakland (Plaquemine Parish), Linwood (Ascension Parish), and Magnolia and Highland Place (East Baton Rouge Parish).

Joseph K. Brown Papers. 1810–1813. 49 items.

Customer accounts documenting the business affairs of Brown, a Jefferson County, Mississippi Territory, blacksmith.

Buckhorn Plantation Records. 1833–1855. 67 items.

Financial records, tax receipts, accounts, and legal documents concerning the operation of Alfred J. Lowry's Buckhorn plantation, Milliken's Bend, Madison Parish, Louisiana.

Burling Family Papers. 1810–1827. 1 in.

Business records, tuition bills, travel expense accounts, and estate records of Colonel Walter Burling, his wife Elizabeth, and their five daughters. Included are bills from the Natchez Academy.

Arthur Carney Papers. 1800–1829. 66 items.

Legal documents, accounts, receipts, and probate records documenting the business affairs of Arthur Carney of Claiborne County, Mississippi.

Elizabeth Jane Caldwell Carter Papers. 1825–1894. 2 in.

Correspondence, invitations, and clippings relating to the social activities and personal concerns of Carter. Most of the papers are contained in a scrapbook indexed and annotated by her daughter, R. G. Carter, in 1894.

Chamberlain-Hyland-Gould Family Papers. 1805–1886. 8 in.

Papers of three Mississippi families containing primarily the correspondence of Ellen Marie Wheaton Chamberlain Hyland (1823–1863), daughter of Oakland College president Jeremiah Chamberlain, and her uncle, brother, husband, son, daughter, and son-in-law. Letters mainly concern personal and business matters and document daily family life on the Hyland plantation Boquedesha (1848–1886) in Warren County, Mississippi.

Rowland Chambers Papers. 1839–1871. 1 in.

Correspondence, legal records, accounts, and receipts documenting the professional and personal activities of dentist Rowland Chambers, whose business practice was, at various times, in Vicksburg and Satartia, Mississippi, and in Madison Parish, Louisiana.

Ferdinand Leigh Claiborne Papers. 1803–1815. 76 items.

Correspondence, legal papers, and financial records documenting the personal affairs and military career of Claiborne, who served as brigadier general of the Mississippi Territory militia during the War of 1812.

Robert Cochran Papers. 1838–1858. 115 items.

Correspondence, accounts, and receipts documenting the business and personal activities of Cochran, an agent based in Natchez for the New York financial house of Brown Brothers.

G. C. Covington Family Papers. 1841–1848. 112 items.

Receipts and itemized accounts relating to the household goods and clothing purchased primarily in New Orleans by Mrs. G. C. Covington. Includes tuition receipts for her daughters Cassandra and Susan.

James J. Cowan Family Papers. 1845–1879. 2 in.

Correspondence, receipts, and accounts documenting the personal and business affairs of the Cowan family of Vicksburg, Mississippi. Materials include James Cowan's description of his train trip to Washington, D.C., in 1859, letters between Captain Cowan and his family written during Cowan's service as an artillery commander for the Confederate Army, and correspondence between family members describing the siege of Vicksburg and their lives as war refugees.

Crutcher-Shannon Family Papers. 1822–1905. 7 in.

Personal and financial records of two Vicksburg families: Levina Morris and Marmaduke Shannon, publisher of the *Vicksburg Daily Whig,* and his daughter Emma, who married William Crutcher. Letters document William's military service on Civil War battlefields, William and Emma's courtship and marriage while he was in the service and she at home in Vicksburg, and the siege of Vicksburg. Emma's career as a teacher in Vicksburg following the war is documented by five school registers and grade books.

Charles Backus Dana Papers. 1802, 1820–1881. 11 in.

Personal and family correspondence and drafts of sermons by Dana (1810–1873), New Hampshire native, graduate of Dartmouth College, and Protestant Episcopal rector of Christ Church in Alexandria, Virginia (1861–1866), and Trinity Church in Natchez (1866–1873).

Joseph Emory Davis Papers. 1824–1880. ½ in.

Correspondence, legal papers, plantation records, and estate records documenting the business and personal affairs of Davis, the eldest brother of Jefferson Davis, including an 1838 loan cosigned by Joseph and Jefferson, government documents concerning actions taken by the Freedmen's Bureau involving Davis's former slaves and plantations, and a printed petition to President Andrew Johnson requesting a pardon and restoration of Davis's land. Also contains letters from Davis describing his experiences in the early years of Reconstruction and an 1866 letter from his former slave Ben Montgomery, to whom Davis had sold Hurricane, his Warren County, Mississippi, plantation.

Elizabeth Dearmond Family Papers. 1827–1848. 30 items.

Correspondence from family members living in Louisiana and Mississippi describing local planting and health conditions as well as the condition of their slaves. Also includes letters discussing the Mexican War and General John A. Quitman's victorious parade through Natchez in 1847.

Mary F. Dunbar Papers. 1859–1860. 28 items.

Literary notebook, accounts, receipts, medical bills, and cotton records documenting Dunbar's Forest plantation in Natchez.

Stephen Duncan Family Papers. 1826–1881. 3 in.

Correspondence, financial records, and legal documents concerning the personal and business affairs of Natchez planter and physician Stephen Duncan and his family, their associates, plantations, and servants.

John Dutton Papers. 1789–1890. 1 ft.

Correspondence, slave lists, financial and legal documents, and public auction records of Judge John Dutton (d. ca. 1849) and other officials of the parish court of Iberville in Plaquemine, Louisiana.

Fielding Fant Papers. 1810–1836. 41 items.

Correspondence, shipping records, accounts, and receipts documenting the business affairs of Fant, a commission merchant based in Concordia Parish, Louisiana.

Benjamin Fuller and Joseph Sylvester Papers. 1817–1824. ½ in.

Day book and receipts of Fuller and Sylvester of Natchez, relating to glazing, paper hanging, carpeting, and painting for various Adams County residents.

Grand Lake Farm Account Book. 1844–1852. 1 vol.

Daily journal of Grand Lake Farm, a plantation in Chicot County, Arkansas, recording the accounts of the household and listing the slaves on the plantation with dates and causes of death.

Greenville, Mississippi, Store Ledger. 1825–1828. 2½ in.

Ledger of a Greenville, Mississippi, mercantile store, containing entries for daily sales of dry goods and groceries.

Harrison and Lewis Mercantile Business Records. 1872–1884. 3 ft., 1½ in.

Business records, including ledgers, of Harrison and Lewis mercantile stores in Edwards and Learned, in Hinds County, Mississippi.

Huston Family Papers. 1835–1860. 53 items.

Will, correspondence, receipts, and accounts documenting activities of the families of Eli Huston and his brother Felix. Contains financial records of Wood-ford Place in East Feliciana Parish, Louisiana, and other papers relating to the brothers' estates.

John Carmichael Jenkins Family Papers. 1836–1900. 5 in.

Papers relating to the family and estate of John C. Jenkins (1809–1855), his son John F., and his daughter Alice, planters in Adams County, Mississippi. Includes financial records, correspondence, a stock book from the family's Elgin plantation, and reports signed by Robert E. Lee while president of Washington College in Lexington, Virginia.

Basil Kiger Papers. 1841–1885. 2 ft., 8 in.

Papers of Mississippi plantation owner Basil Gordon Kiger, his wife, Caroline Isabel Gwin Kiger, and their three children. Correspondence is primarily among family members, especially while the children were away at school, and relates to the operation of the family's Buena Vista plantation, located north of Vicksburg in Warren County, Mississippi.

John Lane Papers. 1821–1855. 121 items.

Cotton records, accounts, deeds, slave bills of sale, correspondence, and legal documents concerning the affairs of John and John A. Lane of Vicksburg, Mississippi. Included are papers relating to the murder trial of the slave Sam, who was charged as an accessory in the killing of his master, Joel Cameron (1832).

Minor Family Papers. 1783–1852. 4 in.

Administrative, financial, and legal records and correspondence concerning the affairs of John Minor, planter, and his brother Stephen (Estevan) Minor, Spanish government official on the Spanish-American frontier in the lower Mississippi valley, planter, and organizer of the Bank of Mississippi at Natchez.

Mississippi Union Bank Inventory. 1846. 2 in.

Trustee's inventory of the property, assets, and debts of the Mississippi Union Bank in Jackson submitted to the circuit court of Hinds County.

Mississippi Woman's Christian Temperance Union Records. 1891–1893. 14 items.

Minutes, reports, and correspondence documenting the administrative activities of the Mississippi WCTU. Included is a forty-page draft of the minutes for the 1892 state convention in Corinth, committee reports, and an 1893 letter relating the history of the WCTU in Mississippi.

NTC Broadside Collection

More than 160 broadsides and handbills published mainly in Louisiana and Mississippi, 1795–1900, announcing or advertising events and services in politics, real estate, law, education, agriculture, and economic, social, and cultural affairs.

NTC Civil War Collection. 1861–1865. 11 in.

Correspondence, military and legal documents, receipts, vouchers, and other financial records relating to the Civil War, organized by document type and arranged mainly chronologically.

NTC Crime and Punishment Collection. 1819–1876. 5 in.

Court records documenting criminal charges and disposition of cases in Warren County, Mississippi, predominantly during the antebellum period. Records are grouped according to particular crimes, including robbery, assault, murder, gambling, dueling, theft, and morals charges.

NTC Ephemera Collection. 5 in.

Tickets, ballots, advertisements, business cards, menus, programs, invitations, funeral announcements, dance cards, and additional papers of everyday life in nineteenth-century Louisiana and Mississippi.

NTC Map Collection

A collection of fifty manuscript maps and eighty-eight printed maps owned or prepared by individuals, families, and organizations represented in the NTC. The bulk of the maps depict Louisiana and Mississippi during the nineteenth century, especially prior to 1861. Cartographic types include land surveys and plat maps, atlases, pocket maps and city guides, and specialty maps, such as Civil War battle maps and railroad route maps. These maps constitute documents drawn or consulted by Natchez District residents as a means of delineating property, planning and guiding travels, recording and depicting natural or man-made structures in their physical environment, and studying the history and geography of their locale, region, and country.

NTC Newspaper Collection

More than two hundred newspaper titles, with special strengths in the decades before the Civil War for titles and issues from Louisiana and Mississippi towns and cities, including Canton, Jackson, Natchez, Port Gibson, and Vicksburg, Mississippi, and New Orleans, Baton Rouge, Donaldsonville, Plaquemine, and Saint

Francisville, Louisiana. All NTC newspapers have been cataloged into OCLC as part of the Center's NEH-funded Texas Newspaper Project. The collection includes issues of the *Louisiana Gazette and Arcadia and La Fourche Advertiser*, published in Donaldsonville, Louisiana, in 1831, the only portion of this newspaper known to exist, with the exception of a single issue housed in the Library of Congress.

NTC Pamphlet and Serials Collection

More than five hundred nineteenth-century pamphlets, paperback novels, and periodicals that constitute the leisure and professional reading of individuals, families, and organizations whose papers are represented in the Natchez Trace Collection. A number of these imprints were written or published by persons and organizations represented in the collections, including Mississippi politician John A. Quitman, cotton planter Stephen A. Duncan, Episcopal bishop Charles B. Dana, Natchez attorney George Winchester, Mississippi's Oakland College, the Vicksburg Athletic Club, and the Planters' Bank. Imprints include sermons, legal cases, funeral orations, speeches, essays, addresses, tracts, college catalogs, almanacs, literary, religious, and fashion magazines, nursery and seed catalogs, diocesan reports, convention proceedings, and annual railroad reports.

NTC Photograph Collection

More than 870 images, 1855–1920, including daguerreotypes, cartes-de-visite portraits, cabinet cards, theater stereographs, lantern slides, and tintypes depicting Natchez and Vicksburg area families and scenes and commercial views. Many images were taken by prominent New Orleans, Vicksburg, and Natchez photographers. This group of photographs is being treated as a single collection. An item-level inventory has been prepared.

NTC Provincial and Territorial Archives. 1759–1813. 3 ft., 9 in.

Correspondence, land surveys, marriage contracts, legal proceedings, slave sales, wills, ordinances, petitions, civil records for posts including those at Natchez, Pointe Coupée, Ouachita, Iberville, and Opelousas, and other legal and administrative papers relating to the French and Spanish provincial and Louisiana and Mississippi territorial eras. Includes documents signed by provincial administrators Bernardo de Galvez and Manuel Gayoso de Lemos.

NTC Railroad Collection. 1837–1913. 4½ in.

Stocks, reports, bond certificates, timetables, and other documents concerning various railroads in Mississippi and Louisiana.

NTC Sheet Music Collection

Approximately four thousand pieces of nineteenth-century sheet music, containing equal amounts of classical and popular music. This sheet music includes music owned and played by individuals and families represented in the NTC as well as the sheet music inventory of a Vicksburg music store. The majority of the compositions are of the genre known as parlor music, including selections to honor a historic occasion or prominent individual, Civil War songs, plantation songs, minstrel and show tunes, and jubilee songs. In addition to its significant musical content, the sheet music is important for its cover illustrations. Fully half of the covers are decorated with engraved or lithographed illustrations that reflect social history through sentiments expressed, events commemorated, heroes celebrated, and attitudes revealed.

NTC Slaves and Slavery Collection. 1793–1864. 1 ft., 10 in.

Primarily legal documents relating to blacks and the institution of slavery in the southern United States, particularly in Louisiana and Mississippi, organized into eleven series: 1) runaway slaves, 2) free blacks, 3) individual emancipation, 4) sales of slaves and slave ownership, 5) estates and sales of land, personal property, and slaves, 6) court cases, civil and criminal, 7) entry of slaves into Louisiana, 8) lists of slaves and slave holders, 9) hire of slaves, 10) financial and other papers, and 11) guards and pickets passes for colored persons.

NTC Steamboat Collection. 1806–1925. 2 ft., 4 in.

Receipts, bills, legal records, correspondence, printed materials, and ledgers documenting steamboat activity on the Mississippi River and its tributaries.

G. W. and Paul A. Oliver Papers. 1851–1861. 44 items.

Business correspondence concerning the affairs of cotton and commission merchants G. W. Oliver of New Orleans and his brother Paul A. Oliver of New York.

T. D. Padelford Mercantile Business Records. 1873–1876. 8½ in.

Business ledgers and journals of Padelford in Edwards, Hinds County, Mississippi, documenting store customers and merchandise sold.

Willard C. Parish Papers. 1874–1926. 9½ in.

Personal and business correspondence, financial records, printed materials, and photographs documenting Willard C. Parish, McComb city and Vicksburg railroad car inspector. Business papers pertain primarily to the construction and delivery of railroad cars, and, after 1912, to pension and travel privileges.

James Rowan Percy Obstetrical Case Book. 1857–1859. ½ in.

Record of obstetrical cases kept by Percy (d. 1877) while he was a medical student at Charity Hospital in New Orleans; contains names and medical particulars for thirty-four women giving birth as well as notes on abortion, miscarriage, and medicines.

Benjamin Roach Family Papers. 1831–1867. 5 in.

Probate records for the estate of Benjamin Roach, Sr., a wealthy planter and slaveholder in several Mississippi counties. Contains financial records related primarily to the management of the estate, which was administered by his son Benjamin Roach, Jr., and includes invoices and receipts for family expenses and for tuition fees paid by Alexander Montgomery, Natchez lawyer and guardian of some of the Roach children.

William Lewis Sharkey Papers. 1823–1881. 3 in.

Correspondence, financial and legal records, speeches, and literary productions pertaining mostly to the political activities of Sharkey (1797–1873), a prominent Mississippi lawyer, jurist, and Whig political activist.

Peregrine P. Sugg Papers. 1847–1877. 1½ in.

Diary and papers of Sugg (b. 1815) documenting his activities as a plantation overseer, slave owner, brickmaker, and lumber hauler in Iberville Parish, Louisiana, and, later, in Rusk, Texas.

Henry Tennent Papers. 1834–1847. 2 in.

Papers of physician Henry Tennent of Pine Ridge, Mississippi, near Natchez, consisting of day book, brief notes, and receipts. The day book records visits with and lists accounts of patients, including, among others, John A. Quitman, William Bisland, and Samuel Chamberlain.

Benjamin Leonard Covington Wailes Papers. 1811–1860. 1½ in.

Correspondence and financial records of Wailes (1797–1862), a prominent Mississippi educator and historian and son of Levin Wailes, concerning the administration of Jefferson College in Washington, Mississippi.

James Campbell Wilkins Papers. 1801–1852. 3 ft., 9 in.

Personal, political, and business correspondence, legal papers, and financial records documenting the life and career of Wilkins (d. 1849), a Natchez cotton planter, merchant, cotton factor, financier, and banker, including his partnership in the Wilkins and Linton Company (1816–1834) and his political interests and activities. Family papers pertain to plantation life and household purchases.

Winchester Family Papers. 1783–1906. 14 ft., 6 in.

Personal, financial, legal, and business records, literary productions, and printed material documenting the lives and careers of Natchez attorney and Whig political leader George Winchester (1793–1851) and his nephew Josiah (d. 1888), an attorney and judge in Natchez, as well as the lives of Josiah's family, including his wife Margaret G. Sprague Winchester and her relatives. The collection's legal and political correspondence, court case files, probate records, and estate inventories chronicle the legal affairs of planters and businessmen throughout the lower Mississippi valley, including Stephen Duncan and John C. Jenkins, from the 1820s to the 1880s. A substantial portion of the personal correspondence is among women in the Winchester family, including Margaret Winchester's mother Frances Sprague and sister Fannie Pugh, wife of a prominent Louisiana planter.

KATHERINE J. ADAMS is associate director of the Center for American History at the University of Texas at Austin. She has focused on processing and promoting the Natchez Trace Collection through publications, lectures, and exhibitions, with particular emphasis on the collection's pamphlets, broadsides, and ephemera. Among her publications are "Archival Resources on the Old Natchez District in the Center for American History," in *Archival Shadows of the Old Natchez District: A Guide to Selected Natchez Holdings*, Southern Research Report #7 (Center for the Study of the American South, University of North Carolina at Chapel Hill, 1996), and "Texas Impressions: Graphic Arts in the Republic of Texas, 1836–1845," in *Prints and Printmakers of Texas* (1997).

SHEARER DAVIS BOWMAN is associate professor of history and associate chair of the History Department at the University of Texas at Austin, where he teaches courses on southern history in the pre–Civil War era. He has written *Masters & Lords: Mid-Nineteenth Century U.S. Planters and Prussian Junkers* (1993). Since the arrival of the Natchez Trace Collection at the University of Texas at Austin, Bowman has directed numerous seminar papers and master's theses based on the new information available in this important acquisition.

RANDOLPH B. CAMPBELL is professor of history at the University of North Texas. He has published numerous books and articles about the slave culture and society of Texas and its impact on the state. His books include *A Southern Community in Crisis: Harrison County, Texas, 1850–1880* (1983), *Planters & Plain Folk: Agriculture in Ante-bellum Texas* (1987), and *Grass-Roots Reconstruction in Texas, 1865–1880* (1998).

LEWIS L. GOULD is the Eugene C. Barker Centennial Professor in American History Emeritus at the University of Texas at Austin. During his career he received awards for distinguished undergraduate and graduate teaching. He is the author of *Progressives and Prohibitionists: Texas Democrats in the Wilson Era* (1973) and *1968: The Election That Changed America* (1993). He is currently working on a biography of Alexander Watkins Terrell.

JOHN D. W. GUICE is professor of history at the University of Southern Mississippi. He has written extensively on the history of Mississippi and the Old Southwest in the early years of the nineteenth century. His books include *The Rocky Mountain Bench: The Territorial Supreme Courts of Colorado, Montana, and Wyoming, 1861–1890* (1972) and *Frontiers in Conflict: The Old Southwest, 1795–1830* (1989).

MORTON ROTHSTEIN is professor of history emeritus at the University of California at Davis. He has written many articles on the Natchez elite and its economic behavior during and after the Civil War, most of which appear in *Agricultural History*. His edited works include *Quantitative Studies in Agrarian History* (1993) and *Outstanding in His Field: Perspectives on American Agriculture in Honor of Wayne D. Rasmussen* (1993).

WILLIAM G. SHADE is professor of history and director of American studies at Lehigh University. He has written on the issue of money and banking in the 1830s, the politics of the anthracite coal region of Pennsylvania, and the history of American women. His prize-winning volume *Democratizing the Old Dominion: Virginia and the Second Party System, 1824–1861* was published in 1996.

INDEX